Playing for Equality

Playing for Equality

*Oral Histories
of Women Leaders
in the Early Years of Title IX*

Diane LeBlanc *and*
Allys Swanson

McFarland & Company, Inc., Publishers
Jefferson, North Carolina

LIBRARY OF CONGRESS CATALOGUING-IN-PUBLICATION DATA

Names: LeBlanc, Diane, 1964 May 15– author. | Swanson, Allys M., author.
Title: Playing for equality : oral histories of women leaders in the early years of Title IX / Diane LeBlanc and Allys Swanson.
Description: Jefferson, North Carolina : McFarland & Company, Inc., 2016. | Includes bibliographical references and index.
Identifiers: LCCN 2016039255 | ISBN 9781476663005 (softcover : acid free paper) ∞
Subjects: LCSH: Sex discrimination in sports—United States—History. | Discrimination in education—Law and legislation—United States—History. | Sex discrimination against women—Law and legislation—United States—History.
Classification: LCC KF4166 .L43 2016 | DDC 344.73/099—dc23
LC record available at https://lccn.loc.gov/2016039255

BRITISH LIBRARY CATALOGUING DATA ARE AVAILABLE

ISBN (print) 978-1-4766-6300-5
ISBN (ebook) 978-1-4766-2698-7

© 2016 Diane LeBlanc and Allys Swanson. All rights reserved

No part of this book may be reproduced or transmitted in any form or by any means, electronic or mechanical, including photocopying or recording, or by any information storage and retrieval system, without permission in writing from the publisher.

Front cover image © 2016 iStock

Printed in the United States of America

McFarland & Company, Inc., Publishers
  Box 611, Jefferson, North Carolina 28640
     www.mcfarlandpub.com

Allys Swanson: For my family, Virgil Swanson,
Susan Swanson, Lori DeAlmeida, and Capri Offield

Diane LeBlanc: For Chick

Acknowledgments

We thank the following institutions and people for their contributions to this project:

Saint Catherine University, Saint Olaf College, and Memphis State University

Giordana Mecagni, University Archivist and Head of Special Collections, and Michelle Romero, Assistant Archivist, Snell Library, Northeastern University

Jeffrey Monseau, College Archivist, Springfield College

Jennifer Motszko, Manuscript Archivist, University Libraries, Martha Blakeney Hodges Special Collections and University Archives, University of North Carolina at Greensboro

Rebecca Parmer, College Archivist, Connecticut College

Jarvis Sheffield, Librarian, Brown-Daniel Library Special Collections, Tennessee State University

Daardi Sizemore, Archives and Special Collections Librarian, and Anne Stenzel, Archives Technician, Memorial Library, Minnesota State University, Mankato

Laura E. Strecker, Periodicals Associate Editor, *JOPERD* (*Journal of Physical Education, Recreation and Dance*) at SHAPE America (Society of Health and Physical Educators)

Dr. Charles W. Crawford, Professor and Director of the Oral History Research Office at Memphis State University

Annie Clement, former president of NASPE (National Association of Sport and Physical Education) for the grant that began the Oral History of Retired American Alliance for Health, Physical Education, Recreation and Dance (AAHPERD) Leaders: Presidents and/or National Award Recipients Project

Carol Johnson, Director Emerita of Libraries, Archives and Media Services at Saint Catherine University, and Emily Asch, Director of Libraries, Archives and Media Services at Saint Catherine University, for their work in publishing many of the oral histories on SOPHIA, an online repository of scholarship and creative works

Wayne Wilson, LA84 Foundation Vice President, Education Services

The late Dr. Sharon Van Oteghen, co-interviewer/interviewer for several of the oral histories that made this book possible

Finally, and certainly, the women featured in this book who shared their experiences

Table of Contents

Acknowledgments vii

Preface 1

Introduction 3

1. Catherine Allen: Building Community through Recreation 9
2. Ruth Schellberg: Guiding Girls and Women through the Wilderness 31
3. Celeste Ulrich: Speaking Out During Title IX Transitions 42
4. Fay Biles: Empowering Women through Fitness and Fundraising 62
5. Dorothy McIntyre: Changing Minnesota High School Athletics 90
6. Willye White: Competing for an Equal Chance in Life 115
7. Doris Corbett: Promoting Human Rights through Sport 130
8. Anita DeFrantz: Making the World More Like an Olympic Village 158

Chapter Notes 193

References 194

Index 197

Preface

"Why focus on Title IX?" We heard that question often when talking with friends and colleagues about this book, and our response was simple: gender equity in physical education and sports is still a work in progress. More specifically, enforcing Title IX remains a critical act as economic recession prompts schools at all levels to cut athletic programming in ways that challenge compliance. In 2016, institutions face new challenges to Title IX and intercollegiate athletics as more women than men attend college. Most importantly, gender inequity and Title IX emerged as common themes when we studied intersections among women's oral histories that chronicle the evolution of physical education and sport from the 1930s through 2015.

The idea for this book emerged during a larger project of interviewing 50 past presidents and national award recipients of the American Alliance for Health, Physical Education, Recreation and Dance. During these interviews, conducted by Allys Swanson and Sharon Van Oteghen, women described similar experiences of gender inequity in their roles as students, athletes, teachers, coaches, and administrators. We identified a group who came of age professionally before and during passage of Title IX. Although some met one another and others never met, their voices intersect to reveal the complex legal and social history of Title IX. We then conducted additional interviews to represent high school athletics more fully and to include the experiences of former Olympic athletes. As a group, the eight women featured in this book have, in distinct ways, promoted sports as an instrument for pursuing human rights.

This collection of oral histories illuminates gender, race, and class inequity in physical education and sport. But they don't end there. These narratives span two generations to document women's leadership, gains in equity, and the ongoing need for Title IX. Six of the featured women began careers before Title IX and indirectly or directly helped to enact, to implement, and to enforce the law. Two of the women featured were in college and graduate school when Title IX compliance mandated equity for women, and both are active in international sports and human rights work. The range in age and experience is intentional to record the momentum and halts that characterize Title IX's far-reaching impact. We believe these voices must be at the table in 2017, when Title IX celebrates its 45th anniversary.

This book occupies a distinct place among three types of studies of Title IX. First, it offers personal context for the objective facts and figures of legendary physical educator Mabel Lee's classic text, *A History of Physical Education and Sports in the U.S.A.* (1983). Second, this book resists repeating and instead complements contemporary and comprehensive portraits of the law's history and implementation, including *Title IX* (L. J. Carpenter and R. V. Acosta, 2005) and *Title IX: A Brief History with Documents* (S. Ware, 2006). Finally, it complicates with lived experience the theorized perspectives in such texts as *Women and Sports in the United States: A Documentary Reader* (Eds. J. O'Reilly and S. K. Cahn, 2007), *A Place on the Team: The Triumph and Tragedy of Title IX*, (W. Suggs, 2006), and *Equal Play: Title IX and Social Change* (N. Hogshead-Makar and A. Zimbalist, 2007). Drawing from some but not all of these texts, this book acknowledges the rich scholarly understanding of Title IX that supports this more intimate narrative.

As oral history, this book's authority resides in the featured women's voices and experiences. At the same time, deviating from oral histories that present uninterrupted first-person narrative, we edited and recast these histories in third person to create coherence and to emphasize contrasting experiences before and after the passage of Title IX. Simultaneously factual and based in memory, personal and collective, this book can be read alone or as a complement to historical reportage. These biographies comprise the cast of a historical drama that played out before some readers were born or when others were too young to understand the social change they were witnessing. As one generation passes the curriculum, coaching rosters, and training logs to the next, we offer these narratives as part of the inheritance.

Introduction

The history of Title IX of the Education Amendments of 1972 is complex, but the law itself fits on a scrap of paper: "No person in the United States shall, on the basis of sex, be excluded from participation in, be denied the benefits of, or be subjected to discrimination under any education program or activity receiving Federal financial assistance" (United States Department of Education). Even though Title IX doesn't mention physical education, athletics, or recreation, its subsequent regulations and policy interpretations demanded a response to gender inequity in athletics. In fact, as women's sport researchers Carpenter and Acosta (2005) note, Title IX "changed the face of American sport forever" (p. 3).

An expansive review of Title IX and its impact on gender equity is beyond the scope of our purpose and would repeat existing literature. Two types of studies—historical presentation and social and political analysis—generally inform the current understanding of Title IX. Although these two categories aren't mutually exclusive, they contribute differently to discussions of Title IX's past successes and future impacts. Within the first category, Carpenter and Acosta's *Title IX* (2005) presents a comprehensive legal and social history of the law's origins, enactment, implementation, enforcement, and impact. Written for a general audience, it engages readers through direct address and includes frequently asked questions at the end of select sections. More of a factual reference than an argument, it is an accessible resource for anyone interested in Title IX. With similar purpose, Y. Wushanley's *Playing Nice and Losing: The Struggle for Control of Women's Intercollegiate Athletics, 1960–2000* (2004) details the conflicts among organizations striving to define and govern women's sport and intercollegiate athletics in the years prior to and after the enactment of Title IX.

Within the second category, social and political analysis, McDonagh and Pappano's *Playing with the Boys: Why Separate Is Not Equal in Sports* (2008) argues that Title IX has mandated positive change but has yet to upset deeply rooted gender codes within and beyond sports. McDonagh and Pappano assert that contact sports remain "sex segregated" and create a "separate but equal" culture, thereby sharing remnants of flawed educational policy that endured until the Supreme Court ruled in *Brown v. Board of Education* (1954) that "separate is not equal" (p. 27). "Females playing sports with males must become standard practice, not the exception," they conclude after offering a manifesto for reforming sport rules and culture (p. 260).

Despite rich discourse and debate about Title IX and women's intercollegiate athletics, many discussions neglect the governance tug-of-war that occupied women's competitive sports in the early 1920s and shaped early responses to Title IX. Sport historian E. Gerber (1975) documents this struggle in "The Controlled Development of Collegiate Sport for Women, 1923–1936." Gerber's primary purpose is to deconstruct the myth that women's athletics weren't competitive before Title IX mandated opportunity for women in intercollegiate athletics. As early as 1896, women played a form of intercollegiate basketball. But that model of competition was short-lived. In 1922, the U.S. War and Navy secretaries founded the National Amateur Athletic Foundation to challenge the high-level competition for women supported by the Amateur Athletic Union (AAU) and the Olympics (Costa and Guthrie, 1994, p. 91). Gerber analyzes the rise of the Women's Division of the National Amateur Athletic Foundation (NAAF-WD), which adopted a democratic, "play for play's sake" philosophy of women's athletics, challenged existing support from women's competitive intercollegiate athletics, and promoted play days that emphasized participation more than competition (p. 4).

These attitudes toward women reflect a larger backlash against women's rights that occurred after passage of the 19th Amendment in 1920. In 1923, the NAAF-WD adopted a platform of 16 resolutions that aimed to protect women. The platform heeded medical myths of the era and cautioned against competition that would threaten women physiologically and emotionally. The resolutions recommended moderate physical education and limited competition to prepare women "to perform their functions as citizens" (as cited in Gerber, 1975, p. 11), assuming their future roles as wives and mothers. The NAAF-WD successfully interrupted women's intercollegiate athletics, but it didn't entirely destroy women's athletic competition. Costa and Guthrie (1994) suggest that NAAF-WD intentions backfired: "The rift between women physical educators and the AAU had the long-term effect of moving more of women's athletics out of education and into the public sector" (p. 91). In short, physical education leaders lost significant control over women's competitive athletics.

Gerber's article lays out more than the critical history of the NAAF-WD's influence. Gerber wrote from the center of Title IX action in 1975 and begins with the observation, "Radical changes are taking place in collegiate sports for women" (p. 1). From this vantage point, the article unveils tension among physical education leadership during the initial implementation of Title IX. Women physical educators did not, by default, support reform. Gerber notes that existing curriculum had not prepared women physical educators to train and coach female athletes for advanced competition or to organize and officiate at intercollegiate tournaments. Similar to earlier conflicts about appropriate level of competition and right to governance, physical education leaders of the 1960s and 1970s faced painful negotiations as philosophies clashed and the National Collegiate Athletic Association (NCAA), which historically governed men's sports, eventually gained control of women's intercollegiate athletics.

This book features women who navigated these conflicts without maps or models. As we accumulated their narratives, we wondered where existing Title IX literature documented the often heroic yet sometimes mundane acts of resistance that our interviews revealed to be essential contributions to the fight for gender equity. We searched for private moments such as this one, when Minnesota State High School League associate director Dorothy McIntyre was organizing Minnesota's first State Girls' Track and Field meet in 1972: "On the Sunday when the state program had to be prepared for the printer, there was a big rain and windstorm and the office lost its electricity. I sat in front of a window in my office, typing in the heats and lane assignments on a manual typewriter" (D. McIntyre, personal communication, 2013). Finding too few of such reminiscences in the literature, we recognized a place for oral history.

The subsequent chapters, organized chronologically according to each woman's birth year, feature Catherine Allen, Ruth Schellberg, Celeste Ulrich, Fay Biles, Dorothy McIntyre, Willye White, Doris Corbett, and Anita DeFrantz. Their experiences collectively span two generations. They reveal experiences of gender, race, and class inequity in higher education and amateur athletics. They depict tensions surrounding Title IX that reached from high school state tournaments to Congress, furor in response to the 1980 Moscow Olympic Games boycott, and celebration of the current mandate that all Olympic Games from the 2012 London Games forward include competition for both women and men in every sport. Each chapter speaks with compassion, laughter, anger, and deep understanding of the importance of physical education and sport in girls' and women's lives throughout the world.

The first six chapters focus on physical educators and administrators born before World War II. They entered their mid-to-late careers as Title IX became law, and three of the six served as president of the American Alliance for Health, Physical Education, Recreation and Dance (AAHPERD).

Catherine Allen (1909–2000) was a lifelong recreation leader. She was equally at ease playing her accordion for folk dancing classes and addressing international audiences through her numerous physical education leadership roles. As a World War II Red Cross volunteer, she organized recreation and entertained military personnel in the Pacific region. She taught at the University of Tennessee, New York University, and the University of Pittsburgh before helping Bouvé-Boston College move to Northeastern University, where she served as a faculty member, a dean, and a special assistant to the president until her retirement.

Ruth Schellberg (1912–2009) opened the wilderness to girls and women. She was a Minnesota State University, Mankato, professor and administrator for much of her 47-year career in physical education. An active leader in Camp Fire Girls, she guided more than 91 legendary canoe trips through northern Minnesota's Boundary Waters. Title IX opened Ruth's eyes to the need for more women in decision-making roles. As president of the Women's Equity Action League of Minnesota in 1974–75, she raised awareness of pay inequity in the Minnesota state college system.

Celeste Ulrich (1924–2011) served as president of AAHPERD from 1976 to 1977. She played a prominent role within the organization as it addressed the question of who would govern women's intercollegiate athletics following Title IX. Her experiences shaped her dedication as a professor at Madison College, University of North Carolina at Greensboro, and the University of Oregon, where she finished her career as a college dean.

Fay Biles (1927–) recounts her formative years as a competitive tennis and field hockey athlete and her determination as a young coach to promote intercollegiate athletics and equal opportunity for women. Fay's teaching, research on physical activity and self-esteem, and dynamic fundraising as the first female vice president for development at Kent State University after the May 4, 1970, shootings coincided with social unrest that contributed to the push for Title IX's enactment.

Dorothy McIntyre (1936–) was navigating her early teaching and coaching career in Eden Prairie, Minnesota, when Title IX reached Congress. She became the first woman to join the executive board of the Minnesota State High School League in 1970 and, during her 32 years as associate director of the League executive staff, organized the first state tournaments in several sports, most notably ice hockey, for girls in Minnesota.

Willye White (1940–2007) earned a silver medal for the long jump at age 16 in the 1956 Melbourne Olympic Games and became the first and, to date, the only five-time female track and field Olympian. Her career as a health administrator, volunteer track coach, and lifelong activist for youth recreation opportunities in Chicago influenced untold numbers of youth over the years. Willye's biography reveals an intersection of race, class, and gender that both challenged and benefited from Title IX.

The two women featured in the final chapters were born shortly after World War II, situating them in the Baby Boom generation, for whom responses to social inequity has become a defining experience.

Doris Corbett (1947–) is the director of the School of Health, Physical Education, and Leisure Services at the University of Northern Iowa. When Doris was elected president of the International Council for Health, Physical Education, Recreation, Sport and Dance (ICHPER-SD) in 1991, a position she held until 1999, she was the second woman and first African American to hold the position. Her chapter details the separation of the National Association for Girls and Women in Sport, of which she served as president in 1980–81, and the Association for Intercollegiate Athletics for Women (AIAW). That defining period in sport history for women shaped and was shaped by Title IX policy and implementation. Doris's specialization in sociology of sport has guided her research and leadership while inspiring her international lectures on ethics, sports, and human rights.

Anita DeFrantz (1952–) began her rowing career at Connecticut College in 1971, an opportunity rooted in response to Title IX, and won a bronze medal in the 1976 Montreal Olympic Games. Her commanding voice for athletes' rights during the U.S. boycott of the 1980 Olympic Games in Moscow established her leadership and opened the door for her tenure on the U.S. Olympic Committee and on the International Olympic Committee. Anita was the first U.S. female vice president of the International Olympic Committee. She was the founding president of the LA84 Foundation, a position she held for 31 years while serving the International Olympic Committee. Through these positions she has advocated nationally and internationally for athletes' rights and women's rights, all in the name of human rights.

As much as possible, we let the oral histories speak for themselves in this book. While editing interview transcripts, we followed the ethics of oral history research and made only minimal changes to clarify language and to correct facts. When talking about the history of intercollegiate athletics and governance, the ubiquity of names and acronyms of professional organizations is unavoidable. Instead of repeating the relationships among these organizations in every chapter, we illustrate them in Figure 1. Likewise, when a chapter draws the biography from a single oral history transcript, we don't repeat citations to the transcript. The references include information

Figure 1: Governance of Women's Physical Education, Sport, and Athletics

```
AAHPERD
1885 - 1886   AAPE    (Association for the Advancement of Physical Education)
1886 - 1903   AAAPE   (American Association for the Advancement of Physical
                       Education)
1903 - 1937   APEA    (American Physical Education Association)
1937 - 1938   AAHPE   (American Association for Health and Physical Education)
1938 - 1974   AAHPER  (American Association for Health, Physical Education and
                       Recreation)
1974 - 2013   AAHPERD (American Alliance for Health, Physical Education,
                       Recreation and Dance)
2013 - present SHAPE America (Society of Health and Physical Educators)
```

↓

```
1899 - 1905  Women's Basketball Rules Committee
1905 - 1917  NWBC (National Women's Basketball Committee)
1917 - 1925  CWA (Committee on Women's Athletics)
             NWBC became one of several sport-specific subcommittees
1925 - 1952  NSWA (National Section on Women's Athletics)
             Governed women's athletics
1952 - 1957  NSGWS (National Section for Girls and Women's Sports)
```

↓

1957 - 1974 DGWS (Division for Girls' and Women's Sports) Added instruction and intramural focus to its role of women in sports

1974 – 2010 NAGWS (National Association for Girls and Women in Sport)

2010 – present *Program for the Advancement of Girls and Women in Sport and Physical Activity*

- - -> 1966 CIAW (Commission on Intercollegiate Athletics for Women)

1971- 1982 AIAW (Association for Intercollegiate Athletics for Women)

↓

1979 CCWAA (Council of Collegiate Women Athletic Administrators) separated from AIAW and embraced NCAA governance

1982 – present NCAA (National Collegiate Athletic Association) began to govern women's intercollegiate athletics

about individual interviews. By minimizing white noise, we hope to simulate the experience of having a conversation with these women whose experiences surrounding Title IX continue to shape physical education, intercollegiate athletics, and recreation in and beyond the United States.

1

Catherine Allen
Building Community through Recreation

Decades before Title IX introduced equal opportunity in physical education and school sports, Catherine Allen spoke her own language of equality through recreation. She studied with some of physical education's most influential practitioners and philosophers during the 1930s, when social and economic forces impacted physical education programming. Her 53-year career included teaching, serving as a department chair, a dean, and president of the American Alliance for Health, Physical Education, Recreation and Dance, and traveling the world to train recreation teachers. But many remember her most vividly, at five feet, three inches tall, pumping her accordion and easing a crowd into a sing-along. Recreation was play, it was a responsibility, and it was her vocation. She wrote in *Fun for Parties and Programs* (1956), "Cooperative group action is our American way of solving our problems. Every person in the group is worthwhile, and his ideas make a valuable contribution" (p. 3). With these post–World War II ideals, Catherine contributed to a democratic culture of physical education and recreation that could not yet imagine the changes Title IX would bring.

Family Influences and Accelerated Education

Catherine Allen's lifelong spirit of interdependence began in early childhood. She was born on December 1, 1909, in Columbus, Georgia, to an immediate family that included her parents, five younger brothers and sisters, her grandfather, her Aunt Edna, and eventually two brothers-in-law, and four nieces and nephews. Her parents were "honest, God-fearing people" who performed traditional roles and ran the family like a cooperative business. Aubrey Davidson Allen earned the family income by working as a salesman while Catherine's mother, Louise Haynes Jessop, cooked, cleaned, and did "all the things that go with loving one's children." Aunt Edna oversaw the children's intellectual development by tutoring them and supervising their schoolwork. In this environment, Catherine learned the importance of cooperation to the well-being of a whole group.

Catherine was a family leader. She became adept at rocking babies, changing diapers, and handling what she called "all those fine things" of childcare. These responsibilities lasted throughout her childhood because, observing the reality of married women's lives in early the 20th century, she said, "When my mother would start feeling free of babies, she'd have another one."

Catherine's mother belonged to a generation defined by gender roles; women's place was predominantly within the domestic sphere. So while Catherine expressed love, respect, and appreciation for her mother, she recognized her father's influence on her later career choice. Aubrey, a supplier for the mercantiles in Georgia and Alabama that sold clothes, food, and farm implements, taught his daughter the art of selling. Catherine boasted,

> No matter what it was, my father could sell it. When I was about five, he would take me with him. My mother always dressed me up before we went. As we drove the unpaved roads in his Model-T Ford, I would sit in his lap and steer. He would take me to the country stores, put me on the counter and say, "Ladies and gentlemen, this is *my* Catherine."

He was successful, Catherine later realized, because he sold what people needed.

Aubrey Allen was also a natural Irish tenor who shared with Catherine his love for singing and playing instruments. When her parents recognized that music came naturally to Catherine, they hired a friend to give her piano lessons. According to Catherine, little teaching or learning went on:

> Mabel used to go to the second floor of our house where she and Mama would talk over tea and a few cookies. I was supposed to be practicing downstairs. Although I was practicing, I was playing by ear what I had heard Mabel play. I always convinced her to play first. I regret every minute of my laziness now that I don't know my notes.

Catherine balanced family responsibilities and music with vigorous play. The children in her neighborhood took advantage of their large families by forming three full softball teams on their block. Catherine also excelled at volleyball, vaulting over fences, climbing walls, and roller skating. "I entered a roller derby when I was ten or eleven," she recalled, "and by golly I won it! I don't know why in the name of sense I didn't break every bone in my body."

Leadership came naturally to Catherine because she was daring. One day, when the children were tired of their neighborhood, Catherine led them to the railroad tracks to see nearby Rose Hill Heights. The train was on the tracks that day, so all of the children climbed under the train to see Rose Hill. "It scares the life out of me when I think about it now!" Catherine exclaimed. "That venture could have killed everyone in the neighborhood. I did some foolish things for thrills, and my leadership wasn't always well thought out."

As early as elementary school, Catherine excelled in academics. After completing half of the first grade she advanced to second grade. But more than the academic work, she remembered the teachers who inspired her. She revered her female teachers: "I remember kneeling in church one day. When the people started to go up for Holy Communion, Miss Mary, my second grade teacher, passed me on the aisle. I couldn't bear it. I reached out and touched her."

Her first male teacher, in contrast, was a distant authoritarian:

> Mr. Drane, my seventh grade teacher, sat up on a platform. We were wild hyenas. To keep order, he rolled a cannonball down the aisle, and if our feet were in the aisle, someone would lose a toe or two. If he didn't like what someone did, he sent that student to the cloakroom.

Catherine did not bow quietly to his authority and made the most of being banished to the coat closet. She said, "It was marvelous because from the cloakroom I could get to the cafeteria and pick up a little extra food, or I could go to the girls' johnny."

Although Columbus was a small town, Catherine developed a sense of the larger world. In 1921, during the sixth grade, classmates chose her to greet President Warren Harding when his train stopped in Columbus. "The whole school went down to the station and gawked as I went up and shook hands with the president of the United States," Catherine recalled. "I didn't wash that hand for days."

Catherine advanced to Columbus High School at age 12. Although she was intellectually prepared, she felt socially and emotionally immature for high school. She found security in her studies, particularly languages, and in tutoring her classmates:

> I had as much Latin as I could get in high school. Aunt Edna was a Latin scholar. She would work with me at night, then required that I teach all the girls and boys in the morning before class. When we got to Miss Rogers' class and Miss Zacharias' class, we knew more Latin than was believable.

Catherine's early aptitude for teaching offered a glimpse into her future vocation.

Early Career Teaching and National Attitudes Toward Females in Sport

In 1926, the United States was sliding deeper into economic recession as Catherine prepared to enter college. Aubrey Allen couldn't pay Catherine's tuition while providing for five other children. Knowing Catherine's academic talents, her mother's sister Edith, who lived in New York City, offered to pay for two years of teacher education, then called normal school, at the University of Georgia in Athens or Georgia State College for Women (GSCW) in Milledgeville. Catherine chose GSCW because it was closer to home than Athens, and she knew many of its alumnae. She entered at 16 and graduated with a normal diploma (teaching certification) in 1928 at the age of 18. "I worked, studied, and played hard," Catherine concluded. "I do everything hard," she added.

Soon after Catherine earned her diploma, two Columbus High School teachers asked her to drive them to New York City. This adventure shaped her adult life. She explained,

> Although I had never driven anywhere but on a country road, and they had a rather nice car, I decided to go.... I remember quite well that I arrived in New York with $5.83. I stayed for five weeks. I didn't live on the streets and I didn't pan handle. I could ride the subway uptown for a nickel.

In New York, Catherine stayed with a relative whom her Aunt Edith had contacted. She explored the city with support from family friends. "I learned a great deal and realized that education was broader than what I had learned in normal school," Catherine said in retrospect. "A person can learn a lot by traveling, and this has become a lifetime pattern for me."

Catherine returned to Columbus flushed with wanderlust. But further travel was out of the question. Her father had died while she was in college; the family was now her responsibility. Catherine earned money teaching shorthand, typing, business penmanship, and business mathematics at Industrial High School in Columbus. The job was a fierce challenge because she had never studied any of those subjects. Every night she took home the books and taught herself the next day's lesson.

Catherine also had not planned to teach physical education or to organize a physical education program. But students wanted organized athletics in place of their sporadic and limited afterschool activities. 1929 was a particularly difficult year for athletic programs at all levels throughout the country. Although the end of World War I had raised the standard of living and increased leisure time, giving people the luxury of attending sporting events, the country was no longer in its prosperous post-war glory. Even fewer sports fans could afford to attend games after Wall Street's economic crash (Freeman, 1987, p. 128). Many colleges and universities cut physical education and sports because they viewed them as "frills" programs. Meanwhile, the Women's Division of the National Amateur Athletic Foundation (NAAF-WD) had declared vigorous competition a threat to female well-being and femininity, thereby limiting women's intercollegiate athletics. During the same year, a Carnegie Foundation report suggested that college athletics were losing sight of their primary objectives and giving in to commercialism, professionalism, and a lack of academic integrity. This report further discouraged public support of school sport programs (Freeman, 1987, p. 129).

Trends in intercollege athletics trickled into high schools, aggravating gender inequity in sport. Girls' already meager programs were allocated even less money than the boys' programs. So, with only piecemeal equipment, Catherine organized softball, baseball, and basketball teams. Despite the lack of financial and moral support, she was dedicated to the girls' basketball team she coached. She recalled,

> My best forward was Zadie Anglin, a big, tall, lanky redhead. She must have been 6 feet, 10 inches tall because she towered over me. Zadie's father ran a vegetable and fruit truck. When we had a ball game, the whole team and I would unload the truck and put the produce where Mr. Anglin wanted us to put it. He didn't give us the gas. We had to put in our nickels and dimes. Then we would drive to the little town where we were going to play. We never accepted games which we couldn't afford to go to.

This stop-gap programming appealed to Catherine's interest in problem solving and to her natural tendency to lead others in play.

After one year at Industrial High School, which was in session 11 months of the year, Catherine requested a transfer to a nine-month school so that she could pursue her bachelor's degree during the summer months. She began a new position as a third grade teacher at East Highland Elementary School, where physical education continued to be her interest and emphasis. She served as the playground director and taught physical education at recess, the only time and place that allowed for it.

Programming, however, wasn't Catherine's greatest challenge at East Highland. With great emotion, she described the school's "tragic" students:

> Some of the children had practically no food and clothes; some were barefoot. This was during the Depression when food was hard to come by, so the teachers made sandwiches for the needy children. There was a crippled boy whom I had to take down the stairs in my arms every time there was a fire drill. We were mainstreaming without knowing it.

Catherine shared vivid memories of a particular student:

> Joe was the best tap dancer I have yet to see on stage or otherwise. His mother and one or two of his teen-aged sisters were prostitutes active on the streets. Joe's mother often took

him across the river to Alabama. Since there were no rules against it at the time, she took him into the bars and made him tap dance for money. The next day he would sleep for two or three hours during school. After I learned what was happening, I let the child sleep. I taught at East Highland as long as I did for this type of child.

Catherine believed that her role as a teacher was to encourage students to develop skills through sports and recreation. She worked for more than a decade at East Highland, at which point the superintendent of schools recognized her success with students. She was then transferred to her alma mater, Columbus High School, to head the junior and senior high school girls' physical education departments. To address discipline problems, Catherine designed recreation programs that would provide an arena for competition and an outlet for students' energy.

Almost 40 years before Title IX challenged gender inequity in physical education and athletics, Catherine addressed gender disparity at Columbus High School. She was concerned about opportunity for all students as she observed stratification typical for secondary school athletics. While highly-skilled boys belonged to basketball, football, or track teams, boys with average skills had no opportunities for organized sports; the boys had no physical education program. The opposite was true for young women, trapped in a long tradition of non-competitive play. In her classic book *The History of Physical Education in College for Women (USA)* (1975), Dorothy Ainsworth, Smith College's Director of Physical Education from 1926 to 1960, defined 1930s sport culture. Women physical educators who supported NAAF-WD philosophies endorsed the idea that women's athletics should foster a healthy attitude toward play rather than instigate competition for the sake of winning (p. 173). The NAAF-WD promoted medical experts' essentialist idea that women were frail creatures who would suffer physically and psychologically if they competed too rigorously (Freeman, 1987, p. 135). Many also feared that modeling women's athletics after men's might encourage the negative elitism and poor sportsmanship that marred men's interscholastic sports. As a result of these prevailing attitudes, most women's colleges offered intramural sports programs but lacked intercollegiate athletics. Conversely, schools saw little purpose in organized sports for boys who were not skilled athletes because that model was reserved for girls.

In *Physical Education and Sport in a Changing Society* (1987), Freeman examined the relationship between changes in physical education, athletics, and recreation and social change in America just prior to the period Ainsworth described. During the Depression, when many schools eliminated physical education and Americans attended fewer sporting events, recreation boomed. Jobs programs employed people to create parks and hiking trails, which provided low-cost, accessible activity in contrast to competitive athletics, which involved only highly skilled individuals. Women's sports followed these trends toward broad involvement and dropped competitive events in favor of play days and recreation (pp. 135–136). This culture of sport still shaped physical education for girls and young women during Catherine's tenure at Columbus High School.

Catherine's philosophy was to provide the most activity for the greatest number. When the boys at Columbus High peered through the door of the girls' gym, she invited them in. "I had rented a jukebox and was going to teach the girls social dance," she explained. "I told the boys that I would be glad to help them. Believe it or not, they came in and loved it."

In fact, Catherine introduced coeducational recreation to high school culture long before it became the norm. Recreation, she observed, shifted students' energy from drinking and racing cars to dancing:

> We had a dance in the gym with the jukebox every Friday night. Admission was 20 cents for those who came with a partner and 25 cents for those who came single. We made enough money to buy archery and fencing equipment, to put a balcony on the gym, and to put table tennis up there.

Catherine added, as an aside, that the balcony was also where some girls sat out once a month. Young women who disliked physical education class used menstruation as a ticket out. As prominent physical educator Mabel Lee recalled in her biography, *Memories of a Bloomer Girl* (1977), no one questioned these truants' long, frequent periods. In contrast, young women like Lee, who loved physical activity, convinced their teachers that they had short, regular periods that fell on Saturdays and Sundays of each month so that they never missed physical education classes (p. 62).

In response to Depression-era budget cuts, physical educators worked to improve public awareness about physical education. Catherine produced shows in the school auditorium to sustain student interest in physical education and to teach that it was more than just throwing and catching. She taught several types of dance—folk, modern, social, and tap—at little cost to the school. In conjunction with physical education classes, Catherine organized an annual May festival with a royal court, horses, and folk dancers. She helped define a new relationship among education, culture, and recreation at Columbus High School.

Catherine also coached girls' basketball. In the 1930s, girls and women played a now-obsolete form of basketball. The team consisted of two forwards, two guards, a jump center, and a side center. Educators and sport administrators argued that full-court running was too much activity for females, so rules restricted play to one third of the court. Although the games were highly competitive according to Catherine, competition was primarily intramural with few interscholastic games. Reflecting on the changes in women's athletics since then, Catherine remarked, "The speed of girls' basketball now is almost impossible for me to believe."

Graduate School and World War II Recreation Work

In 1936, while teaching at Columbus High School, Catherine earned her bachelor's degree and began her graduate studies. Since she had promised her grandfather that she would never live more than five hours away during his lifetime, she went only as far as Peabody College in Nashville. She took courses during the summers after her first and second years of teaching at Columbus High School. The classes in tennis, archery, and track and field disappointed her because she had studied these activities in the past. So, in 1939, shortly after her grandfather died, she drove alone, almost 900 miles, to Teachers College, Columbia University, to study in one of the strongest physical education programs in the country.

Catherine gravitated toward active work in New York City to pay her tuition:

> I threw the *New York Times*. I also taught slimnastics at the YWCA in the Bronx. In all my life I had never seen women as big as the ones in that class. They would meet me at the subway at night and walk me through the streets to the YWCA. As soon as class was over, they would say, "Now let's go eat." I worked them all that time; then we'd go have pie and everything. They also drank a lot of beer, which I never cared for, and they put on as much weight as possible.

No matter where or with whom, Catherine entered community easily through movement and recreation.

After completing her master of arts degree at Teachers College in 1941, Catherine moved to the University of Tennessee, where she taught swimming, stunts and tumbling, folk, tap, and modern dance. That same year, when the United States entered World War II, the university housed troops in its gymnasium. Catherine was undeterred. She took her classes outdoors, played her accordion, and taught simple folk dances, such as the Virginia Reel, on the paved road behind the gymnasium. Her classes attracted neighbors and passersby, and before long the community was dancing among her students.

The war touched Catherine personally. Two of her brothers joined the military and were stationed in active fighting areas. Like many women aspiring to support the war, she took a leave of absence from teaching to volunteer with the Red Cross. She was so adept at working with people that the Red Cross asked her to manage officer personnel. Catherine declined the position.

She preferred to work with enlisted men who needed a morale boost. Her assignment, then, was to set up clubs for service personnel on the Micronesian Islands.

During her six weeks of training at American University in Washington, D.C., Catherine learned how to organize carnivals, sing-alongs, and dances. Despite the fun, training was rigorous:

> I remember taking a swimming test and going off the high board in full regalia, wearing fatigues, heavy shoes, a helmet, and a backpack. We jumped from the high board as if we were on a ship. We would jump into the water, get rid of that junk, and get ourselves back to the surface. It was a fierce test. I appreciated the training, but I'm glad I never had to use it.

Catherine Allen with her accordion in the South Pacific, ca. 1944. Northeastern University Libraries, Archives and Special Collections Department.

On December 1, 1944, Catherine and other Red Cross volunteers began their journey by train to Washington state. En route, they squirreled away both summer and winter clothing since they did not know where they were going. Catherine joked that if Red Cross authorities had known she was a Southerner, they surely would have stationed her in the eternal wind and cold of the Arctic Circle.

Catherine still didn't know her destination when her group of volunteers boarded a ship in Washington. Gender segregation on the ship mirrored larger social roles. Women recreation volunteers traveled on the ship's upper level while men in the troops occupied the lower deck. Catherine often sat at the edge of the upper deck and played her accordion while the men below sang. The music, she said, created a wonderful sense of unity among volunteers and troops.

This unity also temporarily blurred differences in social class. Affluent volunteers, including Helen Merrill of Merrill, Lynch, Fenner, Bean, and

Smith and Margaret (Maggie) Vanderbilt, accepted only one dollar a year for their services. And regardless of socio-economic differences among volunteers, the Red Cross treated everyone the same. Catherine recalled,

> One night, I was with eight people in the stateroom. Everyone was seasick except me. While we were in there, we heard a knock on the door. It was Maggie, who asked, "Cat, can you help me?"
> I said, "Of course."
> "Come in and close the door," she said. "Cat, they make us polish our shoes every day, and I have never polished shoes. I have to learn to polish my shoes."
> So we sat on the floor and polished our shoes. She had the shiniest shoes in the Pacific!

As volunteers neared their various Pacific destinations, they celebrated Christmas in 1944 at Maggie Vanderbilt's house in Hawaii. "Christmas was warm," Catherine remembered, "so we went swimming and sang 'Jingle Bells' to the accordion. We even decorated a palm tree or two."

Catherine's training in physical education and recreation served her well in her new role as the recreation director for executive officers and troops on Guam. She and her assistant Kay Brennan adapted entertainment for different locations and varying size crowds. For instance, they established a club on Guam where they performed music and skits for men coming from Iwo Jima and the South Pacific Islands. Catherine and Kay worked closely with Madge Caperton from Texas, whose husband was an army pilot, and volunteer Lorene Wharton from Alabama. Although much of their material, Catherine admitted, was foolish and corny, even the executive officers and the captain would join in and allow themselves to be the butt of jokes. Catherine recalled, "The boys would fall off their chairs as if we were the funniest thing they had ever heard." The shows drew crowds from five to 1500.

Catherine described the accordion as a "marvelous come-on" during their shows:

> We would sing, then ask, "Boys, is anybody here from Texas?" Their hands would go up, and they would hoot and call out, "San Antonio!" "Dallas!" "Fort Worth!" At that, I would bring out Madge, who came from San Antonio. She would banter back and forth with the boys. I'd never heard such a slow, Southern voice in my life.

Shows progressed with this call and response, bringing out the other volunteers from different cities. These shows made the homesick men feel at home. The goals were entertainment and community building. "There was never a pass made by either the men or the women," Catherine emphasized.

For large crowds, Catherine organized carnivals. She would station women in what she considered to be "psychologically good spots." One woman read the men's palms. Catherine admitted, "Of course she was told what to say because we didn't know how to read palms. She would say positive things like, 'You're going to go home and have five children.' I'm convinced that even in very disastrous circumstances, recreation had a lot to do with high morale."

If officers and troops couldn't reach the entertainment, then Catherine and her volunteer crew brought the entertainment to them in the jungle and on ships. One night, Catherine, Lorene, and Madge went into a rain forest battery with a picnic for the men. While a group of men watched the shore for approaching enemy fire, the volunteers told tales and talked about home. Catherine remarked, "I don't know why those boys hadn't lost their minds. All they heard was DRIP, DRIP, DRIP." On a different occasion, when Catherine ventured into a battery, a young man spotted a Japanese soldier aiming to shoot at the base of her spine. The young man knocked her flat on the ground just as a shot rang out. She has always been grateful to that stranger who saved her life. It was not easy to distinguish between enemies and allies. Although she wanted never to relive those days, she would not have missed a minute of the experience.

Catherine's accordion became the heart of recreation when volunteers entertained on ships in the Pacific Ocean area. The war hovered at the edge of their shows, but Catherine carried on. One night during a blackout, she gathered the women on the lower deck and told them to hold hands and lie low in case something serious happened. She then went upstairs to maintain morale among the troops. "When I got up there," she said, "everything was blacked out and I stepped right in the middle of a huge frosted cake. There I stood when it was all over. It was perfect because in the laughter everyone forgot their fear, and believe me, they were afraid."

News of the shows on Guam reached the *Evening Independent* in St. Petersburg, Florida, in August of 1945. The article simultaneously praises their involvement and prescribes their place. It opens with a declaration: "Three single girls from the South who never saw the back of footlights before they came to war are doing professionally competent jobs of entertaining here on the jungle island of Guam" (Wiley, 1945). But after describing the shows and noting Catherine's leadership, it concludes, "So successful has been the program of these three amateur show girls, whose phone rings constantly with requests for more shows, the Red Cross is organizing similar units" (Wiley, 1945). Identifying highly-educated volunteers as "amateur show girls" illustrated prevailing social attitudes toward the volunteers and their work that conflicted with Catherine's deeper philosophy of recreation as a community-building and social-equalizing activity.

Catherine had no doubt that Red Cross volunteers and the activities they organized served a vital role in World War II:

The servicemen would talk to me as if I were a mother, a grandmother, a girlfriend, or a wife. Once a young man who had been badly wounded said to me, "Georgia, you know except for you and a bulldozer we would have lost this damn war." He was not talking about Catherine Allen; he was talking about recreation.

Doctoral Studies with Legendary Physical Educators

When Catherine returned to the United States in 1946, doctors detained her in California because of fungus in her lungs. She took advantage of her location by auditing courses in philosophy of physical education, dance, theater, and speech at UCLA. "I was not going for credit," she emphasized. "I was going to learn." When her health improved, she returned to the University of Tennessee. For six months of the year, she worked exclusively with physical education and recreation majors and graduate students.

During the other six months of the year, Catherine taught recreation in rural Tennessee and in other Southern states. She developed the Tennessee Statewide Recreation Leadership Training Program to educate teachers in rural areas. Her programs included all ages in order to accommodate entire families who arrived at workshops together. Program leaders taught methods for organizing folk dance, simple, quiet games, and active games. This training relied on Catherine's talent for innovation:

> In Tennessee we taught in strange places as we had done in the Pacific. We taught them how to get farmer Jones to let his field be used for outdoor sports, how to dam a creek to get enough depth to teach swimming, and how to sew together potato sacks and string them between two trees to made a volleyball net. We used what we had, taking leadership where it could be found and giving what training we could. During the interim, trainees had obligations to go back and teach in their churches, garages, or organizations, such as the Future Farmers or Homemakers of America.

Despite the challenges and rewards of this work, Catherine yearned to learn more. In 1954, she took a second leave of absence from the University of Tennessee to pursue her doctorate at New York University (NYU). New York City was the hub of progressive concepts in physical education that had been evolving since the 1920s. Physical educators Dr. Jesse Feiring Williams and Dr. Thomas D. Wood at Teachers College, Columbia, and Dr. Jay B. Nash at NYU were advocating exercise for women that was more natural than the previously required gymnastics, stunts and tumbling, and other activities deemed appropriate for women. They introduced games and sports into women's physical education curricula.

Catherine described Nash as a fine host in the city.

> When I arrived, he called me and said, "I hear you're from the South." When I said that I was, he invited me to breakfast. I wore a red suit, which he loved. When I arrived at their

apartment, they had a rocking chair for me, and Jay had planned a Southern breakfast of grits, scrambled eggs and fish eggs. Where he had gotten the idea for fish eggs, I don't know.

Nash then mentored Catherine during the summers of her doctoral program when they worked together at Camp Sebago, a retreat in upstate New York where graduate students traditionally spent a summer quarter. Catherine taught classes, planned programs, and organized trips. She believed that she was chosen for the job because she could "sell" physical education to the country as masterfully as her father had sold flour and cotton to the old mercantiles.

Although Catherine studied under many qualified physical educators, Jay B. Nash captivated her utmost respect. She viewed Nash as "one of the greatest philosophers of recreation":

> He was a precious man. He should have been solely an orator because he was an eloquent speaker with a spiritual quality. He used to prop his foot up on a boulder on Sunday nights and deliver what would have been a magnificent homily in any cathedral. He spoke of values, love of our fellow men and women, fair play, and the ultimate importance of physical education, recreation, and youth work.

Nash's values reinforced Catherine's belief that recreation was integral to community, as she had experienced as a child, as a young teacher, and more recently as a Red Cross volunteer.

Nash's philosophy of sport embodied his legacy to Catherine's generation. Nash encouraged the participation of individuals at all skill levels. As early as 1928, following women's increasing participation on Amateur Athletic Union teams and in industrial leagues, Nash ideologically opposed the separation of athletics from a school's education program. In his article "Athletics for Girls," he argued that the results of this schism were, in many cases, "the earmarks of bad athletics ... *intensive coaching of a few, neglect of the many, spectators, gate receipts, State and National championships*" (432). He believed that all learning was acquired through mental and physical activity. Athletic teams that allowed only the most skilled to perform for crowds created passive onlookers who had nowhere to perform at their own capacity. Nash further insisted that "every child in the school be given an opportunity to take part in *activities adapted to his capacities*" (433). Developing women's athletic teams according to men's rules would alienate some women just as men's elite sports had alienated recreational athletes. Nash argued that activities designed to meet young girls' needs would provide the foundation for proper physical development.

Although Nash's theory about girls' and women's physical education and sport was radical in the late 1920s, his general beliefs about female ability mirrored dominant social attitudes. For instance, Nash speculated that young women's physical abilities were inherently limited by their sex. Enumerating the factors necessary for girls' development, he stated that with the adaption of activities to needs, "the programme of activities of girls will differ very decidedly from that of activities for boys" (Nash, 1928, p. 434). He reasoned that girls had been less active than boys up to that time, so plunging them into sudden vigorous activity would be dangerous. Nash was even more concerned about the physiological changes a girl experienced at adolescence. He wrote,

> The dangers which are involved in throwing a girl suddenly into the highly charged emotional situation of an athletic game, where she is a representative of the school and there are many spectators, is well pointed out by the experience of Dr. St. Clair Lindsley, who has had wide experience in her capacity as advisor for girls in connection with the Los Angeles public schools: "The entire endocrine balance is being established and the adolescent girl who is subjected to highly emotional situations is but sowing the seed for a nervous breakdown later on by putting undue stress on these glands of internal secretion, which are trying to adjust themselves to the physiological changes taking place at that time" [1928, p. 435].

Catherine didn't say whether or not she believed the prevailing myths about female physiology. Nash nevertheless influenced her to advocate for physical education and recreation for all, as well as moderate competition through intramural sports.

During her doctoral study at NYU, Catherine became nationally recognized for her teacher training and was invited to speak and teach at seminars throughout the world. She traveled to the 1952 Olympics in Helsinki for the first World Seminar on Health, Physical Education, Recreation, and Youth Work, where educators from around the world discussed issues in their field and exchanged ideas about working with various groups. Catherine's presentation on her recreation experiences during the war was a unique contribution.

The most memorable event of the trip occurred during the return to New York through Denmark, Norway, Sweden, and Finland. Catherine was one of 17 Americans aboard the Anna Salén, a Swedish passenger ship that accommodated approximately 600 passengers. On August 13, the ship was diverted to pick up 300 people displaced throughout Europe. Catherine, who was in charge of recreation, recalled the terrifying events of that tour:

> We went through the Kiel Canal at night and didn't really know where we were. Instead of going through the English Channel, we went through the North Sea. We were rammed at midnight by a Norwegian mother whaler loaded with oil and blubber. I remember the exact time because I was running recreation and I stopped activities every night at midnight. It's impossible to know how we stayed afloat because there was water coming in at the bottom and there were flames at the top of the boat.

Several people considered jumping overboard into the icy North Sea. Catherine observed,

> It's strange what people do when they expect to die, and we expected to die. One lady put on her brand new outfit from Paris. Some people got on their knees and prayed. Other people sang. The American boys played table tennis. Our problem with them was that they were smoking and flicking their cigarette butts over the side of the ship onto the oil. But somehow we made it through the night. At daybreak, the captain gave the "all clear" signal, and we were towed slowly around the north end of Scotland.

Catherine once again drew from her eclectic leadership experience to help maintain morale during the crisis.

On the Move: Mid-Career Administration

Catherine's doctoral course work and professional activities were superior. Recognizing her strengths, NYU appointed her chair of its women's physical education department after she graduated. Her specific missive was to rebuild the women's department and to speak throughout the country about women's physical education. In 1955, Catherine resigned from the University of Tennessee and devoted her attention to the needs of NYU.

The new position offered considerable responsibility but limited resources. "We didn't have the best facilities," Catherine recalled, "so we went to a YMCA for swimming, and somewhere else to play field hockey." While the department offered dance, sports, theory, and practice, Catherine described her focus as simply "good physical education." In that mindset, she accomplished her main goals at NYU within two years. She rebuilt the women's department into a strong educational program, raised morale among students and faculty, and promoted new ideas in physical education throughout the country. She also published *Fun for Parties and Programs* (1956), a step-by-step guide to leading social recreation programs that reflected her expertise in recreation. In 1957, she felt the time was right to leave NYU.

Catherine's personal life contributed to her decision. Living in the city and entertaining family and visitors had left her heavily in debt. So when the University of Pittsburgh offered to double her NYU salary, Catherine could not refuse. She accepted a dual appointment to teach physical education and to coordinate special activities.

The move introduced Catherine to another physical education legend: Minnie Lynn. Minnie, who had been at the University of Pittsburgh for 19 years, mentored Catherine. Through the years, they developed a close friendship that would further shape Catherine's career. Catherine described Minnie as a brilliant scholar and a personable, petite, attractive person. A graduate of Oberlin College, Minnie was the first woman to receive a Distinguished Alumna Award. Although Minnie was best known as a health educator, she played professional basketball before she was a teacher. "She was so tiny that she would run under the other players' arms," Catherine recalled. When circumstances called for it, Catherine noted, she had "a backbone of steel." She added, "There were things that she had to do that a brave man with a sword wouldn't have tackled. I have the greatest respect for Minnie Lynn."

One pivotal incident in their relationship occurred shortly after Catherine returned from Mexico, where she had studied Mexican culture and dance under the auspices of a Pan-American Scholarship. Minnie invited her to speak at McKinley High School in Canton, Ohio. "My speech was about Mexico and was full of dancing, laughing, and clapping," Catherine explained.

> It seemed like a great speech because everyone was laughing and shaking my hand afterwards. Then Minnie came up to me and said, "Cat, I never want to hear that speech again."
> I asked Minnie if she had seen the reaction of those people.
> She said, "Yes, but I've heard that speech five times."
> I said, "Well, I didn't invite you; you just came."
> She replied, "You know, I think it's time for you to broaden your base. Use examples if you like, but learn to speak about...."
> She then gave me a list of all the subjects I was to explore. Minnie was my second tutor, after Aunt Edna.

Catherine and Minnie became an invincible professional duo. When the executive committee of Bouvé-Boston School, an outgrowth of the Boston School of Physical Education, offered Minnie the director's position in 1960, she had no difficulty securing Catherine a position as her assistant. The decision to move was difficult for the two women because they were happy in Pittsburgh. The ethnic mix of people in the city introduced great variety to the folk dance, music, and crafts programs they taught. The deciding moment came when Felix Pereira, chair of the executive committee of Bouvé-Boston School, told Minnie they were desperate and needed a leader who would guide them into the 21st century. The executive committee had already voted to close the school if it could not hire a national figure to direct its future. Minnie's dedication to the history of Bouvé-Boston School and to the school's continuity prompted her to accept the challenge. When Minnie asked Catherine to go as her assistant, Catherine told her, "Sure! Young people are young people. It doesn't matter where I am."

On May 6, 1960, Catherine and Minnie arrived at Bouvé-Boston School on the campus of Tufts University. They had barely unpacked when Tufts' provost asked Minnie if she would release Catherine part-time to coordinate special activities for students and to develop unity among various groups on campus. Once again, Catherine found herself building community through recreation.

After assessing the state of the School, Catherine and Minnie concluded that it would never thrive at Tufts. Tufts had proposed to merge Bouvé-Boston School with Jackson College, Tufts' women's college. Minnie fiercely opposed this merger because Bouvé-Boston's faculty would have been released and its buildings closed; she refused to let the School give up its traditions. Catherine and Minnie searched for an institutional atmosphere that would suit the changing needs of the school. They were interested in Northeastern University for its cooperative education plan. Students attended classes for one quarter, and then worked at a job in their field for the next quarter. They earned tuition money *and* experience. This plan extended the typical four-year college plan to five years, but, according to Catherine, students were "beautifully educated." She favored a cooperative plan because she valued her own college work experience and wanted the same for Bouvé-Boston women.

As Catherine and Minnie crafted Bouvé-Boston's future, the Civil Rights Movement and the second wave of U.S. feminism initiated social changes that would impact physical education and athletics across the country. During 1962 and 1963, Catherine and Minnie commuted between Tufts and Northeastern to oversee plans for the consolidation. Northeastern granted all of Minnie's requests. New facilities included a dance studio, a recreation room, a gymnasium, a swimming pool, and an outdoor center. The most radical directive, however, came from Northeastern's President Asa Knowles. He wanted Northeastern's men's department of physical education and Bouvé-Boston's women's department to become a single, coeducational program. Still ten years before Title IX, separate physical education and athletics departments for women and men were the norm. Minnie conceded, and Catherine credited her with the congenial and effective merging of the departments: "In spite of the possibility of real conflict over maintaining a four-year curriculum, Minnie was able to introduce the women's program into a complex situation at Northeastern."

Bouvé-Boston was still transitioning in 1964 when Catherine was elected president of the American Alliance for Health, Physical Education, and Recreation (AAHPER). Her highest priority as president was to inspire and support creativity in physical education and recreation programs. She invented the term "creative-innovative intelligence" to define the conception of new ideas, particularly new methods of doing old or familiar things. According to Catherine, this creativity has empowered many leaders, for good or for bad, including John F. Kennedy, Al Capone, Richard Nixon, and Ronald Reagan. Her presidential activities encouraged educators to be creative with existing resources and programs. Of equal importance were her efforts, in conjunction with President Lyndon Johnson's Elementary and Secondary Education Act, to ensure that physical education facilities were included in all new schools built in the United States. Her continuing emphasis on access, inspired by Jay B. Nash, contributed to physical and philosophical infrastructures that would later support changes effected by Title IX.

Expanding International Influence and Late-Career Administration

Fully immersed in her work, Catherine cultivated lifelong friendships through professional liaisons. Her bond with Dorothy Ainsworth began in 1960, as Dorothy was completing her 34-year tenure as Smith College's Director of Physical Education. A world traveler, Dorothy was a founding member of the International Association of Physical Education and Sport for Girls and Women (IAPESGW) and the International Council on Health, Physical Education and Recreation (ICHPER). Dorothy had invited Catherine to lead recreation and singing at the 1960 World Congress of IAPESGW in Washington, D.C., where the two first met, and to facilitate international groups through ICHPER. This relationship deepened Catherine's world view of physical education and recreation.

Catherine's favorite stories about Dorothy recalled their travels:

> I carried her pocketbook practically everywhere we went. She had one the size of a man's suitcase, and she had a horrible habit of setting it down and leaving it. She carried a mint of money because she always bought gifts when we traveled; she was very generous. She left her pocketbook on the counter in a gift shop in Atlantic City once. When we got back to the hotel, she said, "Cat, where is my pocketbook?"
> I said, "You didn't give it to me. You must have left it in that last gift shop."
> I was glad I had track and field practice, but I still nearly broke my neck getting down there to pick up that pocketbook. They remembered me because of all the gifts she had bought. Her pocketbook was the heaviest load I have ever carried. It was worse than an accordion, and that's heavy.

As Catherine traveled, she dismantled language and culture barriers with music and song. In 1965, she attended a conference in Ethiopia co-sponsored by ICHPER and the World Confederation of Organizations of the Teaching Profession. The meeting was held in the Center for African Unity, which was patterned after the United Nations building. Representatives from around the world gathered to exchange ideas on contemporary issues in their fields. They were seated in a semi-circular pattern with their names and countries on a placard in front of them, and everyone had access to a translation machine. During one session, Catherine donned her accordion and taught the group "Kumbaya." The song was translated into French and Swahili. As groups sang each of the different languages together, participants were moved by what Catherine described as a "deeply spiritual experience." According to Catherine, the Ethiopian conference was "the epitome of the influence of music and movement."

Catherine's traveling programs established her as an international recreation liaison. When jogging became a U.S. fitness trend during the 1980s, interested Czechoslovakian physical educators contacted Catherine. They asked her to help one of Czechoslovakia's outstanding physical educators escape from behind the Iron Curtain to observe and study fitness in the United States. Catherine was uncertain exactly how, but the Czech educator made it to the United States. Serving as ambassador, Catherine noted that he was "wide-eyed over the types of freedom and the great diversity of programs we had." Catherine considered such a visit a vital part of international relations.

Catherine's international efforts were honored in 1989 when she received the Dorothy Sears Ainsworth Award. Receiving the award was "a very humbling experience":

> The fact that it is international means that there is a lot of understanding among us whether or not we speak the same language, whether or not we worship in the same way. We all worship the same God, a creator greater than we are, but we have chosen different avenues. To me, it was a great tribute to Dorothy Ainsworth's philosophy and vision in founding IAPESGW. She wanted to give more opportunities to women, particularly in developing countries. She felt that in this way, delegates from these countries could take back ideas on health, physical education, recreation, and the implementation of dance into schools. It certainly was one of the greatest honors every bestowed on me.

Although traveling consumed considerable time and energy, Catherine remained dedicated to Bouvé-Boston School. In 1964, the School was renamed Boston-Bouvé College to reflect its roots in the Boston School of Physical Education. Three years later, at the age of 58, Catherine became dean of the College and acting chair of the newly established recreation department.

As dean during the tumultuous 1960s, Catherine confronted students protesting the Vietnam War. She noticed that the people most agitated by current affairs were students and graduates of prestigious schools, such as Harvard and MIT, in the Boston area. Activities were fierce at Northeastern because its dormitories were located near those of the many other colleges and universities in downtown Boston. Catherine was close to the conflict:

> While I was dean, some of our students picketed and threw bricks and bottles at the police. I lived in my office for a while because students threatened to bomb the ROTC building, which was right behind our building. It's not that I could have done much alone, but the closet with brooms and buckets was right next to my office. If a fire started, at least I could have put water on it.

In the same way that she had emphasized group unity during World War II and in her rural teaching program, Catherine encouraged faculty and students to work together. She met with them daily in the recreation room to calm their tempers, to talk about the war, and to discuss the directions they should take. "During that time we cemented our relationships," Cather-

Catherine Allen, Conference for Teachers and Supervisors of Elementary School Physical Education, Washington, D.C., October 1968. SHAPE America.

ine recalled. "One important aspect of being a dean was to understand the faculty, staff, and students. I let them know that I cared for them and that if I had to discipline them, it was because I cared." In an effort to prevent riots that were destroying campus communities throughout the country, Catherine established a student advisory board whose main task was to solve problems before they exploded. "I guess I'm a problem solver," she said in retrospect.

Catherine served as dean for ten years. As in the past, she left the position when she had accomplished specific goals and felt the work no longer demanded her particular talents. She then moved from the gym into the administrative building in 1977 to work as special assistant to Northeastern President Dr. Kenneth G. Ryder. In that role, she wrote a history of Boston-Bouvé College and did administrative work until her retirement in 1981, at age 72. She continued to serve the university as professor emerita for several years.

Reflecting on Work and Play

Catherine came of age professionally when higher education did not require overspecialization:

> I enjoyed the thrill of working at every level, with the very young to the very oldest. When segregation still existed in the South, I taught illiterate blacks and whites together at night at a black school in Georgia. It was a real challenge to learn and an even greater thrill to see a person write his or her name, instead of an X, for the first time.

Lifelong interest in and activity through recreation and physical education reflected Catherine's philosophy of work: "A person has a right to stop, but as long as she is alert, has experiences to share and young people to guide, she should stay active." Likewise, her advice to young professionals was straightforward. She recommended that anyone interested in the field should get involved immediately. She reasoned, "When we realize that we are at the core of total health and well-being, I can think of no greater missionary work than ours."

Rather than viewing retirement as the end of her career, Catherine anticipated the time when she would "be able to dream, write, think, listen to music, garden, visit with friends, and travel." She added, "I also saw it as a time to continue my professional commitment." Although various surgeries, including a hip replacement, limited her physical activities as she turned 80, she rose early each morning to listen to music and prepare for a day of research, writing, and work in various professional associations. She no longer played her accordion as much as she wanted, primarily because of its weight, but she had entertained colleagues and students at conferences well into her late seventies. Catherine shared her secret of longevity, which would sustain her until her death at the age of 91. "My mind governs my body, and I can keep myself completely calm," she confided. "I don't have any problem with diet or stress management. I balance active times with quiet times, my public life with my private life."

As Catherine reflected on a full career, she articulated a philosophy of living that synthesized all of her stories:

> My family and some teachers, in English for example, never understood why in the world anyone would need to go to college to learn how to play. Perhaps they had forgotten that our profession is based in the sciences: biology, physiology, kinesiology, and motor learning. Perhaps they had forgotten that the human body is the greatest instrument that has ever been created. It has a soul. If a person's greatest capability is to play, that's magnificent. What could be greater?

2

Ruth Schellberg
Guiding Girls and Women through the Wilderness

Ruth Schellberg was an environmentalist before the word, as we know it today, existed. As a longtime Camp Fire Girls leader and a professor of physical education, Ruth shared her love and respect for canoeing with students and colleagues. Her teaching empowered women by instilling in them the courage to confront and find a place in the natural world in ways that were traditionally prohibited. At the time of her interview in 1988, more than 400 women had experienced one of Ruth's week-long sojourns; some accompanied her on as many as eight trips. The reason, perhaps, is as Ruth said: "Once you have gone on a canoe trip with someone, you have a friend for life."

Childhood Adventures

The oldest of four children, Ruth was born in Omaha, Nebraska, in 1912, "in the day of horse and buggy doctors." When the doctor failed to arrive in time for her birth, her grandmother delivered her. Ruth's father, Otto Emil Schellberg, managed an office for the Western Union Telegraph Company. At a very young age she observed women working as secretaries, nurses, or teachers. She also noticed that most women's careers ended when they married.

Early childhood camping experiences inspired Ruth's lifelong involvement with the Camp Fire Girls of America, which is now the co-ed organization Camp Fire. "My father was very interested in the Boy Scouts because of his three sons," Ruth explained. "Before they were old enough to be in the scouting program, he became a volunteer for the Boy Scouts. He would take the family to stay in the weekend cabins operated by the Boy Scout camp before I was eligible for Camp Fire camp."

Already a seasoned camper at age 11, Ruth attended Camp Iwaqua at Little Sioux, Iowa, 50 miles from her home. She became so fascinated with canoes that she chose *gaonouh*, a Native American word for canoe, as her Camp Fire symbol. But she was forbidden to ride in a canoe until she learned to swim.

A boating accident during Ruth's third summer at Camp Fire Girls camp turned out to be a pivotal incident in her life:

> As we entered camp, we had to be taken by rowboat across the lake, and the boat capsized. I blacked out and didn't know what was happening to me, except that I was in the water. I was later told that I had been a problem to one of my friends, who was a fair swimmer, because she couldn't get away from me. Somehow someone got me to the side of the boat, and when I became conscious I was grasping the boat. I was frightened by the experience.

Ruth Schellberg, ca. 1970s. Courtesy University Archives at Minnesota State University, Mankato.

A physical education major who witnessed the accident took Ruth back to her cabin, collected her swimming suit, and brought her back to the lake for a swimming lesson. On that day, Ruth learned to float face down in the water, more commonly known as the "dead man's float." She recalled, "This experience taught me that I had a mission in life, and that mission was to teach the world how to swim!" More importantly at the time, learning to swim entitled Ruth to get in a canoe.

Ruth saw glimpses of her vocation during her summers at Camp Iwaqua:

> I met many college students in physical education from the University of Nebraska and the University of Iowa. Each of these people seemed to have a very exciting professional life ahead of them. I decided that I would like to go to college, even though it was not a part of my family's background. That's when I determined that I would be a physical education major.

Up to that point in her life, however, Ruth had relatively no experience with organized physical education. "They *tried* to teach me to skip in kindergarten," she joked. During high school, in the mid–1920s, she was a member of the intramural basketball and swim teams and captain of the senior class water polo team. More than formal education, her Camp Fire experiences and her innate love for outdoor activities led her into physical education.

College and Early Career

Ruth's decision to attend college challenged the Schellbergs' assumption that only their sons would pursue higher education. As a member of Midland College's Board of Directors, Otto Schellberg was certain that his sons would attend Midland. He had never even considered that Ruth would want to go to college. Her family, nevertheless, supported her decision. "My father thought that I could attend Midland College," she explained. "I told him that I couldn't major in physical education at Midland and that I would have to go to the state university. He accepted that and was very supportive."

In September of 1930, Ruth enrolled at the University of Nebraska–Lincoln as a physical education major. The University of Iowa offered more courses in swimming and canoeing, but the out-of-state tuition was prohibitive. She paid her room and board costs by caring for children and doing domestic chores in the off-campus houses where she lived during her first three years at the university. During her senior year, she lived in St. Elizabeth Hospital Nurses Home, where she directed recreation for student nurses.

Ruth had no regrets. As a first-year student at the University of Nebraska, she experienced the influential mentoring of Mabel Lee. Throughout her years at summer camp, Ruth had heard countless stories from counselors who were Lee's former students. Lee's Orientation of Physical Education course gave Ruth an arena in which to ask questions about her expectations of the major and the physical education curriculum. While inquiring about the major, Ruth developed a better understanding of the profession. Then, when Lee served as the first woman president of the American Physical Education Association (APEA) during Ruth's junior year, news of the annual convention furthered Ruth's commitment to her major. She explained,

> I still recall the seniors who came back from the convention at which she presided. They were very supportive of all of her activities. They acted as her telephone people and took on other responsibilities. It was very exciting to have them come back and tell how it was to be students of the first woman to be president of APEA.

As Mabel Lee guided Ruth into the profession, she also inspired her philosophy of administration.

> I didn't think in terms of administration when I was an undergraduate. As I moved forward in my curriculum, I simply was thinking of being a teacher at the college level. But one of

the things I remember copying very carefully into my notebook was that an administrator is expected to set the stage so that other members of her staff can function. That idea stayed with me through all of my years of college administration because I've seen so many administrators who are not interested in what their staff members are doing but only in how they can promote themselves and their research.

On her commencement day in 1934, Ruth interviewed for her first teaching job with the Nebraska City superintendent of schools. She recalled,

> The interview was very interesting because the superintendent had had some bad experiences with English teachers who taught physical education. He wanted to be sure that he hired a physical education teacher. She might have to teach seventh grade grammar, but he believed it would be more fair to the student body if the school had someone with expertise in physical education.

When Ruth arrived in Nebraska City the following Monday, the superintendent informed her that although he supported her hire, she would have to sell herself to the board of education. Armed with a map of Nebraska City's business district, Ruth visited several businesses owned by school board members to introduce her qualifications. She was convinced that she received the appointment because of her Camp Fire Girls experience:

> All of the school board members had daughters. The president of the school board had three daughters, and the middle one didn't have a leader for her Camp Fire club. I became the volunteer executive director for the 13 Camp Fire groups in Nebraska City.

During her first year in the Nebraska City public schools, Ruth founded a Camp Fire Girls group for blind girls. According to Ruth, it was the first and only one of its kind. Since the Depression had forced the school to eliminate home economics classes, administrators moved students from Nebraska's School for the Blind into the abandoned home economic rooms where they could learn to cook. Under Ruth's supervision, sighted Camp Fire girls assisted the blind girls. "They were very enthusiastic and wrote letters to the school administrators concerning their experiences," Ruth recalled. "The blind children enjoyed many Camp Fire experiences that were possible only because we were able to match them with sighted Camp Fire girls." After a year and a half of this activity, the superintendent joked with Ruth, "You know, you have the school board convinced that Camp Fire is a school subject!"

Although Ruth realistically did not view Camp Fire as part of the curriculum, she supported it as a vital part of her students' education. After her first year in Nebraska City, she escorted 60 girls to Camp Fire camp in Lincoln where they enjoyed the same outdoor activities that boys experienced in Boy Scouts. She also worked at Spokane Camp Fire camp during those summers.

Graduate School and New Career Goals

After completing the two years of teaching experience that Mabel Lee had recommended, Ruth enrolled in New York University's master of physical education program. Ruth asserted that every major in her era had to choose between Columbia University, where the renowned Dr. Jesse Feiring Williams taught, and New York University, where the equally respected Dr. Jay B. Nash taught. Again prompted by Mabel Lee's advice, Ruth chose to study under Nash at NYU. Like Catherine Allen, Ruth described Nash's courses as "the most influential." Her coursework focused on camp leadership experiences and "anything that had to do with camping, canoeing, and swimming." Her study culminated in a master's thesis on camp leadership training courses.

In 1937, after receiving her master's degree in physical education, Ruth was eligible to teach college as she had so long aspired to do. During the 1937–38 academic year, she filled a one-year sabbatical replacement position at the University of Minnesota for a salary of $1200. She explained, "I went

Ruth Schellberg leading a canoe trip in the Minnesota Boundary Waters Canoe Area. No date. Courtesy University Archives at Minnesota State University, Mankato.

to Minnesota because a Camp Fire counselor had once told me that if I liked canoeing as much as I did, then I had better go to Minnesota."

The following year, Ruth became the director of physical education for women at Macalester College in St. Paul. She described her eight years in that position as "a very, very satisfying experience" through which she combined her professional activities and personal recreation interests. She taught canoeing and hiking to college classes that, like many across the country, were driven out of the gymnasiums by the Army Air Corps during World War II. Many of those activities remained in the curriculum after classes returned to their indoor facilities. And, as leader of the Women's Aquatic League, the College's extracurricular swimming club, Ruth enthusiastically supported the tradition of canoeing the St. Croix River.

Ruth's wilderness sojourns were cutting edge adventures because "there were no other women in canoe country." She believed that women took to the sport because it offered them adventure:

> So often things that were hardships were best remembered, and they were often the very reasons that people wanted to go back. We always said that the most excitement came when we had problems with the weather or problems with wild animals. Those two things just made the trip! The number of portages you took and/or how many men you met also were memorable.

In July 1941, Ruth's canoeing classes attracted national interest through a *Life* magazine feature story. Gasoline shortages during the War had forced the classes to be moved from the St. Croix River to the Minnesota River under the Mendota Bridge. When the Minnesota Tourist Bureau contacted *Life* regarding women and canoes, it discovered that Macalester College was the only school in the state offering canoeing classes for women. *Life* then sent Wallace W. Kirkland, accompanied by Vic Johnston of the Minnesota Tourist Bureau, to determine which two of the 53 Women's Aquatic League members would represent the group in a feature story about outdoor vacations.

Ruth described the selection process as "very interesting." It went without saying that the two chosen should be strong swimmers, senior life savers, and water safety instructors. But *Life* and the Tourist Bureau were looking for more than ability:

> At the Tourist Bureau, they put pictures of all fifty-three women along-side one another and then selected the two who had even teeth and vivacious expressions. That's how they selected the two, and then for eight days Wallace Kirkland and two commercial guides from Border Lakes Outfitting took the trip.

As happy as they were to be featured in the article, Norma (Penny) Penschuck and Floreine (Flo) Kelly were dissatisfied with the roles delegated by the male organizers. Ruth, who chaperoned, explained,

> We didn't get to do any of the things that we believed were the most fun except when they were taking pictures. As soon as the pictures were taken of us paddling stern, putting up a tent, cooking over an open fire, or catching fish, we were immediately detained to wash dishes or blow up the guides' air mattresses.

The article's real agenda was tourist promotion, so it emphasized the adventure and beauty aspects of the trip. It claimed,

> The girls set up their tent every night, caught and cleaned their own fish, cooked their own food. As they went along they saw a porcupine nibbling happily on a small tree, watched a fawn dart back to its mother from the stream bank, made friends with a baby tern ["Vacations," 1941].

Although these statements described a typical trip, the male crew from *Life* appropriated these tasks on this particular outing. The article also reminded readers that these were "girls" in the wilderness by including a photo of them curling their hair. Its caption read, "Far from the haunts of men, the girls nevertheless applied cream and curled themselves every night by candlelight" ("Vacations," 1941). Ruth remarked, "The pictures were posed. They only curled their hair when they knew their picture was going to be taken."

Vocation, Avocation and Leadership

Ruth knew what she wanted in 1946, when she left Macalester to join the faculty at Mankato State Teachers College as an assistant professor in physical education:

> I moved to Mankato State Teachers College because I wanted to teach to a major in physical education. Mankato State offered a major, and I was able to continue offering classes in camp administration, camp leadership, and many of the other courses that I had developed at Macalester.

Despite the opportunities at Mankato State, Ruth stayed only two years. She then took a leave of absence to earn her doctorate in physical education at New York University. Again melding her vocation and avocation, she wrote a doctoral dissertation entitled "Evaluation of the Camping Program of Camp Fire Girls in Terms of the Characteristics and Needs of Girls 7–17."

As Ruth was completing her dissertation, Mabel Lee offered her an associate professorship at the University of Nebraska–Lincoln. Ruth would replace Aileene Lockhart, who had supported Lee's work as director of the department of physical education for women. Ruth accepted the position knowing that Lee was planning to retire in three years; she viewed it as a short-term effort to help a respected colleague. Meanwhile, her heart remained in Minnesota's canoe country.

In return for Ruth's allegiance, Mabel Lee helped Ruth establish an outdoor recreation program at the University of Nebraska. Lee had accompanied Ruth on a canoe trip in 1943, so she was well acquainted with her love for the Boundary Waters. Although Nebraska had no canoeing areas, the women improvised: "Mabel Lee purchased from the 'towel fund' five Grumman aluminum canoes and a trailer which we took to an artificial pond near the Lincoln campus. We taught canoeing during the week, and on weekends we took students on the Blue River."

In 1952, following Mabel Lee's retirement, Ruth returned to Mankato State Teachers College as the first chair of the new women's physical education department. Prior to her appointment, physical education did not exist as a department and was governed by the division head for health, physical education, and recreation. The enticing offer came from Mankato State President C.L. Crawford, a former school superintendent in Council Bluffs, Iowa, who knew and respected Ruth from her early teaching days. Ruth described Crawford as "a very ambitious man who collected faculty members with doctorates."

As a department chair, 20 years before the passage of Title IX, Ruth faced common challenges created by the evolution of women's physical education and athletics:

> I discovered many women coming to major in physical education from a cheerleading rather than a sports background. I was on national and state "sport for every girl" committees fighting for gymnasium, pool, and field time. With the eventual restoration of women's interscholastic teams, I faced the problem of credit loading for coaching for some very dedicated and effective women coaches.

The challenge was further complicated by the reality that many of the women coaching newly-formed intercollegiate teams had never played on one. They had come of age participating in play days and intramural sports. Ruth found herself guiding a first generation of coaches through unknown waters.

Despite the energy she devoted to her administrative duties, Ruth remained passionate about teaching, particularly through the summer school canoe trips she led. Although she initially disliked the idea of teaching summer school in the Boundary Waters, the president convinced her to develop the first outdoor education course for graduate students. Once the course was established, she led many canoe and camping trips for which students received academic credit. She concluded,

> I found that through all of my extracurricular involvements, particularly the ones of a camping nature, I came to know those students better than the students I had in traditional classroom courses. We still exchange Christmas cards, and I hear about all of their families and their trips to the Boundary Waters and to Europe.

In the early 1970s, during Title IX's nascent implementation, the burgeoning women's athletic program at Mankato State College[1] suffered from a lack of funding. Ruth explained her frustration:

> The Title IX impetus to gain equity for the women's program became so difficult that I discovered that I was fighting for more than just women's athletics. If we had women administrators to make all of the decisions about where the funding was to go, we probably would have fared much better than if we simply fought for more athletics for women.

Like so many women physical educators of that era, Ruth pursued higher leadership roles to initiate necessary changes for women.

To that end, Ruth joined the Women's Equity Action League and served as state president during 1974–75. The group filed complaints regarding the lack of women administrators in Minnesota's college system. It called statewide attention to the fact that few women were making judgments regarding the administration of women's athletics and curriculum.

Through her involvement with the Women's Equity Action League, Ruth discovered that women faculty were not paid as much as their male colleagues with the same experience and responsibilities. She then became active in statewide class-action lawsuits seeking back pay for women faculty at all of the Minnesota state colleges. The difficulty was to identify women and men with equal responsibilities on each of the six state campuses. According to Ruth, the male administrators did not cooperate in identifying women and men with equitable experience and responsibilities. She noted that Mankato State's president fully supported their efforts. After pursuing the lawsuit for almost a year, Ruth and other plaintiffs settled out of court and received half of the original claim.

Ruth retired in 1974. Reflecting on her career at MSU, she said her greatest accomplishment was to stimulate women students' interest in intercollegiate athletics. This increased interest was important for Title IX compliance, which requires institutions to demonstrate that current programs accommodate the interests of both female and male students (Carpenter & Acosta, 2005, p. 227). Serendipitously, increasing interest at MSU coincided with the construction of a new men's athletic facility. During space reallocation, the women's program received its own facility. Access to three gymnasiums enabled the physical education department to expand the number of courses and athletic opportunities for women.

Ruth's legacy lives on. In 1981, seven years after she retired, Mankato State University memorialized her successful development of the women's athletic programs by inducting her into the Mankato State University Hall of Fame and Distinction. A decade later, its North Highland Arena was renamed Schellberg Gymnasium to honor the "Woman of the Waterways" (Sloan, 1994).

Ruth acknowledged three individuals who most influenced her professionally. The first was her camp canoeing counselor, Aileene Carpenter, who told her that if she liked canoeing as much as she did, then she belonged in Minnesota. Years later, Ruth and Aileene became reacquainted as professional associates. Another great influence was Mabel Lee, who gave her pride in the profession and served as a guiding mentor during Ruth's early career.

Although Ruth never met her third influence, she expressed profound admiration for Luther Halsey Gulick, a physical educator and co-founder of the Camp Fire Girls. At the University of Nebraska, Ruth had read Gulick's *The Philosophy of Play* (1920), which many physical educators have considered his philosophy of life. Her teaching and recreation pursuits modeled his idea that "the individual is more completely revealed in play than in any one other way; and conversely, play has a greater shaping power over the character and nature of man than has any one other activity" (p. xiv). Ruth elaborated:

> I first knew him as the founder of Camp Fire Girls, during my experience in Camp Fire. I knew him as the person who wanted for his daughters something more than a finishing school education. He was interested in girls' education far in advance of the modern equal rights movement. He made outdoor play significant in the education process and applied it to girls as well as boys. I've read everything he has written, and I count him as the person who started my commitment to equal rights and to the importance of women being a part of an administrative team.

In later years when Gulick enthusiast Gertrude Moulton accompanied Ruth on eight canoe trips, the two women often discussed the philosophies of Gulick and Jay B. Nash:

> Before a canoe trip, we'd travel along the North Shore getting ready to go up the Gunflint Trail or one of the roads that would take us into the wilderness, and she would see all of the tourists who would stop, observe the waterfalls, and get back into the car and go on to the next stop. Gertrude said that those people didn't really know the waterfall. They have to live with it to know it. That was a theme of Nash and Gulick.

Moulton specifically recalled Nash quoting Robert Louis Stevenson and often, during strenuous paddling, repeated, "To travel hopefully is a better thing than to arrive."

Ruth didn't retire her paddles when she left MSU in 1974. In the summer of 1988, at age 76, Ruth guided a group of friends through Europe. At 83, she still guided tours through the Boundary Waters and British Columbia. Ruth led more than 91 canoe trips, all of which are carefully catalogued and some archived at the Minnesota State University, Mankato, Memorial Library. Although she did not portage her own canoe during later trips, her spirit remained powerful.

Ruth's teaching and professional service were widely known and respected among colleagues. She chaired the American Alliance for Health, Physical

Education, Recreation, and Dance (AAHPERD) Archives Historical Advisory Committee for 14 years. She also was an active member in the International Council for Health, Physical Education, and Recreation (ICHPER).[2] In 1993, at the 12th Congress of the International Association of Physical Education and Sport for Girls and Women (IAPESGW) in Melbourne, Australia, Ruth received the Dorothy Sears Ainsworth Award. Established to honor Ainsworth, who "exhibited a profound interest in the teaching and coaching of the world" (Sloan, 1993), the award had been given to only two American women: Catherine Allen (1989) and Ruth Schellberg (1994). Mette Winkler, IAPESGW secretary/treasurer from 1977–89, said in her nomination of Ruth, "I know of nobody who has been more devoted to the work for international understanding and women's rights and who has shown this devotion in practical work in many fields" (Sloan, 1994).

During retirement, Ruth was involved with many community agencies, among them United Way, the senior citizen board, the Camp Fire Council, and the Southern Minnesota Historical Center. She began these activities as a young teacher because they extended her community involvement beyond campus: "I felt that I knew businessmen who shared my concerns about youth in the community. I related well to senior citizens and to the history of Mankato. All of these things meant a great deal to me." She added that her ongoing involvement brought her joy through contacts with former students.

Ruth confided that the secret to her sustained energy and good health was friendship and former students: "There is nothing as mentally invigorating as students and to have people in touch with you over a period of years. Every day I meet a former student who remembers me as being a person who has helped her have a happier life." She also emphasized the importance of staying physically active. Her daily regimen included swimming and walking as long as she was able. She concluded, "I feel that happiness in retirement is related directly to your ability to continue to contribute to your community and to your profession." Ruth stayed active until her death in 2004 at the age of 92. Traveling hopefully, she was thrilled with the journey.

3

Celeste Ulrich
Speaking Out During Title IX Transitions

Celeste Ulrich encountered an unusual challenge as an assistant professor of physical education at the University of North Carolina at Greensboro in 1972. The university had recently merged its women's and men's physical education departments, thinking that Title IX compliance would eventually mandate the change. Without warning, Celeste's fear case swimming course, for students petrified of swimming, became coeducational. She suddenly faced a dilemma:

> I had always taught women. They would cry because they were so frightened. I would sit down, put my arm around their shoulders, and talk to them as a big sister might. I had a great degree of success, but I couldn't use my standard method with a young man. It would have been absolutely devastating for him to have a woman see him cry. And putting my arm around his shoulders would have created a terrible situation.

Celeste visited classes taught by male instructors to see how they encouraged young men in difficult situations. There she observed "the most affectionate of all male gestures":

> They patted the male student on the behind and offered words of encouragement. There was a limit to what I could do, so I devised my own technique: I hit myself. I'd say, "John, I think you can get in there," and *bang, bang, bang*, I banged away at myself. That was acceptable and almost the same as patting the student. So, I tried to use techniques that would challenge him and appeal to his masculinity.

Both the daily challenges and incremental social change involving the enactment of Title IX defined Celeste Ulrich's career. As a result, she became a problem solver and an outspoken advocate for gender equity in physical education and sports. When introducing Celeste at the Ninth Amy Morris Homans Lecture (1975), University of Georgia Professor of Kinesiology Ann E. Jewett boasted, "No speaker in the physical education profession is more in demand to keynote…. Her over 500 major addresses have excited, intrigued, and stimulated us to catch brass rings, to savor old wines, and to listen to new tones." With such intriguing speech titles as "The Mystery of the Invisible Female," "The Demise of Minnie Mouse," and "You Can't Put Backspin on a Beanbag," Celeste's indisputable reputation earned her the nickname "The Silver Tongue" ("Adele Celeste Ulrich," 2013). Interviewed at age 66, the former professor, dean, and active participant in many professional organizations spoke about the current status of women and sport as brightly as when she helped define and implement changes in women's intercollegiate athletics after the passage of Title IX.

Childhood and the Value of Work

Born in Baltimore in 1924, Celeste identified her family, which included her parents, one younger brother, an adopted cousin, and both grandmothers, as "typically middle class." Her father, Frank Ulrich, had gone to work as an errand boy for the Baltimore Gas and Electric Company at age 12, after his father died. He worked full time after high school while attending night school to become an engineer. Although he never completed a degree, he earned a position of great responsibility and always spoke with reverence about "the Company" because of the opportunities it had given him. Frank managed to retain his job throughout the Depression, enabling the family to live frugally but quite well. Celeste grew up observing and emulating his dedication to a profession.

Celeste's mother, Adele Seidewitz Ulrich, excelled in high school science and hoped for a career in chemistry. But when her father died, the economic reality of caring for her mother forced her to find work with little regard for her own advancement. Choosing among the positions most readily available to women—teaching, nursing, and stenographic work—Celeste's mother worked as a mathematics stenographer. She defied tradition at the time when she resumed work as a comptometer operator two years after the birth of her youngest child. She computed so efficiently with newly emerging computers that she eventually became vice president of a company that manufactured slipcovers. She worked steadily until her retirement.

It seemed natural to Celeste that her mother worked, even though her position initially caused family tension. She explained,

> At first, my father was a bit embarrassed to have his wife work because her employment was obviously necessary to support our extended family. But he slowly took pride in her talents because she did so well. I don't think he would have been able to accept the idea that she could earn a bigger salary than his, but since she didn't, he never faced the situation.

Adele Ulrich often told Celeste that a person's mission in life was to serve other people and "whatever God you believe in." Celeste admired her mother for being both selfless and smart:

> Although Mom was not there to kiss my scraped knee when I was growing up, I never felt neglected because on weekends we did marvelous things together. Quite honestly, I felt sorry for my peers who had housewifely mothers. My mother was vibrant, alert, and alive. When she came home, we discussed the economy and our opinions on national problems. My friends' mothers talked about which pair of socks they should wear.

Her mother's words resonated in Celeste's memory: "You must also serve your job, your family, or whatever is most important to you. After that, you worry about yourself. Always put yourself third."

In response to their parents' dedication, the Ulrich children worked hard to help the family and shared in its governance. If they neglected the daily grocery shopping and laundry, then the family went without food or clean clothes. Celeste gained confidence by participating in decision making: "We had a good opportunity to discuss our ideas and to bring our hopes and dreams to arguments. As a result, I learned that my opinions had some merit."

Celeste's early confidence was reinforced at Howard Park Elementary School. Her greatest training was in public speaking. "We had to stand in front of the class and speak on a given topic," she recalled. "It was all extemporaneous. As a result of those assignments, I learned to express my ideas and accept criticism." Despite its richness, the curriculum lacked physical education. The teacher who visited once a week to supervise games did not teach sport skills. Celeste's greatest physical opportunities as a child came from playing with her brother and the neighborhood boys. When not doing chores, they played cowboys and dragons, and they dug a landscape of ponds and ditches for their adventures. Celeste was enamored with active, imaginative play.

Her love of play did not, however, compromise Celeste's studies. The Ulrich family joked about how she skipped the second grade:

> The school faculty decided that I was bright enough to skip the second grade, although they never talked to my parents about this. Skipping a grade didn't particularly impress me. The principal told me to go home and tell my parents that I had skipped. So I went home and said, "Guess what, Mom? I skipped today." When I told my father, he said, "Honey, that's swell." They didn't realize that I had advanced to the third grade. A year later, my mother and I argued about what grade I was to be promoted to. I was ahead of myself and didn't even realize it!

In addition to school, Girl Scouts influenced Celeste. She became a Brownie at the age of eight and was an active Scout throughout college. She admitted,

> As we got older, it wasn't cute to be a Girl Scout. But we persisted because we thought it was a good program; we believed in what we were doing. Scouting made it possible for me to believe that I could do anything I wanted to do if I were willing to work hard and to suffer, to some extent, social ostracism.

Since the organization's main concern was human welfare, many of Celeste's Girl Scout experiences shaped her viewpoints and values: "We worked with ethnic minorities, and I learned to appreciate that international pattern. As far as ecology was concerned, camping and understanding nature were an integral part of Girl Scouts."

Reports of administrative scandal within the Girl Scouts, particularly concerning the distribution of funds received from cookie sales, left Celeste skeptical. She nevertheless maintained high regard for the organization:

> It seems to me that Girl Scouting still follows its essential purpose of trying to empower young girls to believe that they are capable of leadership and that they are not restricted by social restraints. To that extent, I think that it continues to do what I consider a very good job.

Discovering Gender: Adolescence

Two incidents during junior high school made Celeste aware of gender and confirmed her passion for physical education. "It doesn't seem possible now," she recalled, "but the women wore tunics and long black stockings." Then two young instructors, alumnae of Sargent College and Bouvé-Boston College, initiated bold change:

> One day, our teachers came to class in socks. I was in the seventh or eighth grade, and I couldn't believe that could happen. I had been running around in shorts and socks because that was acceptable dress for young girls, but here were my grown-up teachers without their long black stockings!

Celeste's reaction represented a general attitude shift in the 1930s as women transitioned from full, and oftentimes restricting, exercise dress to lighter clothing conducive to greater movement.

On another day, her teachers were called from the gym during class. One of them gave Celeste her whistle and told her to take charge. "She put the whistle around my neck, and I felt as if I were being knighted," Celeste recalled. After deliberating for a moment about what to do, she blew the whistle. To her surprise, everyone stood at attention. When she commanded her peers to line up, they obeyed. "It was like being empowered all of a sudden with that whistle," she said. "At home I was just one of the gang, and no one really cared. I liked the concept of being boss."

Celeste first experienced the fair treatment of female athletes at Baltimore's coeducational Forest Park High School in 1941. Practicing against the boys' teams gave her an edge in women's athletic competition. Still 31 years before Title IX would mandate equal opportunity, the girls felt privileged that the boys' head coach, Fess Marx, paid any attention to them. Although Celeste was never close to Marx, his personal guidance inspired her. She viewed him as a model coach and physical educator because of his insistence on proper dress, behavior, and gender equity.

During high school, Celeste played on the field hockey, badminton, basketball, and tennis interscholastic teams. The school provided the girls' teams with uniforms, officials, and a coach, but it did not offer the conveniences or the luxuries that the boys' teams enjoyed. Girls in these programs throughout Baltimore traveled to games on streetcars rather than in school buses, and they bought their own hamburgers after the game.

Celeste never viewed her high school athletic experience as extensive until she later enrolled in the University of North Carolina. She explained, "My teachers were appalled that I had participated in such a broad interscholastic experience even though it had been done under the aegis of very finely developed women physical educators." Such reactions guided Celeste's later research and professional choices, most of which she dedicated to creating opportunities in athletics for girls and women.

College, Stereotypes and Forces to Be Reckoned With

In the mid-1940s, parents with Depression-era values hoped education would ensure their children the professional and economic opportunities they never had. Frank and Adele Ulrich were no exception. So when Celeste announced her decision to major in physical education in college, her father asked if she planned to be a playground instructor. Teachers told her, "You're bright. You don't have to go into physical education. If you want to teach, why don't you teach science or language?" But her father was a fair man and told Celeste to research schools and potential careers in physical education. The two obvious choices, Sargent College and Bouvé-Boston College, were beyond the Ulrich budget. Celeste finally chose the Women's College, University of North Carolina at Greensboro, because of its affordable tuition and high placement rate for graduates.

As a physical education major, Celeste faced a more subtle but insidious stereotype: the myth that women physical educators were lesbians and therefore socially deviant.

One time I said something positive about Babe Didrikson and my father demanded that I not view her as my idol. I didn't know what she had done. She was an Olympic athlete as far as I was concerned. Dad explained that he had once seen her lick her hands before a golf shot. He thought that such a gesture was coarse. He wasn't afraid that I would behave like that; he was afraid of the homosexuality accusation.

Celeste felt confident enough with herself and her decision to follow her dream and disregard what people thought she *should* do. She rejected the stereotypes because she viewed her physical education teachers as attractive, dedicated women.

Celeste Ulrich. 1959. Celeste Ulrich Photograph, UA 104.9, Photographic Print Collection, Martha Blakeney Hodges Special Collections and University Archives and Manuscripts, the University of North Carolina at Greensboro, NC, USA.

One of Celeste's teachers was not just dedicated to the profession; she was a legend. The "iron handed" Mary Channing Coleman headed the physical education department at UNC at Greensboro from 1920 through October 1947. Celeste described Coleman as "principled, disciplined, tenacious" and "a force to be reckoned with," as the following incident illustrates:

> Apparently English Professor Dr. Friedlander, when registering a student, called Miss Coleman and said that he would like to have a student excused from physical education. He explained that she had a horse stabled near Greensboro and rode often. He offered to confirm that she had ridden for a least one hour every day and added that she was willing to take instructions from the stable master. He believed that would substitute for a physical education class.
>
> They say Miss Coleman didn't bat an eye and replied, "That certainly sounds reasonable. And while I have you on the phone Dr. Friedlander, let me tell you that I have a student in my office right now who has read extensively. She has promised me that every day she will read for an hour. I will personally guarantee you that she will read at least ten books of any subject you choose. Can she be excused from English?"
>
> To that, Dr. Friedlander responded, "I understand your point Miss Coleman."

Coleman's strict attention to standards guided Celeste's professional behavior:

> We did not walk across campus in our gym suits, which in those days were tunics. We worked very hard as far as our academic subjects were concerned because the department's reputation depended on our success. We had a very difficult schedule ahead of us, but she didn't want to hear any complaining. She expected us to be on time. If we weren't, that suggested to her that we were slovenly. It was up to us to shape up or ship out.

As an afterthought, Celeste joked, "Those who survived Miss Coleman could survive anything."

The physical education curriculum did, in fact, require majors to be above-average students. While enrolled in an 18-hour liberal arts program at UNC at Greensboro, majors also were required to take four hours of activity courses. Some, like Celeste, took as many as ten additional hours but earned only two credit hours per semester for activity courses, regardless of the number in which they were enrolled. The department did not award full credit for activity courses until after Celeste graduated.

Like most of her college peers in the early 1940s, Celeste experienced the impact of World War II. Travel was restricted, so when a sociology class required students to observe individuals with disabilities living in institutions, Celeste and her classmates bicycled 50 miles to complete the assignment. Rather than focusing on the inconvenience, she viewed the trip as "a very meaningful experience."

Meanwhile, many of the men being sent to Europe stopped at the Overseas Replacement Depot near Greensboro. The college hosted a dance every Saturday night where, according to Celeste, young women "met hundreds of boys who were on their way to be killed." She confided,

> Every one of them became very important to us because some of them would never come back. All of that haunted us continually. I wondered if I should start thinking about my personal life instead of my professional life and make some decisions about marriage. However, I decided then that it really was not a good time. Everything was tenuous, and my decision would not be based upon reason and logic, but upon emotional factors beyond my control.

The more deeply Celeste engaged in teaching and research, the more clearly she saw her future: there was not one special person proposing marriage at the time, and the longer she said no to marriage in general, the more definitive that decision became. Ultimately, she would choose to remain single to pursue her career.

As Celeste approached graduation, Mary Channing Coleman advised her that a future in physical education depended on graduate school. Coleman recommended the physical education master's program at the University of North Carolina at Chapel Hill, where Celeste enrolled in the fall of 1946. She described the unusual atmosphere on campus after World War II ended:

> The boys started to come back, except they were no longer boys; they were now 26-year-old men. Instead of an institution with a collegiate atmosphere, our institution had a very

grown up atmosphere. I was going to teach men who were my age and older and who had seen a lot more of the world than I had.

In her typical fashion, however, Celeste accepted the challenge as a learning experience that could strengthen her teaching.

Early Career and Mentors

In 1947, after finishing her master's degree in physical education, Celeste began her first full-time teaching position at James Madison College in Harrisonburg, Virginia. She secured the job, in part, because Mary Channing Coleman routinely informed students about the politics of the American Alliance for Health, Physical Education and Recreation (AAHPER). During the interview, the department head Elizabeth Rodgers interrogated Celeste about the profession rather than discussing her strengths and qualifications. Rodgers pointed brusquely at two pictures on her desk and asked Celeste to tell her about the men in the photos. Celeste had attended professional conferences as an undergraduate, so she recognized the legendary physical educators Jesse Feiring Williams and C. H. McCloy. Like Coleman, Rodgers put the profession before the individual and was seeking new faculty who would do the same.

As a very young and poorly paid assistant professor, Celeste still heeded Mary Channing Coleman's advice to attend professional conventions regardless of the personal sacrifices required. Attending the 1957 AAHPER convention in Portland, Oregon, however, seemed impossible for Celeste. She had all but given up on the idea when Caroline Sinclair, then head of the physical education department at Madison College, recommended Celeste as a speaker and loaned her $100 of her own money to get to Portland.

Despite several obstacles, the conference changed Celeste's life:

> The situation at the convention was a mess! It rained for the duration of the convention. The convention center was out of town, and we were staying in town. To top things off, Senator Neuberger of Oregon decided to talk to our profession about the health of the nation. The only time he could talk was during our session. I was told to cut my speech short. The psychologist was from outside of the profession, so we couldn't ask him. I was only 33 years old, so I did what I was told.
>
> When we arrived to hear Neuberger speak, we were drenched. They told him that he could have no more than 10 minutes, and he honored that. No one listened much to his talk because he was boring. But those 10 minutes gave us a chance to shed our wet clothes and set our umbrellas to drain. *Now* the audience was ready to listen.

Celeste's talk followed Neuberger's. Then, according to Celeste, the psychologist presented as speakers from outside the profession often did:

> They would come unprepared, thinking that anyone could address an association of dumb jocks. The psychologist didn't have any notes, and he was terrible. With Senator Neuberger on one side of me and this guy on the other, I appeared well-prepared and excited with the new ideas I was generating.

In fact, Celeste's professionalism impressed Dr. Delbert Oberteuffer, a highly respected professor at The Ohio State University, who then invited her to help him revise *Physical Education: A Textbook of Principles*. Caroline Sinclair encouraged Celeste to accept the offer. Obie, as close colleagues called Oberteuffer, worked out a schedule for the two of them to spend four weekends in Columbus, Ohio, discussing revisions. During their two-day work sessions, they talked non-stop and discovered each other's beliefs regarding principles of physical education. Celeste described the experience as "taking a class with Obie all by myself."

Working with Oberteuffer also taught Celeste how to write professionally and to collaborate. She explained,

> We agreed that I would write on one subject, he would write on another, then we would exchange chapters. I worked particularly hard on one chapter and thought it was extraordinarily good. I sent it to Obie, and he returned it to me edited in ways that I didn't believe possible. I thought that one paragraph was an absolute gem until he replaced the entire paragraph with one sentence. If he was going to do that to mine, then I was going to do that to his. We were ruthless in our editing. As a result, I have no idea what I wrote and what he wrote. We respected one another a great deal. That was one of my lucky experiences.

Following this period of personal and professional growth, two factors prompted Celeste's resignation from James Madison College in 1956. First, ongoing disagreements between Celeste and Elizabeth Rodgers had characterized Celeste's nine years at Madison College. Celeste could not stand by passively as her department head lied to students, treated well-qualified junior faculty as children, and demanded that her opinion not be challenged. During one tense episode, Rodgers became enraged and threw a paperweight after Celeste challenged her opinion. Shortly after that incident, the staff delivered an ultimatum: either they or Rodgers had to leave. Without much debate, administrators asked Rodgers to leave. This formative experience taught Celeste to be more compassionate about mental illness, which she suspected affected Rodgers' behavior. She learned to interact with students and colleagues in a more mature way than she might have otherwise.

In addition to facing this professional conflict, Celeste had realized that career advancement would require further graduate education. In the early 1950s, she had again gravitated toward her role models and enrolled in a summer session at the University of Southern California to study with physical education legend Mabel Lee. After her summer experience, and a warm reception by the faculty, Celeste enrolled in USC's doctoral program where she would study further with her intellectual role models Eleanor Metheny, Aileene Lockhart, and Craig Davis.

Eleanor Metheny, a mathematics major from Wellesley who had earned a Ph.D. at the University of Iowa under C.H. McCloy, influenced Celeste most profoundly. While team-teaching with Metheny at the University of Southern California, Celeste observed how methodically she worked with students at all levels of ability. Celeste considered Metheny's movement research "on the cutting edge of everything new that was happening." Because Celeste's specialty was stress physiology, Metheny's small circle of physical educators invited her to join their movement research. Celeste hoped to prove the mind/body relationship using Hans Selye's stress theory. His theory, she summarized, "was that life involved adaptation and as we met the stressors of life, we used adaptive energy to keep the human being in equilibrium." When she proposed a dissertation exploring physical education's effect on psychological behavior, Metheny urged her to find a more academic topic. Celeste would not concede. She convinced Metheny that Selye's theory was important to physical education, and Metheny eventually became her strongest ally.

Celeste's relationship with her mentors inspired her "cascades of heritage" principle. She believed that an individual can trace her professional heritage through the lineage of her teachers. Most of Celeste's early lineage stemmed from Columbia University and the Boston Normal School of Gymnastics. She felt fortunate to have met some of the great leaders who shaped physical education, particularly Jesse Feiring Williams and Jay B. Nash. They believed that physical education contributed holistically to mental, emotional, social, and physical development. Celeste felt closest to Williams, whose philosophies she shared. All of her teachers had studied under Williams and talked about him often. "As I grew older," Celeste reflected, "I found myself literally saying some of the things that these leaders said, because that was where my indoctrination had been."

Celeste concluded, "I went through Southern Cal during a golden era. I think that most institutions have highs and lows, and that was one of the high periods at Southern Cal." During her years at USC, Celeste deepened her roots in the profession. She exerted a major leadership role as secretary of the National Section for Girls and Women's Sports (NSGWS). When illness forced Aileene Lockhart to resign her position as NSGWS chair in December 1954, Celeste had organized Lockhart's files and briefed incoming chair Mable Locke on NSGWS activities. At the same time, she studied and worked with E.C. Davis, Francis Coleville, and John Nixon, with whom she later co-authored *Tones of Theory* (1972).

Expanding Opportunities for Women in Sports

One of Celeste's most notable contributions to physical education and athletics was equity for women in sports. She explained,

> The role of women in sports was much more important in the 1950s and 1960s than it appears to be now [1990]. It governed almost all of our lives. Most women in physical education were partially drawn to the field because of their own sporting experiences. Most of us were a little bit above average as far as our skills were concerned, and most of us coached and officiated. If I had any kind of feminist consciousness at all, it was through sports.

Women's athletic departments did not exist before the 1970s; women's athletics depended on physical education departments for resources. Discussion about expanding women's athletics resurrected familiar arguments that females weren't strong enough to do certain activities. Celeste pointed out hypocrisy within the debate:

> Women were allowed to do certain activities in tennis, badminton, golf, and other individual sports that no one even considered they could do as part of a team. Many people believed that if we allowed women to play basketball on an interscholastic, intercollegiate level, then we would unleash the hounds of fury. We were floundering around in a morass of unintelligent responses guided only by the fact that we honestly believed that girls should have a chance.

The extent to which women could participate in athletics remained a vague argument until Katherine "Tyke" Ley took a dramatic step into the men's world of sports research with her study of women's basketball. At a National Section on Women's Athletics (NSWA) conference in Chicago in the late 1950s, she presented data that revealed inconsistencies in the regulations governing women's athletics. The general thinking at the time, Celeste explained, was that women were not allowed to play full-court basketball because they were too weak to endure an entire game. At the same time, in field hockey, which Celeste described as "the one pure and unadulterated women's sport," women played two 30-minute halves of hard running without substitutions. Tyke Ley measured the number of minutes played in field hockey and calculated the energy expenditure. She contrasted these data with the expenditure of energy in women's basketball and concluded that women were performing only one-sixteenth of the activity required in field hockey. Ley's study set in motion changes that created contemporary women's basketball.

When Celeste heard Tyke Ley's presentation, she thought, "Hey, I like this gal! She's with it." Shortly after their introduction, they formed a productive professional liaison. They later served together on the executive committee of AAHPERD in 1975 through challenging years: "Many times we spent our own money to get to Washington for a weekend to work on women's sports issues, which I don't think women particularly appreciated. We did it because we believed in the Alliance."

Before hearing Ley's study, Celeste had not questioned women's physical limitations because her respected mentors had upheld the myths that interrupted women's intercollegiate athletics in the 1920s. But the profession was beginning to replicate those debates. When she joined the move to dispute these myths through research, some colleagues told her that she did not fully understand the current problems and how change could exaggerate them. Others feared that women's athletics would develop the same problems of commercialism and obsession to win that had hurt men's athletics. Celeste countered with another option: "We could create a new model of women's sport. We wouldn't have to follow the men's model." She heeded Bouvé-Boston School Professor Minnie Lynn's prophetic statement to the National Association for Physical Education of College Women: "We dare not back into our own future."

Celeste's highest priority as an educator and researcher in the late 1950s and 1960s was to develop a new model of women's sport. After completing her Ph.D. in 1956, she returned to her undergraduate alma mater UNC at Greensboro as an assistant professor. She taught courses on the philosophy, history, and significance of physical education. One of her favorite courses, His, Hers, and Ours, focused on gender discrimination in sports. Meanwhile, she continued her research on stress physiology with hopes of redefining leading perceptions of women in sports. What is common knowledge today was startling to the public in the mid–1950s: "It certainly was a powerful platform to suggest that women were capable of performing at high levels in sports. Research indicated that women were not as weak as they had been characterized to be. Our research proved that we didn't drop dead during our menstrual periods."

Eager to create change, Celeste became an active member of the Division for Girls' and Women's Sports (DGWS), the National Association for Physical Education of College Women (NAPECW), and the Athletic and Recreation Federation of College Women (ARFCW). Members from each of the three groups met at the 1957 Piney Lake Conference and established the National Joint Committee on Extramural Sports for College Women (NJCESCW). Their first model for women's intercollegiate sport events was cumbersome. Event coordinators needed a permit, and the application called for laborious details regarding the event, participating teams, officiators, transportation, and health standards. In Celeste's words, the Committee concluded that "the weight of the mechanism was so great it failed."

Although it did not produce the future model of women's athletics, the Piney Lake Conference gave Celeste and her colleagues the opportunity to envision a national organization that would support women in collegiate sports. That organization took shape in 1965 when NJCESCW passed its leadership to DGWS. The following year, DGWS formed the Commission on Intercollegiate Athletics for Women (CIAW). CIAW ultimately became the Association for Intercollegiate Athletics for Women (AIAW) in 1971 (Carpenter & Acosta, 2005, pp. 104–105). AIAW was the first step toward visible national support for women's intercollegiate athletics.

Title IX and Restructuring Women's Athletics

As consciousness raising swept through many women's lives following Betty Friedan's *The Feminine Mystique* (1963), a classic study of suburban housewives' boredom and search for identity, Celeste pursued equal rights through the channel she knew best: women's national sports organizations. First-generation leaders such as Mary Channing Coleman, Mabel Lee, and Eleanor Metheny had established NSWA and NAPECW to support female colleagues and students. Celeste and her peers were the second generation of "a family situation in which the parents were telling the kids that they had better get along."

Celeste's involvement with women's sports organizations put her at the heart of the most historically significant change for women's athletics: Title IX. She shared an insider's perspective:

> A common misunderstanding about the purpose and adoption of Title IX is that it is all about athletics, yet it wasn't about that at all. There were several bills in Congress about higher education and the way in which contracts were to be let. Congress wanted to ensure that there was not discrimination, particularly concerning blacks and other minority groups, with regard to institutions that received federal money. But there was a group in the Senate that didn't want the non-discriminatory clause written in. They believed that all men of good will would naturally do the right thing. Of course, omission gave them the permission to do the wrong thing.

Physical educators felt Title IX's impact locally as colleges and universities began to merge women's and men's physical education departments. In her introduction (1992) to *JOPERD*'s Title IX anniversary issue, Connie Fox explained,

> Although Title IX would not be interpreted as mandating the merger of men's and women's athletic departments, the leadership in many schools erroneously anticipated that it would, and a large number of men's and women's athletic departments began the process of merging [p. 34].

Whether or not Title IX was responsible, Celeste strongly supported unified departments to end program replication and intradepartmental competition. She argued,

> For the most part, the merger has been advantageous to our field. There still remain some special discrimination patterns that, for the most part, do not favor women. However, we're working through the problems. During my career, I saw evidence that there is greater strength in unity than in divisiveness.

The merging of departments also introduced Celeste to a whole new cadre of colleagues. After working primarily with women, she relished the chance to work with men. "A lot of them were wonderful human beings who shared my philosophical beliefs," she remarked.

Title IX's ability to transform opportunity for girls and women came with similar power to force discussion of difficult issues, particularly athletic scholarships. The Division for Girls' and Women's Sports favored broad participation of players. This philosophy would eventually conflict with AIAW's goals. While the two initially agreed that financial aid for athletes may lead to abuse of athletes and resources, AIAW changed its position after surveying member institutions (Carpenter & Acosta, 2005, p. 105).[1] Celeste witnessed the tension in subsequent years: "The AIAW was caught in a very interesting situation. Philosophically they didn't think that there should be scholarships, but at the same time they believed in equality."

Higher education was still responding with trial and error to Title IX in 1976–77 when Celeste became president of AAHPERD. As a mid-career leader, she pushed to expand sport opportunities for women. But AAHPERD was "a sleeping giant" according to Celeste. "It had more power than we envisioned, and we weren't utilizing it, particularly in the athletic circles." When she organized a meeting for representatives from all of the major sports associations, they "came as though they were waiting to be called." Her goal was to push AAHPERD into an unprecedented leadership role. A related focus was the governance structure that oversaw all of the associations within the Alliance. While AAHPERD was swayed heavily by district concerns, the associations were accomplishing the "nitty-gritty" as far as Celeste was concerned. She wanted to achieve a balance of governance among these groups. In short, she said, "I hoped to bring to AAHPERD a sense of mission concerning the future."

Celeste viewed the AIAW's response to scholarships and other controversies as tragic. It hired Washington, D.C., attorney Margot Polivy for counsel regarding financial problems and a lawsuit challenging AIAW's opposition to athletic scholarships for women (Wushanley, 2004, p. 111). Polivy, a high-profile advocate for women's rights, appeared to be the perfect candidate. She had taught physical education at the college level and knew sports issues and NCAA policies intimately. Celeste, however, believed that Polivy's ultimate goal was to achieve fame, status, and money:

> I talked with her for some time about her qualifications. I quizzed her about some of the legal patterns, and she quizzed me about the history of women's athletics. Then she invited me to talk more with her the next time I was in Washington. During my next visit to Washington, we met at a restaurant and spent the whole evening talking about the legal implications and the history of women's sport. It was a marvelous conversation. I enjoyed it and had the impression that she did, too.

When Celeste returned from Washington, AIAW executive director George Anderson showed her a $200 consultation bill from Polivy's law firm. Celeste was shocked. She immediately countered with a $200 bill for educational consultation that stalemated the attorney's fee. Whenever Celeste and Polivy talked after that incident, Celeste jokingly asked if the meter was running.

Celeste attributed many of the AIAW's poor decisions to its "green" leadership.

> It seems that AIAW's leadership skipped an entire generation. The new leaders were young women with experience in athletics but very little knowledge of or interest in the history of AIAW. Instead of having a smooth and natural transition, we found ourselves plopped in the middle of a high-powered women's sports organization that was faced with all kinds of possible lawsuits. We were being strongly conditioned by a law firm.

The sudden expansion of women's intercollegiate athletics also created conflict with the National Collegiate Athletic Association (NCAA) leadership. Rumors alleged that AIAW President Judith Holland informed NCAA Board of Directors that she would "deliver" AIAW to the NCAA. Celeste described Holland, UCLA's first full-time athletic director, as "a very strong feminist but an even stronger individual who was determined to make her name." Until AIAW could create an agenda to define women's athletics and to articulate its needs and wants, it was, in Celeste's opinion, better left separate from the historically-male NCAA. She speculated,

> I think I became AIAW's greatest deterrent primarily because I had some clout in the field of women's athletics. I had worked in it for such a long time that people couldn't say that I knew nothing. I spoke publically in many places, and they were furious that I talked about women's sports. From their point of view, I wasn't the elected AIAW, so I didn't have any right to talk about that.

In retrospect, Celeste said that she should have been a little softer and a little bit more giving toward AIAW leadership. But AIAW's allegations against AAHPERD infuriated her. "We had knocked ourselves out to make money available for them," she declared. "Once they started to make a little bit of money and we started to charge overhead fees, they became incensed."

To end the feud, Celeste and LeRoy Walker, past president and member of the AAHPERD executive committee, honored AIAW's request to end its status as an AAHPERD association.

The tension marked a particularly difficult professional moment for Celeste:

> It was like a Greek tragedy to me. I knew it was going to happen, and there was nothing I could do. I tried to insulate myself. I decided that my days of working with women's athletics were over and that it probably didn't make any difference anyway. AIAW had been caught up in the NCAA swell.

Like previous-generation physical educators, Celeste worried that the male model of intercollegiate athletics, which prioritized athletics and money over education and participation, wasn't a healthy one for women's athletics. But she admitted in retrospect that AIAW may not have done any better than NCAA was doing for college athletics:

> The ethos of sport is such a powerful male-oriented model that there is no way women can break into it. It wasn't so much that women were trying to be like men; they were trying to be good basketball players or whatever kinds of players they were naturally.

Celeste said modestly that perhaps her greatest contribution to the whole sports picture was to help define AAHPERD's association with the NCAA. She was the first woman to speak on the floor of the NCAA annual convention. In addition, she made friends with the presidents group of the NCAA, which was trying to move toward a more ethical pattern for the NCAA. Celeste also has been credited for introducing Robert's Rules of Order into NCAA procedure, in place of its own meeting rules that privileged only those whom it allowed to speak. The adoption of Robert's Rules of Order made possible the discussion of women's issues at NCAA meetings.

Higher Administration

In 1979, after 23 years at UNC at Greensboro, Celeste felt she had done all she could do for the university. So when colleagues encouraged her to apply for a position as Dean of the College of Health, Physical Education, and Recreation at the University of Oregon, where she had spent three summers as an adjunct faculty, she applied.

Celeste was stunned when the University of Oregon offered her the job; she had assumed they would never hire a female dean. The position would enable her to initiate much needed change for women in physical education, athletics, and recreation. Meanwhile, her live-in mother was very ill and "it was a miserable time to consider leaving." Celeste felt a familiar tension between her career goals and family. Her mother insisted, "If you're hesitating because of me, that's the wrong reason. You have your own life. We'll find ways that I will or won't fit in. I think you have to eliminate consideration of me." Adele Seidewitz Ulrich died shortly after Celeste accepted the position in Oregon.

Working with the all-male dean's council was a challenge, but Celeste implemented ideas for change that she might never have realized as a faculty member:

> My best contribution was to help the administration understand the real meaning of physical education, that it was not just a group of activity classes that people were doing in order to have some fun or in respite from their real day of work. I helped them see that we were interested in understanding human movement and that it was a discipline worth pursuing.

Celeste admitted that she never felt equal satisfaction from administration and teaching. An illustrative incident occurred shortly before she retired:

> I looked up from my office desk, and there stood a student I had taught at Greensboro. She explained that she and some friends were on a bicycle tour of the Oregon coast. This student had pedaled 50 miles out of her way to say hello. I thought to myself, "There's not a single faculty member here who would pedal 50 miles to visit me!" Yet whatever I had done for this student made enough of a difference in her life that she was willing to bike 100 miles to see me.

She believed, nevertheless, that her work to create gender equity was part of her life's mission.

The University of Oregon's 600 Hours Plan offered faculty the option to teach in a one-quarter position for five years after retirement. In 1990, Celeste opted to teach in the College of Education because, she said, "I don't think it's a good idea to have the former dean in the college where the new dean is trying to take her place." She also created a series of seminars on subjects related to education, such as the effects of athletics on gender roles. Even after retire-

Celeste Ulrich. No date. Source: Celeste Ulrich Photograph, UA 104.9, Photographic Print Collection, Martha Blakeney Hodges Special Collections and University Archives and Manuscripts, the University of North Carolina at Greensboro, NC, USA.

ment, she continued to create public relations materials to serve the university.

Retirement and Reflection

Retirement never worried Celeste because she planned for it. At 45, she realized that she would remain single and be responsible for her life. Although she knew that she would have to alter her spending habits, she didn't anticipate having to live through the "severe austerity" that she experienced as a child and again as a young professional. She advised, "Start to plan as soon as you can afford to. When you're 30 you don't think you're ever going to be 50, and at 50 you're not sure you're ever going to retire. Then all of a sudden, it's time."

With age, Celeste developed concerns about her exercise and nutrition habits. She admitted a tendency to gain weight, saying, "It gets away from me very easily."

Although by age 66 she had stopped participating in sports because she was no longer agile enough to perform at her level of enjoyment, she walked and swam to stay fit. Her busy academic schedule had made it difficult to stay conscious of nutrition, but after retiring she stayed more attuned to her eating habits.

Stress research taught Celeste that stress is productive as long as a person can control it:

> I don't try to avoid stress. I try to make sure that I can handle the stress I have. If stress becomes so great that I can't handle it, then my eye starts to twitch. That tells me to do something else. There are certain times when to flee from a situation is the best thing that one can possibly do. When I have to, I flee from a stressful situation in the most socially acceptable way I can.

Despite her separation from many of the issues in athletics after her retirement, Celeste remained concerned about women entering the profession. She observed young women who no longer wanted to coach and officiate, which were once the obligatory duties of physical educators. Experience taught her that coaching is demanding work because of the time that coaches must spend with student athletes; they act as counselors, big sisters or brothers, mothers or fathers. They also must recruit. Many women simply don't want that kind of life, or, in Celeste's opinion, "won't make that sacrifice." As a result, she saw women's teams coached by men with family support who could more easily devote the time. She warned young professional women,

Athletics is a dead end street. What is happening to college athletics overall is not good. We won't ever get rid of collegiate athletics, but we need to straighten out the increasing mess concerning transgressions, student athletes, and coaches. I don't pretend to know the answer, but I know that we are reaching a crisis point.

So what did such change mean to educators like Celeste who initially fought for intercollegiate athletics as an extension of physical education? She concluded a bit wearily, "I wake up three days a week feeling guilty that I no longer provide any kind of leadership for women's sports. I wake up the other four days thanking God I don't."

The roots of Celeste's ambivalence pushed beyond the profession. As in other areas of feminist gain, women physical educators of her generation faced difficult decisions about their personal lives. She explained,

> It was pretty hard to merge family and marriage with a profession. For the most part, women of my era who chose to be professionals remained single. A woman's work became her life. I look around now and see that many people are married with families and various types of relationships. Women are finding ways to identify support systems. They hire people and do other things that I had never thought possible, in terms of either money or what society allowed or approved.

Celeste is careful to clarify that the tension was not just between women and men. Some of her most difficult encounters in higher education involved faculty members' wives. At that time, fear of nepotism denied spouses the opportunity to teach at the same institution. She acknowledged that many highly qualified women gave up their professional lives to become full-time wives and mothers. But some viewed Celeste as their nemesis. "They didn't like me very well," she stated. "They weren't afraid that I might steal their husbands. They resented that I received perks that their husbands might have gotten if I had not been there." Celeste remembered faculty wives chastising her for working long hours while their husbands limited their working hours to spend time with their families. Celeste conceded,

> That was true. I was willing to work weekends. I accomplished more because of that, and I gained more credentials and career opportunities. However, the husbands had their children, and I didn't have any children. There were times when we were jealous of each other, but that's how things worked out.

Celeste's early 1990s view of the roles of working women was prescient:

> Women who have to make choices and who are trying to do everything aren't going to be able to do it all. Those who are not willing to do it all must make choices or view themselves as failures. They are setting themselves up for failure. I advise my graduate students to know their limitations.

If individuals make personal decisions thoughtfully, Celeste believed, then they should be able to live with the consequences of those decisions. She advised,

> It's important that we try as much as we are able to change our own behavioral patterns and not act in certain ways or knock ourselves out just because those are the social niceties of the era. We must not be frightened or intimidated to choose a different course and to defend those who do the same.

This message, her effort to empower women, is her legacy to Girl Scouts, students, younger colleagues, and senior peers.

"The world is not a perfect place," Celeste came to realize long before her death in 2011, at the age of 87. She tempered disappointment by reevaluating goals she did not reach. Conflicts with AIAW disappointed her the most. She concluded, "My hope for women's sports wasn't realistic. Some of the things I might have hoped for just didn't work out. There was almost always a good reason why they didn't work out, so I don't feel that the world turned against me.... I have no regrets at all."

4

Fay Biles
Empowering Women through Fitness and Fundraising

As many Americans tuned their televisions to news of anti-war protests erupting on college campuses on May 4, 1970, Fay Biles watched students gather near her office building at Kent State University. "I could feel that something was going to happen that day," she recalled, "but I never thought it was going to be a shooting." She watched with horror as the tragedy unfolded, never imagining the role she would play in social and economic recovery efforts.

Fay's life story is a chronicle of a woman who made things happen in challenging circumstances. She came of age as a physical education teacher in the 1950s, 20 years before Title IX created opportunities for girls and women in physical education and sport. After years of organizing intercollegiate competition with little institutional support, Fay was one of the first women to address Congress in support of Title IX. As she moved into administration, serving as vice president for public affairs and development at Kent State after the May 4 shootings, she brought with her a spirit of teambuilding and the love of a challenge. In all of her leadership roles, the stakes were high: people's lives and livelihood depended on the opportunity to participate, to be heard, and to be taken seriously.

Knowing the stakes, Fay has put her heart into her work and play. And considering that her accomplishments as a professor and scholar, administrator, and internationally-recognized health enthusiast span four decades, she is the perfect advocate for healthy hearts and lifestyles. Her fundraising and educational outreach for the American Heart Association are best known through the lucrative Jump Rope for Heart program that she was instrumental in developing. At times, the pace of her lifestyle has seemed to move in fast-forward. The secret to her energy is perhaps best summed up when she reminds audiences of all ages, "You gotta have heart."

Childhood and Family Influence

The youngest of three girls, Fay Reifsnyder was born in 1927 in Reading, Pennsylvania, to Tom and Dora (Weaver) Reifsnyder. Tom was a hosiery manufacturer whose work employed the entire family. "We got up at five o'clock in the morning and we worked all day," Fay recalled. "He was a typical German father. His philosophy was that you never played until you finished work, but we never finished work!" Dora challenged her daughters and encouraged them to "take the hard road." Their combined influence would inspire Fay's lifelong work ethic and commitment to fairness.

Fay's father was her first and most impressive role model in work and play. Although his Brethren faith made him a harsh disciplinarian, intolerant of name-calling, lying, and off-color language, Fay described him as a kind man who was always fair with people. He loved innovation and had a talent for putting ideas to work. "The future always had movement," she said. "It was never static, never still, and always improving. My father was very much that way, and I got that from him."

As early as the first grade Fay worked obsessively to earn the highest grades in her class. She recalled that her aggressive personality also caused trouble in elementary school:

> My fourth grade teacher was not very knowledgeable. I used to interrupt her and say, "That's wrong." The teacher would then call my parents and tell them that they had to stop me from doing that. They would tell her that I had read about what she was teaching and probably knew as much about that subject as she did. The teachers didn't appreciate that, so I spent a lot of time in the cloakroom because I wouldn't shut my mouth. I received good grades, but I wasn't good in deportment.

School rules further irritated Fay. In the sixth grade, she led a riot against the requirement that students go home after school and change clothes before playing on the playground. She considered that a waste of valuable playtime. When teachers discovered that she was bringing her clothes and changing at school, they complained to her parents. Fay then gathered all of the children on the playground and declared, "We're not going to obey these rules. We're going to fight them!" They marched en masse into the principal's office carrying placards scrawled with their riotous message. In retrospect, Fay considered her behavior rather radical and perhaps misplaced leadership for that age.

In 1940, the Reifsnyders moved to West Chester, a college town with a more sophisticated school curriculum than Reading's. Fay enjoyed the new academic challenge, but the lack of organized physical education disappointed her. She hungered for instruction in *all* sports. School playtime was "recess," not the physical education she desired. Her father, an avid swimmer and professional tennis player, had taught Fay to play tennis when she was barely old enough to hold the racquet. As an aside, she noted that he advocated and practiced physical fitness but smoked several cigars a day. His death from a stroke at age 55 would later influence her healthy heart fundraising interests.

Fay's first experience in organized play was at a summer sports camp in Maryland. She prioritized play above all other activities to the point of dramatic consequence:

> To keep my hair out of the way, I wore thick, long pigtails. I wouldn't let the counselors take them apart and comb my hair because I knew it would take time when I'd rather be playing. When my parents came to pick me up in August, the counselors told them, "This kid hasn't combed her hair since she came to camp." I said, "That would take hours. Just cut it off." I really didn't care that I should look like a girl. So my mother took a pair of scissors and cut my pigtails right at the nape of my neck.

One sister, whom Fay described as "a perfect lady," went so far as to ask Fay when she was going to act like a girl, walk like a girl, or even *know* she was a girl. But Fay was so oblivious to gender rituals that when she was asked for a date to the movies, in the ninth or tenth grade, she asked the boy, "Why would you want to go to the movies when you could play baseball?"

Meanwhile, Fay had been working in her father's stores or the mill since she was ten. By the age of 12, she was managing all of his creative advertising. One avant-garde hosiery ad, in which she had positioned the model's legs upside down, won a national award in 1943. But she hesitated to go to New York to receive the award because she couldn't imagine herself, then 16, appearing in front of a crowd. Her father, however, insisted that she go. Both parents wanted their daughters to develop self-confidence, and they viewed work as one way to ensure that. When Fay went to New York to receive the award, the audience gasped when they saw that the recipient was a young woman. It never occurred to Fay that people would assume a young man had created the ad; she believed that hard work, not gender, yielded success.

During adolescence, sports deepened Fay's understanding of gender dynamics. "I lived to play sports," she said. "Field hockey, lacrosse, basketball, swimming, tennis, volleyball, and also head cheerleader. I did everything I could get my hands on. Our high school hockey team was undefeated." She attended field hockey camp in Pennsylvania's Poconos Mountains each summer, from 7th grade through high school, where she was coached by the famous Constance Applebee. Miss Applebee, as her students called her, introduced field hockey to numerous women's colleges in the United States in 1901. Her aggressive coaching style and lack of adherence to "proper" women's behavior made her a role model for many of her players. According to Fay,

Miss Applebee ran up and down the field during games screaming commands at the players. "I played left inner and used to cut into the goal, just missing the goal post, flick across, then go out," Fay described. "She'd scream at me, 'Someday you'll run right into the post and kill yourself.' She'd even stop the game and shout, 'You can't do that!'"

Their acquaintance didn't end during those summer camps:

> Years later, when I was coaching at Kent State, I took my hockey team to Miss Applebee's camp in the Poconos. I was also playing club hockey at the time. There I was playing as an adult coach when Miss Applebee stopped the game and screamed, "There's only one person I've ever known who did that, and her name was Fay Reifsnyder.... You've got to be that same idiot!"
>
> And I thought, "Yes, the same one."

The strength and competitive spirit that athletics demanded, and the self-confidence that they inspired, eventually influenced other aspects of Fay's life. She was elected the first female vice president of the student body and organized women's rights groups at West Chester High School. As a student leader, she encouraged her female peers to participate in student government and to question their role in society. "I was never a bossy captain or leader," she said. "I was more of a leader through group process and consensus. I still believe in that methodology. I was always very conscious of other people's feelings."

College Athletics & Leadership

In 1945, Fay was one of only two Philadelphia area students to be accepted to Duke University. Her awkward admissions interview set the tone for the challenge that lay ahead:

> When I walked into the room, the interviewers motioned for me to sit in a certain chair, which I swear was five feet deep. I looked at it and wondered if I should sit on the edge or lean back with my feet not touching the floor. I assumed it was a test to see how people adapt and how self-esteem helps in such situations.

Fay's awareness typified her scrutiny of other people and her own behavior modification in response to others' cues. This kind of careful observation would prove crucial to her lifelong success in motivating people.

Fay experienced "a rude shock" during her freshman year at Duke, where most of her new peers were high school valedictorians. She was accustomed to being at the top of her class with minimal studying and recalled that her freshman year was difficult. "I socialized too much," she admitted. "I was away every weekend playing sports. It finally dawned on me that I had to start balancing my work and play habits because I was falling behind." Early morning, late night, and weekend study sessions became routine as she pursued pre-medicine with hopes of becoming a doctor. Her goals changed, however, after her internship at Duke Hospital. She realized, "I didn't want to be around sick people!" Her deeper interest was prevention rather than crisis treatment, so she pursued a degree in physical education.

Meanwhile, men returning from military service were entering college with the help of the 1944 G.I. Bill. Just after World War II ended, Durham headlines announced, "War hero Returns to Duke Campus." Fay was curious to meet the former Duke freshman who was a paratrooper returning with two Purple Hearts and a Double Cluster, so she went to a baseball game to watch him play:

> As I was going on and on about the catcher, still wondering who the hero was, a guy sitting next to me said, "That's the hero you came to see. That's Bedford Biles."
> I thought, "What a name!" At any rate, I was impressed with the way he threw and ran. I was such a nut for athletic ability.

After the game, Bedford asked his fraternity brother, who had spoken with Fay, about the young woman in the pink dress. When he learned that her name was Fay Reifsnyder, he declared, "God, what a handle! But I want a date with her."

Drawn to Bedford's athleticism and war-hero mystique, Fay remained nevertheless pragmatic. A relationship was possible as long as she could balance it with work and play in order to thrive in both the personal and academic spheres.

Throughout college, Fay promoted athletic opportunities for women. As a freshman member of the Women's Athletic Association (WAA), she encouraged her dormitory to get involved in intramural sports. Once they did, she proposed intercollegiate competition. She and another field hockey player from New York formed Duke's first field hockey club. According to Fay, they played hockey "around the clock" and eventually competed against other schools. Duke was ahead of its time because in the mid-1940s, 30 years before Title IX, women's intercollegiate competition was still a radical concept, largely forbidden since the 1920s.

Equity between women's and men's athletics was as important as opportunities within women's athletics. As president of Duke's WAA during her senior year, Fay led the group's revision of its constitution's bylaws to allow for a women's intercollegiate athletics program. She held back nothing when advocating for equitable physical education facilities. To demonstrate the dramatic inferiority of the physical education facilities at Duke's women's campus to those on its men's campus, she printed pictures of the women's swimming pool in the school newspaper with the caption, "How Can You Possibly Allow Duke Women to Swim in This Pool?" She also wrote letters to the local newspaper voicing the need for additional funding.

Fay was certain that her extreme methods embarrassed the physical education department. At one point, Department Chair Julia Grout told her, "You know, you really ought to calm your voice a little bit. Women don't need to come on quite that strong." Fay disagreed.

Although Grout's advice seemed counter to feminist ideologies, she and her colleague Elizabeth Bookhout were strong role models for Fay. Their high ethical and moral standards resembled those of her father. Fay recalled Bookhout admonishing, "Listen, young lady, you have a lot of talent, and you're not using it to your full extent. We expect big things." In response, Fay pushed herself to meet their expectations and graduated with a triple major in biological sciences, health and physical education, and English. Even after graduating, she continued her letter-writing campaign to help raise money for a new women's physical education building.

"Studies and sports were my life," Fay concluded, reflecting on her years at Duke. "I realized how much sports give a person. You learn teamwork, tactics, and strategy." She has observed that some women who do not play sports, or who were never part of a team, do not understand those concepts. "Even in the business world, they don't understand how to be a member of a team, and how to change tactics and strategy when the ball's in the other court." For Fay, athletic achievement always transferred into greater power in the business world, and opportunity was essential to enabling women's achievement in all areas.

Marriage and Graduate School

After Fay and Bedford married in August of 1949, she stepped from Duke into the gendered middle class postwar America that Betty Friedan would later chronicle in *The Feminine Mystique* (1963). War veterans displaced women in factory jobs, creating economic shifts that resituated middle class women in roles as wives and mothers. Even Fay's childhood work experience and advocacy for women's rights at Duke did not fully prepare her to navigate 1950s American gender ideologies.

Fay never anticipated that sports would threaten her relationship with Bedford. But shortly before the wedding, Bedford announced that he was going to work as a terminal manager for Roadway in Atlanta. Fay was adamant: "Never! I'll never be able to play field hockey in Atlanta. They don't have any teams. No, I won't go!" Bedford snapped back that he wouldn't ask her to go anywhere. Fay was certain that she had destroyed their relationship until Bedford compromised by taking a job in Akron, Ohio. Now Fay could continue to play field hockey on a club team in the Akron area and during the summer commute to field hockey camp in the Poconos. Many of their early "compromises," Fay admitted, were not compromises at all; Bedford gave in to her demands because he wanted her to be happy.

Marriage demanded adjustments beyond field hockey. Living on Bedford's salary was her first major challenge. She recalled,

> When I wanted money as a child, I just went to the cash drawer either at the mill or at the store. I never knew what living on a salary meant. I always had access to money. The first week we were married, I went downtown and spent our only 35 dollars. Bed told me that there was no more money until payday. I was absolutely shocked. It scared me so bad that I made pennies squeal.

Despite hardship, they never told their parents in an effort to make it on their own.

Bedford's "Southern chauvinism" caused even deeper tension. The women in Bedford's family had traditionally stayed home, in the kitchen. So, of course, Bedford believed that's where women *should* stay. Before they married, Fay had been blunt: "You and I are going to have some problems. I'm not going to live like that, and you'd better know it now or we won't get married." Despite her resolve, Fay spent eight hours a day during their first year in Akron learning to cook, for lack of anything else to do. Her specialty was elaborate desserts. Within a year, she was bored, miserable, and several pounds heavier from eating her desserts. Bedford, who gained 16 pounds, had literally had enough. She recalled him saying, "I can't stand this. You're driving me crazy. Go get a job. Do something!" Fay immediately called the school system, which hired her as a substitute and then as a full-time teacher.

Like many middle class women in the 1950s, Fay separated career and family ambitions. She quit teaching in 1953 to have a baby. Her pregnancy ended with pain and grief when her father died unexpectedly. Fay explained, "Doctors told me that I was pregnant, but they couldn't find the pregnancy. They thought that the emotional shock stopped the fertilized egg very high up in my tube. They couldn't feel it, and they had no instruments to find it." Five doctors examined her, but at the time none could explain the ectopic pregnancy. Fay was educated enough about health not to follow one doctor's instructions to douche with a special powder, which could have ruptured the egg and killed her. Finally, a female doctor referred her to a doctor who found it and operated just before it burst.

In 1955, after two years at home, Fay was predictably restless. She and

Bedford still planned to have children as they continued to build their careers. Bedford entered law school with a great deal of support and direction from Fay. At the same time, Fay entered the master's program in physical education at Kent State University and had a part-time appointment directing intramural sports at the University of Akron. The pace would have daunted the average student. She worked in Akron until four o'clock, drove 14 miles to Kent State to attend classes at seven, and then returned to Akron where she typically spent several more hours in her office.

Kent State University was a perfect fit for Fay, and being back in an intellectually stimulating atmosphere inspired her. In 1955, while in her master's program, she accepted a full-time position as instructor in the women's physical education department at Kent State, where her teaching career would unfold over the next 16 years.

Even the busiest days couldn't override Fay's yearning to coach field hockey. She started intramural clubs at Kent State in hopes of establishing a varsity team to compete against other schools. But she met an obstacle: Hester Jane Johnson, the field hockey instructor, believed that women's intercollegiate varsity competition was a ludicrous idea. Johnson argued that it turned girls into boys. When Fay announced in a faculty meeting that her club would compete against Lake Erie College, Johnson was furious. According to Fay, "She was so upset I thought she was going to hit me. She said that a club is just for girls who want to play hard and learn more about sports. I told her that she was old-fashioned. Times were changing and women needed more experience." Fay refused to yield, and during the next year her club played eight intercollegiate games despite ongoing opposition from colleagues like Johnson.

Fay then formed and coached basketball, volleyball, and tennis teams. She explained, "We developed a cadre of students who were pushing for the opportunity to compete in interscholastic sports, and in that era changes started to happen." To help build her hockey program, she took her players to Constance Applebee's field hockey camp in the Poconos every summer, noting, "I drove them all the way to Pennsylvania in a station wagon!" Fay speculated that perhaps her greatest accomplishment was that the young women she coached learned to love sports as much as she did.

Since the Women's Division of the National Amateur Athletic Foundation had redirected women's intercollegiate athletics toward intramural play, such competition had been non-existent or informal at colleges and universities. As long as women weren't building programs and asking for resources, no one paid much attention to them. But, Fay recalled, the men began to take notice when women started to "push and shove" for greater freedom and financial support for their teams. Years earlier, male colleagues had ostracized Gladys Palmer and other women at Ohio State for trying to establish intercollegiate programs. According to Fay, Ohio was "ultraconservative," and "aggressive leadership was sorely needed during that era."

One experience crystallized sexism toward women athletes:

> A graduate student in my class at Kent State was a very conceited, chauvinistic male. One day he marched into my office and said, "I hear you think you're a pretty good tennis player."
> I said, "I don't know about that. I've played a lot of competitive tennis, and I play in a lot of tournaments."
> "I just want you to know that I'm not a tennis player," he said, "but I'm athletically inclined and I can beat any woman. I don't care how good she is."
> I answered, "Buddy, I'll meet you at five on the tennis court this afternoon."

After Fay "beat the tar out of that guy," he scheduled a second match for the following evening, convinced that her victory was a fluke. News of the match spread through the department:

> By five o'clock, the court was surrounded by enough spectators to fill an auditorium. I served hard and I hit hard so that I could put the balls right at his feet. A couple of times he fell down on the court.

Although Fay won, her body paid for her victory. "For the next six weeks I couldn't raise my arm to comb my hair or brush my teeth," she said. "I really wrecked my arm with tendonitis. I was such an idiot to do that for sheer vanity, but I had to beat the living daylights out of that egotistical male."

Fay's struggle to develop intercollegiate athletics for women generated her concern about public awareness and understanding of physical education and athletics. She realized that some educators were notoriously poor communicators:

> We're active people who get involved in a lot of things. But we weren't taking time to educate people about the value of our profession. Other departments within the university looked down on the physical education department, and I resented that. I didn't like being at the bottom of the totem pole.

Fay was elected to the faculty senate and other political groups through which she began to improve physical education's image. Although she gave many talks on the relationship between sports and a positive self-image, she was convinced that there had to be a better way to convey her message.

Television was just emerging as an educational vehicle in the 1950s, and Fay saw it as her opportunity to reach the public. She interpreted data from a Kent State physical education department survey on women's attitudes toward physical education. A majority responded that the sport aspect of physical education was fun but there was not enough emphasis on fitness. Fay believed that the first step in public relations should be to define clearly what it meant to be physically educated. While educators were striving to produce well-educated students, Fay urged them to go a step further to tell parents and the community who they were and what they did, and to identify their objectives and values. She wrote a television script to present the goals, the objectives, and the long-range values of being a physical education major. All incoming women students then viewed the program before enrolling in physical education classes.

Professional Service and Doctorate

After completing her thesis and earning her master's degree with a 4.0 average in just nine months, Fay continued to teach and to coach at Kent State University. At that time, in 1956, she also joined the board of the National Section for Girls and Women's Sports (NSGWS), an organization that promoted sports through play days and sports days. Her first undertaking for NSGWS was to develop skill charts and rulebooks for tennis, badminton, and other sports. Although executive director Rachel Bryant praised her efforts, Fay wanted to break tradition:

> I wanted to do more training and formalize the educational backgrounds of physical education teachers and coaches. I wanted to organize conferences and write more detailed training books for coaches. This was the beginning of coaching for women, and I wanted to get in on the ground floor.

To her disappointment, NSGWS was not ready to support her ideas, so she continued to produce skill charts.

Another of Fay's objectives was to improve the quality of secondary physical education programs. She observed, "In this country we worship professional athletes, big money, and Olympians. Physical education was at the bottom of the totem pole while the Olympic athletes we revered were at the top." In order to create a greater balance of recognition between fitness training and its ultimate development of highly skilled athletes, fitness had to become a focal point for educators and for the general public. To that end, Fay emphasized movement education, which taught correct skill development and fundamental movement in individual sports.

The biggest challenge was to define the concept of fitness. A big boost for physical education had come in 1953 when Dr. Hans Kraus and Ruth Hirschland (New York University, Institute of Physical Medicine and Rehabilitation) published "Muscular Fitness and Health" in the *Journal of Health, Physical Education and Recreation*. Their study of youth fitness was based on a test developed by Kraus and Dr. Sonja Weber that measured the minimum strength and flexibility of key muscle groups. Administered to approximately 4,400 U.S. children and 3,000 European children, the test revealed a much higher failure rate among American children than among their European peers (Russell, Oria & Pillsbury, 2012, p. 26; Our History).

According to Fay, Kraus and Hirschland's article alarmed physical educators and inspired revolutionary change. The NSGWS formed a task force to meet with Dr. Kraus and President Dwight Eisenhower. Sharing Kraus's concern, President Eisenhower and Vice President Richard Nixon organized the President's Conference on Fitness of American Youth in June 1956. The President's Council on Physical Fitness and related conferences evolved from this initiating event. During these conferences, physical educators established guidelines for improving youth fitness in the United States (Our History).

Despite national interest in fitness, Fay encountered physical educators who rejected the fitness movement. They believed that their responsibility was to teach sports skills and motor performance, not fitness. Fay argued that healthy, physically fit, and highly skilled physical education majors would be role models for students in other fields. Her radical position caused a disruptive rift between her and a colleague who argued that because fitness could not be defined, its results could not be measured. Fay still possessed the competitive drive that had earlier compelled her to accept her male peer's tennis challenge, so she would not let go of her vision. She was determined to integrate fitness into physical education.

Fitness Research and Teaching with Technology

Several forces directed Fay into the next phase of her life. While the fitness controversy threatened to polarize the field of physical education, television was becoming a prime medium for educating the general public about fitness. Perhaps most importantly, Fay and Bedford knew, in 1963, that they would not have children. Fay had suffered six sports-related miscarriages since her first pregnancy in 1953. She explained,

> I never knew I was pregnant because I never missed a period. One miscarriage happened when I jumped and bent over backwards during a volleyball tournament. I felt excruciating pain and started to hemorrhage. Another happened during a tennis match. My last miscarriage was in November 1963. I was in bed with my feet up watching the Kennedy funeral.

One doctor prescribed the synthetic estrogen DES (diethylstilbestrol) according to the popular belief that it helped prevent miscarriages. The U.S. Food and Drug Administration later advised against DES use after studies linked it to cancer and other serious health complications.

The miscarriages left Fay emotionally and physically devastated. "I blamed myself," she confided. "If I had known when I was pregnant, I would have slowed down. I probably would have carried a child to term." Her guilt was compounded by the social pressure for women of her generation to have children. People who knew that she was married often asked her why she had no children. Although she explained her miscarriages, she felt that people did not accept her and Bedford's lifestyle. Some insinuated that Fay was selfish. Yes, she and Bedford lived comfortably with two salaries, but money was little compensation for their loss. Fay had a great deal to offer and cared for her nephews and students as if they were her own children.

Despite her grief, Fay's work ethic buoyed her goals. In 1964, while still teaching at Kent State, she enrolled in The Ohio State University's doctoral program to extend her fitness research. First, she designed a program of study that combined her interests in physical education, health and fitness, and public relations. She also studied psychology to better understand perception and self-concept, and she took courses in communications to strengthen her background in television production. Her advisors tried to discourage her from pursuing a multi-disciplinary dissertation topic by insisting that she complete twice the required hours if she wanted to incorporate so many fields into her degree.

As Fay had done so often in the past, she approached her newest goal with zealous enthusiasm. After she finished teaching and coaching, she literally raced from Kent to Columbus in her new Corvette, a gift from Bedford:

> I loved speed. I drove to Columbus going 100 miles per hour down Route 71. The speed limit was 75 miles per hour at that time. I memorized 1,500 French idioms by holding the cards up in front of me as I drove. It doesn't say much for my good sense, but it worked.

When Fay began her qualitative research on self-concept in 1964, the field of physical education had traditionally valued only quantitative studies. She focused her research on self-concept because positive self-image had so distinctly impacted her own success. But physical education researchers at Ohio State argued that her survey data did not reflect legitimate laboratory research. They questioned how she could ask people how they felt and compare their answers to laboratory test data. Fay countered that objectivity was not necessarily a measure of validity. Her groundbreaking dissertation, the first on self-concept at Ohio State, eventually paved the way for other qualitative studies. In fact, her dissertation was so popular that it disappeared from the university library five times before being archived on microfilm.

The fitness controversy inspired Fay to co-author *Foundations for Movement* (1964), which argued that physical education, while rooted in basic sciences, branches into health and fitness, motor skills, intramurals, sports, and highly organized competition. Many colleges and universities adopted the book for their required first-year physical education fitness courses, making it a bestseller. At the same time, Fay learned a valuable lesson about professional relationships.

> I was nuts in those days. I was young and inexperienced. I let my colleagues talk me into all kinds of agreements. They used me. I was so eager to prove that I was bright that I wrote the book that included six other colleagues as co-authors. The royalties were divided among seven of us, so no one made very much money from the book.

Curriculum development was another inevitable outcome of Fay's research. She designed Foundations for Fitness, a course required of all first-year women at Kent State that combined motor performance skills with health-related fitness skills. The course was designed to study every measurable physical parameter. Instructors taught students how to walk, lift, push, and pull properly. Fay studied posture photographs and conducted physical fitness testing. Some of the women faculty were horrified when she suggested that they wear leotards just as their students did. She admitted that she was brazen when she told those who refused, "You're not proud of your body image, and you don't deserve to be in our profession."

In order to meet the course's heavy teaching demands, Fay created a series of 10 television lectures that all students viewed on Wednesdays. The two-hour course then combined a Monday or a Friday laboratory activity class with the common Wednesday television lecture class to reduce teaching hours. Creating the series was an exhausting but memorable experience: "We worked with a very creative television director, sometimes until four or five in the morning because there was no replay in those days…. We had to memorize pages and pages of script." The design of the university's new television studio allowed trucks to bring in extra props and materials. Fay recalled, "Once I even brought in an elephant. There was a circus in the next community, and I asked the circus manager, 'Can I borrow your elephant for about fifteen minutes?' This guy looked at me as if I were crazy." The elephant was part of Fay's innovative teaching strategy to discuss nutrition, obesity, and self-concept while vividly illustrating that anyone who felt like an elephant didn't really look like one.

Although the amount of work was traumatic, Fay enjoyed the chaos of working with student television crews:

> I'd look up and see a ball flying through the air while we were filming. I'd have to reach out and catch it. Students were fun, and I was, too, but sometimes we worked until four o'clock in the morning. In some of those tapes, I look awful with deep circles under my eyes. That's how I became involved with television.

In the 1960s, educators were still debating the value of television as an educational tool when Fay produced her instructional series. Some faculty insisted that students disliked television instruction. Fay asked if students had told them they disliked it or if that was the educators' assumption. These kinds of questions appealed to Fay's research interests. Seeking a valid answer, she conducted tests to measure the self-concepts of the students taught with television, the students she taught personally, and a control group who didn't take the course. Although the three groups scored relatively even at the outset, the test averages of the young women in the television class and in the personally taught class rose significantly. In fact, the scores of the television class were a bit higher. The control group showed very little increase. Fay conceded, "They may not like it, but they learn." Her use of television and the evidence that students learned through technology hinted at 21st century teaching technologies. Fay's television course was so successful that Kent State's regional campuses still taught it 25 years after its original production.

Leadership in an Era of Social Unrest

The most difficult stories for Fay to tell describe the fatal clash between student demonstrators and the Ohio National Guard at Kent State University in May of 1970. Since the 1950s, after Russia launched Sputnik, she had watched the educational system pour knowledge into American students to compensate for math and science deficiencies. A decade later, she perceived a dangerous trend among students:

> Kids were rebelling against this authoritarian type of teaching. Everyone had become a number. Enrollment jumped from 6,000 to 13,000, and the university used computers for the first time. I refused to call them by number and memorized all of my students' names. Many were dropping out of college, and they started to speak out and to hold demonstrations. The Vietnam War was in full swing, including the Cambodian invasion. Kent State's Black students marched off campus en masse. They claimed discrimination to the degree that the campus was becoming almost inhumane.

Fay pleaded with colleagues to listen to students and warned them that anger would escalate if they ignored student concerns. Students confided in Fay because they knew she would listen. Her role as mediator between students and administrators was not an official position but a role she felt morally obligated to assume. From her perspective, the administrators' attitude was to "keep 'em down" and to punish students for what school authorities defined as deviant behavior. Fay concluded that University educators were unaware of students' deep emotions because they were interested only in the intellectual life at Kent State.

On Friday, May 1, 1970, Fay watched as approximately 500 students gathered on the campus Commons to protest the Cambodian invasion. That evening, downtown Kent was paralyzed with vandalism as protestors shattered the plate glass windows of North Water Street businesses. Kent Mayor LeRoy Satrom closed the bars at 12:30 that morning and declared a state of civil emergency. He then phoned the governor's office, which summoned the National Guard.

The Guard had restored order by Sunday, May 3, without significant confrontation with students. Also, Mayor Satrom had declared a curfew for students and prohibited outdoor demonstrations and rallies. Sociology professors who challenged the concept of martial law urged students to demonstrate regardless of regulations. Assured that the Guard did not have live ammunition, students gathered on the Commons at noon on Monday, May 4. Fay observed an obvious dichotomy of values between the guardsmen, "clean-cut, military All-American types," and the protestors, "hippies with beards." She recalled,

> The tension was building to a climax. There were no administrators in sight. Someone should have taken a bullhorn, sat down, talked, and listened. There was absolutely no authority and no control at all. Almost everyone had abandoned campus.

Countless newspapers, books, websites, and court documents have described the series of events that occurred on May 4. Fay offered her own account of the shootings, which she witnessed from behind Taylor Hall:

> The Guard made a wedge and moved through the crowd on the Commons. Protestors simply folded out and surrounded them. Some thought students were going to attack the Guard, but for some reason they didn't. The Guard regrouped, marched over the hill by Taylor Hall, and went down to the practice football field. They huddled, then turned around and moved back toward Blanket Hill and the Commons. When they got to the top of the hill, they turned, knelt and fired. Some people on the other side of the Commons said they heard a loud crack just before the shootings. One hundred and fifty people testified later that there was in fact a crack. It could have been a cherry bomb, a firecracker, or a pistol shot. To this day, some think that's what caused the Guard to fire. Most of their guns were pointed in the air, but obviously some weren't.

From Fay's vantage point, the guards appeared to be marching up the hill to form another wedge and try to dismantle the demonstration. Something still untold happened when they reached the top of the hill: "They fired, 'dah-dah-dah-dah,' and it was over. Thirteen students were lying on the parking lot pavement. I was like a statue. My blood ran cold. Students started running around, trying to regroup, apparently wanting to attack the guards en masse."

Shock and horror followed the shootings that killed four students and injured nine. "Some of the protestors were carrying Viet Cong flags," Fay recalled. "They dipped the flags into the blood of one of the killed protestors and did a crazy dance, screeching at the top of their lungs."

Minimal order was restored when geology professor Glenn Frank grabbed a bullhorn and shouted for students to gather and sit down. Fay described Frank as a "gentle, mild-mannered" man whom no one would have suspected of taking charge as he did. He warned students that they would be killed if they tried to attack the Guard. The school closed, and Frank sent the students home.

In the aftermath of the tragedy, Fay faced personal and professional tensions:

> The faculty went either far right or far left. Some people thought that the Guard had willfully murdered the students. People on the other side thought that the students were at fault and deserved to be shot. Helicopters hovered over the campus all day. At night, they flew very low and scanned the campus with searchlights. To this day, I get a chill when I hear a helicopter.

To help restore order on campus, Fay summoned the endurance and the motivational techniques that had made her a winning athlete and coach. She had stepped into a new and difficult role when she attempted to mediate between students and administrators. Although she was no longer the radical or the underdog confronting authority for change, she still found herself at odds with authoritarian leadership. She challenged herself with new leadership goals to respond to the university's immediate needs.

Rebuilding Kent State

Leadership shaped Fay's career as she assumed new, visible roles at the national level of physical education administration and at Kent State. She relished the story of how one led to the other. It began in fall of 1970, as the national recession prompted secondary schools and colleges to cut physical education programs. As a member of the Secondary Physical Education Council of the National Association for Sports and Physical Education (NASPE), Fay urged AAHPERD to protect these programs. Ross Merrick, AAHPERD representative to the United States Olympic Committee, responded by asking Fay to propose a program to meet national physical education needs. She met with "the best minds in physical education," listened to their needs and concerns, then distilled recurring themes into five major concepts for her Physical Education Public Information (PEPI) project. When NASPE approved the project, Fay arranged a one-year leave of absence from Kent State to plan and direct PEPI.

In 1971, when the Division for Girls' and Women's Sports established the Association for Intercollegiate Athletics for Women (AIAW), a multi-sport governing body, Fay was elected president of the Ohio College Association of AIAW. At this time, she advocated for Title IX and led a strong movement toward intercollegiate athletics in Ohio. With a single vision to promote physical education, fitness, and gender equity, she bridged her local and national work.

The PEPI report she delivered at the 1972 AAHPERD convention in Houston was a media spectacle. Her presentation featured animated figures projected onto a large screen. It caught the attention of Glenn Olds, the new president of Kent State, who happened to pass the meeting room on his way to an unrelated meeting. He asked someone in the audience for details about this dynamic speaker. He had no idea that she was a Kent State faculty member. After her report, Olds approached Fay and invited her to visit him as soon as she returned to Kent. If Olds had been surprised to learn that Fay was from Kent State, he was even more stunned when she asked, "Oh, who are you?" Neither knew the other because Fay had been on leave working on the PEPI project.

Their first meeting at Kent State ended with an offer. President Olds asked Fay to serve as Vice President for Public Affairs and Development. Fay hesitated. She would be the first woman vice president at an Ohio university and the first woman in the country at that level in the field of development in higher education. She insisted that the Board of Trustees, the faculty, and the students approve her appointment to ensure community support for Olds' decision.

All of the groups favored Fay's appointment, but she faced sex discrimination common for women entering traditionally male professions during the 1970s. Her nemeses were a medical doctor and an older single man on the Board. "They fought me on everything I did," she recalled. "The vote was always nine to two for anything I suggested. These two men were just vehement in their dislike for women, particularly married women."

According to Fay, their prejudice excluded her from an equitable annual raise: "When the issue of raises was presented, the doctor jumped up out of his chair and said, 'Absolutely not! I will never give that woman the same raise as a man. Never! She's a woman, and besides that, she's married.'" His statements came more than a decade after Title VII of the Civil Rights Act of 1964 prohibited employment discrimination "based on race, color, religion, sex and national origin" (U.S. Equal Employment). Fay warned him that she would sue if he ever made such statements in a public meeting. He retracted his statement and claimed instead that Fay was incompetent and did not

Fay Biles, ca. 1980s. SHAPE America.

deserve an equitable raise. So, regardless of President Olds' "glowing report" of her accomplishments, she received only a three percent raise to the men's eight percent.

The antagonism between Fay and the medical doctor worsened when President Olds appointed both to a committee so that the doctor could witness Fay's capabilities. According to Fay, the doctor had little concern for her abilities.

> By the time we got to his country club, where he insisted that we meet, he would have had three martinis. When I gave reports of our meetings at the public board meetings, he never remembered what we had discussed and what he had agreed to. Finally I couldn't take any more. I made up my mind that if women were going to get ahead, then we had to learn to operate in a man's world.

The most obvious defense against overt sexism was a lawsuit, but Bedford advised against legal action. He warned Fay, "You're the first woman. If you cause trouble, they'll never hire another woman." So, instead of taking legal action, Fay assumed the offense in order to gain control. Alienated from clandestine breakfast meetings where the vice presidents discussed their agenda and made agreements on upcoming issues, Fay developed what she called an "information gestapo." She instructed her secretary to lunch with their secretaries and find out what would be discussed at upcoming meetings. She gathered research to offer information that they might not have considered. When she discovered that they were weak in finances, she made that her area of expertise by attending seminars and studying. Playing the "men's games" meant much more work for Fay, but she pushed herself in the interest of advancing women in business.

Despite her tactics, Fay could not make those two vice presidents see beyond the fact that she was a woman. Two incidents stood out in her memory:

> They all smoked heavily during meetings. One day I stood up to open a window. The room was suddenly quiet. When I turned around, they were all staring at me. One vice president said, "Hey, Fay, you should wear sweaters more often." I was speechless with anger. I was always searching for either a smart answer or something that wouldn't put them down but that would at least make a point clear. It was a chore.

During a different meeting, President Olds called for a break just before the vote on an important issue. The men went directly to the men's room. Fay followed them in and said, "Look, I know the decision's going to be made right here. I want to be here when it's made." They were shocked. But Fay was not the only woman to see the inside of a men's room during an era of radical social change. Either women crossed boundaries or they were excluded from important business decisions.

Meanwhile, the May 4 shootings had devastated Kent State socially and financially. Fundraising dropped almost to zero because, Fay observed, no one wanted to contribute to such a radical institution. Enrollment plummeted from 21,500 to 16,500 students as parents in northeast Ohio told their children that they could attend any university *except* Kent State. When the campus closed in May of 1970, the university had refunded all student housing fees. In an effort to compensate for the loss, the legislature authorized a substantial fee increase for out-of-state students, who usually occupied three new dormitories built specifically for them. Fay perceived a hidden agenda in the increases:

> The legislature knew that East Coast kids led the 1970 riots. They were much more likely to be activists than Midwestern kids. So the legislature declared that *all* out of state students would pay a hefty out-of-state fee. In other words, they kept them out of Kent State.

Fay's first initiatives as vice president were to replenish exhausted reserve funds and to fill the vacant dormitories. Fundraising during the first phase pursued the three largest corporations in Ohio: Goodrich, Goodyear, and Firestone. While researching the needs of each corporation, Fay discovered that Goodyear President and CEO Charles Pelloid was a strong advocate of free enterprise. So with a quarter of a million-dollar grant from Goodyear, the College of Business endowed a professorship to hire a retired businessperson to spend at least one semester discussing the free enterprise system with students. Fay envisioned a non-traditional approach to teaching that would give students a realistic view of business. The endowed professor would teach classes, bring in visitors from the business world, and, if necessary, sit on the floor of the dormitory and talk with students until three o'clock in the morning.

Sustained funding would require measurable evidence of the endowed professor's impact on students, so Fay designed a pre- and post-course survey for first-year business students. The survey asked questions such as "How much of the business dollar do you think goes for profit?" Students generally answered 33 to 35 percent, when in fact profit was sometimes only two to three percent. At the end of the semester, students answered the same survey with more realistic answers. Pelloid was so thrilled that Goodyear awarded Kent State a five-year grant of $50,000 per year.

Next, Fay created and hosted a luncheon group of all the CEOs in northeastern Ohio. They met once a month in Kent State's Board of Trustees suite. Fay got to know the corporate leaders on a first name basis and invited speakers to discuss cutting edge business developments. She also wrote a newsletter for the CEOs to introduce recent research. Kent State eventually received a gift from each one.

A significant problem remained: Kent's three new dormitories were still sitting vacant. Fay learned that B.F. Goodrich Company held its training programs at a very expensive resort, so she suggested converting the upper three floors of one dormitory into a training center. She negotiated meal fees to boost the Student Center's sagging revenues and secured unlimited use of the library and fitness facilities. She reasoned that if the community interacted with Kent State students, they would see beyond the violent rebel stereotype conjured by the May 4 tragedy.

Goodrich's CEO had only one problem with the plan. He believed that male trainees would never agree to share bathrooms. Fay recalled bartering with him:

> Goodrich, in addition to manufacturing tires, also manufactures plastic products and wallpaper. Why don't you convert the two top floors and use it as a gift, a tax write-off, to Kent State? You could put beautiful wallpaper on the walls and install nice carpeting. We'll have new draperies, fluffy towels, and expensive soap. You can have a lounge with a bar where people can congregate.

Goodrich liked the idea, but insisted that the communal bathrooms would be a problem. Fay convinced Goodrich to pilot the plan for one year. If the men disliked the accommodations, she would terminate the agreement.

As Fay had anticipated, the program was a huge success and subsequently raised three million dollars a year. Goodrich offered Kent State researchers the use of its sophisticated computer center and in turn Kent offered to house Goodrich's administrative offices in unused library space. Some disagreed with the arrangement. One professor telephoned Fay and shouted, "How dare you bring a business into the inner sanctum of the library circle!" Fay knew, however, that Kent State could not afford the luxury of such academic elitism. She asked the professor if there had been faculty raises or an increase in library holdings that year. When he said no, she explained that rent from Goodrich paid for library publications. She made her point and ended the conflict.

Fay's fundraising and image development transformed Kent State into a media magnet. The news media were particularly interested in Kent State's plans to build an addition to its gymnasium next to the football field. The field was adjacent to the parking lot and the hill where the shooting had occurred. This news caused violent public reaction. Fay explained,

> The protestors feared that when people came to see the area, the new building would make it look as though the area was closed in. In actuality, the area where the students were shot was wide open. In fact, at the moment of the shootings there were no students close to the Guards.

Fay's job was to convince the public that the building was not on the spot of the killings as the protestors claimed.

Like a haunting déjà vu, protestors swarmed Kent State. They vowed that the annex would not be built in that area. Students called their own press conferences to counter Kent's public information releases. Eventually, the university erected a fence around the building area. According to Fay, protestors climbed the fence to demonstrate on the grounds. They demonstrated every Saturday for two years during the building's construction. On one particular Saturday, the University of Michigan's vice president for development warned Fay that Kent State students were recruiting Michigan students for a big demonstration at Kent State. The University of Chicago then called to say that students were renting a bus to come to Kent. Although Fay warned Kent security to expect a big crowd that day, they envisioned a manageable crowd of about a hundred people. To their shock, 2,000 demonstrators arrived and, Fay noted, caused extensive damage:

> They tore down the fence, wrecked machinery, and painted signs and symbols all over campus. They were going to repeat the demonstration two weeks later, so more police came in on horseback with tear gas. They were right across the commons from where the students were sitting. It was worse than May 4.

As Kent State's spokesperson, Fay became the target of student anger:

> Every time they saw me, they'd sing, "Fay Biles you can't hide. We know you're on the murderers' side." The minute my husband left for work in the morning, they'd come out in Jeeps to picket around the cul-de-sac in front of our house.... They would follow me in cars. I had to have a security guard escort me from campus to the Ohio Turnpike so that I could get safely onto the road home. They would call me every day with threats like, "We're gonna cut you up in pieces and send you home in a box."

If these students were identified, Fay revealed, they would have become FBI targets. So they created a radical image for themselves. They wore handkerchiefs around their faces and hats pulled low so that only their eyes showed. They planned weekly bomb scares, giving authorities until 4:00 p.m. to find four bombs—one for each student killed. But the protestors didn't scare Fay. "They were my students," she said, "so I'd laugh at them. I tried to figure out something that would get to them. Finally I told them, 'You look ugly.' They hated that. We lived through a violent two years."

Although Fay believed in freedom of expression and standing up for one's beliefs, she perceived a basic hypocrisy in the students' actions and their way of life. During one telephone threat, she asked the caller how students could afford to protest for a living. The student said that they received $80 a week to protest at Kent. When she asked who paid them, the phone went dead. She called the FBI, which had orders to stay out of Kent State business. They would investigate only if Fay could identify the source of funding. She wanted the chaos and violence to end, but she was never able to collect enough evidence to warrant an investigation.

Public support for the protestors ended abruptly after Fay debated the leader of a radical student group on television. Before the show, the mediator told Fay that he planned to ask her why the administration was repressing students. Fay reminded him that his position was supposed to be neutral. So during the program he asked what she would do if the courts ruled against Kent State in favor of the students whose families were suing the National Guard, the Governor of Ohio, and the state of Ohio. She said that the university would obviously obey the courts. The mediator then asked the student leader what his group would do if they lost the court battle. The student said that they would continue to protest. Shocked by this response, the mediator said that the students' actions sounded Communist. According to Fay, the student replied, "You're damn right we're Communists and we're damn proud of it."

That afternoon, Fay received hundreds of messages from people who had heard the program. Most were shocked at the student leader's final comment. As a result, the flow of contributions to students dried up, the campus atmosphere settled, and Kent State built the annex to the gymnasium.

Moving Forward: New Initiatives for Women

Two years of daily conflict had taken Fay away from her primary interests in program building, self-esteem research, and gender equity. In the calmed environment, she turned her attention to non-traditional women students and initiated the Development Opportunities Vocational Education (DOVE) project for women over 30. A major component of DOVE was confidence building. Some women who had successfully raised their families returned to school to finish a degree they began before marrying, to get an advanced degree, or to see if they were even capable of earning a degree. Between 1974 and 1980, approximately 3,000 women enrolled in the DOVE program. To Fay's disappointment, DOVE would become a minor program after her tenure as vice president. She remarked frankly that the program suffered because subsequent vice presidents would not hire another woman to maintain it.

Many of Fay's program ideas were rooted in her experience. She explained her development of Kent's graduate and undergraduate gerontology degree programs:

> Before my mother died, we had to place her in a nursing home where she could have around-the-clock care. When I went to the nursing home, I was shocked by the conditions and how

the residents were treated. The most traumatic incident was when I asked where her teeth were. The caregivers looked at me as if I were an idiot and said, "We had to take them out. She might swallow them." I then realized how little I knew about the aging process and what happens to people in the terminal stages.

After her mother died, Fay asked that memorial donations be sent to Kent State to start a gerontology center. To her surprise, representatives from 14 academic departments came to the organizational meeting. Some colleagues warned her that 14 departments were too many. They were wrong. The graceful interworking of these departments created the first interdisciplinary program at Kent State. Fay concluded, "If people are creative, innovative and perceptive, and if they can see trends and determine what's needed, then they can work together in a meaningful way."

Fay's immersion in program building did not detract from her commitment to physical education leadership. In 1979, as she completed her service as Vice President for Public Affairs and Development, Fay was elected president of AAHPERD and spent a year as president-elect struggling with the Alliance's half-million dollar deficit. She wondered what kind of fundraising could possibly alleviate such a deficit. At a PEPI regional meeting in Chicago, Jean Barkow had spoken about doing a rope-skipping project with the American Heart Association (AHA). "That was always in the back of my mind," Fay explained. She recruited Executive Vice President of NASPE George Anderson and AHA administrators to help her develop Jump Rope for Heart.

Fay Biles, speaking for AAHPERD Projects, ca. mid-1970s. SHAPE America.

This national fundraiser focused on elementary school children and emphasized health education while participants jumped rope for fun. Although the AHA supported the project, it hesitated to share fundraising income. Fay negotiated with the AHA for a year before addressing its Board of Trustees directly. She was well aware of its resistance, at that time, to preventive health spending. To add to the stress, she entered the meeting and found a hundred trustees, all cardiologists, seated around a table as if it were a United Nations meeting. Fay emphasized AAHPERD's concern for education at the kindergarten through college levels while the trustees reiterated the AHA's need for crisis intervention and coronary care units. Compromise seemed impossible until Fay suggested that the project would raise millions of dollars. Her description of Chicago's pilot project, which raised over $400,000, piqued their interest. She offered to organize a nationwide program if AAHPERD received a portion to fund wellness and education. The Board of Trustees refused.

Unwilling to concede, Fay met with AHA auditors, treasurers, and CPAs to define exactly how the money would be spent. She and George Anderson provided background on numerous Alliance programs. These efforts secured Fay a meeting with the 4,000-member AHA delegation at its annual convention. She and her colleagues resurrected the PEPI figure with moveable arms and legs. As the figure exercised on a large screen behind her, she assured the audience that the rope-skipping project would raise millions of dollars, making the AHA's largest fundraising total to date, $150,000, look like peanuts. And, in return for only five percent of the funds, AAHPERD would administer the project.

Fay recounted the lively response:

> At the end of the fifteen minutes, everyone stood up. They clapped, they hammered on the table, and they stamped their feet. *Good Morning America* host David Hartman was there as the AHA's national honorary fundraising chair. He picked me up and swung me around. Meanwhile, the PEPI figure was off and running across the screen. The AHA folks went absolutely wild, and the vote was one hundred percent in favor of the project.

Jump Rope for Heart raised between five and six million dollars in its inaugural year. The program continues to thrive internationally and to involve school children in fitness activities for fun, health awareness, personal development, and fundraising (About Jump Rope, 2014). One participant particularly embodied the concept of fitness that Fay had long been promoting:

> When Cuyahoga Falls, Ohio, had a Jump Rope for Heart Day, a man called and said, "I've jumped rope all my life. May I come over and jump with the kids?" He was 80 years old, and he did great tricks. I called the newspapers and all the radio stations immediately. He was interviewed over a period of three hours, and he never stopped jumping.

To ensure the program's educational impact, Fay served on the AHA Health Education of the Young Committee and contributed to the publication of manuals, songbooks, and videotapes about heart health. She advocated the benefits of fitness beyond heart health. "I think the best kept secret in this country is the fact that we could prevent the drug culture if we could teach our children to become more physically active," she insisted. "Activity offers a natural high and gives them self-confidence."

Each of Fay's achievements led to new opportunity. In 1981, at age 54, Fay became a consultant for the United States Olympic Committee Education Council to introduce Olympic education programs into the schools. She reasoned,

> If we can get our very young, our youth, and our adults to look at the beginning values and ideals of the Olympic games and the Olympic movement, then we might convince them to practice good sportsmanship, to stay away from cheating, violence, gambling, drugs, and everything else that's negative about our sport scene. I feel that we must return to the moral, ethical values in sports.

To that end, she developed curriculum and supplementary activities based on the concept of "Olympism," which celebrates the ideals, values, and strengths of the ancient Olympic games. Working with the United States Olympic Committee, Fay planned activities to promote the harmony of body, mind, and morals. In 1980, she was appointed to the United States Olympic Committee, which she then served for 16 years.

Fay accepted a subsequent appointment from 1984 to 1988 as Director for the Olympic Day in the Schools. This program expanded the ideals of "Olympism" into activities in all subject areas. Its festival events simulated Olympic opening and closing ceremonies to teach students the meaning of Olympic symbols through activities such as art, poster and writing contests, and field events. It was one of the most exciting programs Fay had ever participated in because it stimulated ingenuity and creativity in teachers and students. She added that the committee was trying to reach young people with values that the United States desperately needed.

As an AAHPERD representative and North America's vice president of the International Council for Health, Physical Education and Recreation (ICHPER), Fay took part in World Congresses in Israel, London, Italy, Vancouver, and the United States. Her participation in the Israel Congress resulted in another first for her. Just prior to the conference, Israeli President Uriel Simri asked Fay if she would give the opening keynote address in place of Menachem Begin, who was ill. She was the first woman to deliver this address, and she has never forgotten the audience reaction.

> In Israel, they ask the keynote speaker to sit at the top level of the auditorium. As the M.C. announced my name and invited me down to the platform floor, I had to walk down steps, cross over, descend to the ground floor, walk up the steps and across the stage, and sit down. Everyone stared at me to see what a *woman* was going to do. When I began to speak, many

> in the audience kept talking. I wondered if I should wait until they stopped or tell them to be quiet. So I just kept talking about the changes in health throughout the world. After a while, they picked up their earphones and started to listen. Then they leaned forward with sincere attention and interest.

A standing ovation confirmed her impact on the audience.

Full-time teaching and university committee work occupied Fay until 1985, when Kent State offered faculty incentives for early retirement. She gratefully accepted the offer in order to give full attention to her research, which inspired a successful consulting firm. She and Virginia Bowman founded FAVA, which specialized in self-concept therapy. "I wish I could give many women a shot of self-confidence to take risks, to compete equally with men, and climb the ladder to the top where they deserve to be," she confided. FAVA conducted programs to help people think creatively and be more perceptive of their environment. It also offered workshops on different styles of personality, communication, leadership, and team-building. The firm was a culmination of all of Fay's deepest commitments and interests, and she continued as president well into her retirement.

Empowering people has always motivated Fay's work. After moving with Bedford to Marco Island, Florida, in the early 1990s, she became president of the Marco Island chapter of the American Association of University Women (AAUW). Earlier in her career she had directed an AAUW study of self-concept among boys and girls in elementary school and in high school. The results were shocking. While first grade girls' and boys' self-concept measurements were almost equal, high school girls' scores had fallen to 1/3 of boys' scores. Although many factors, including teacher and peer behavior, affected the plummeting scores, Fay was convinced that public awareness and education regarding self-concept would be key factors in maintaining and improving girls' self-esteem. With the Marco Island AAUW chapter, she fought for women's rights in business and in public office participation.

Fay attributed much of her success to her husband's support. Bedford once admitted that since retirement he kept busy taking Fay to and from the airport. Fay elaborated,

> He meets me at the gate. He reaches out and takes my purse and my briefcase and carries them out to the car. I keep telling him that he doesn't look very good carrying a purse. He was a very masculine football player and is extremely confident. It doesn't bother him to be nice. He helps me in every way.

Fay has never forgotten the compromises he made early in their marriage, some that required him to change his beliefs and values. In return, Fay helped him build his dream home on Marco Island overlooking the Gulf of Mexico.

The death of Fay's beloved Bedford in August 2013 shifted her foundation. Yet, at 86, she continued her leadership and public relations work as president of the Marco Island Taxpayers Association. Her lifelong interest in the relationship between fitness and self-confidence has made her a brilliant leader and created new ways of defining and responding to women's needs. Her vision for equity and the ethical values and legal possibilities expressed through Title IX aligned powerfully. Fay has always been a force ahead of her time.

5

Dorothy McIntyre
*Changing Minnesota
High School Athletics*

One of Dorothy McIntyre's formative experiences occurred on a Sunday afternoon in December 1941:

> I was five years old and playing on the living room floor after a Sunday dinner at my grandparents' home in Hawkeye. Suddenly all of the adults stopped talking as the radio announced that Pearl Harbor had been attacked. I didn't know where Pearl Harbor was, but I knew it must be very serious. My uncle said he was going to enlist the next day.

From that day forward, World War II impacted Dorothy and her peers. As an imaginative nine-year old, she climbed with friends among the branches of a favorite schoolyard tree, pretending to pilot a B-17 destined for adventure. Meanwhile, Windsor #3, the one-room schoolhouse Dorothy attended, was only a mile from the McIntyre family farm near Hawkeye, Iowa. The world was simultaneously unknown and familiar to her.

This childhood nurtured Dorothy's early roots of lifelong service and leadership. She taught physical education and social studies for 13 years, and then served for 32 years as the first woman associate director of the Minnesota State High School League executive staff. An advocate for opportunity for girls and women, she guided the development of statewide sport clinics where teachers learned how to train girls and women. She also led efforts to organize the first girls' state tournaments in a variety of team and individual sports. Much of this work occurred during contentious national debate leading to and following the enactment of Title IX in 1972. After retiring from the League, Dorothy co-authored two historical accounts of women's basketball in Minnesota and co-founded McJohn Publishing as a means to share women's stories.

In the spirit of team effort that her work has promoted, Dorothy insisted that she never acted alone. She relied on a trusted crew of friends to advise her and to approve her ideas with thumbs-up. Improving sports for girls and women required teamwork, and Dorothy McIntyre's life is deeply rooted in community effort.

Midwestern Roots

Dorothy was born in 1936, the eldest of two daughters. Her parents shared the farm and family chores, regardless of gender. "Our mother milked cows alongside dad, drove tractors, grew big vegetable and flower gardens, as well as raising the children, making meals, plus tending to her church and community responsibilities," Dorothy explained. "She was a strong woman. Every day I read a piece of paper taped to the edge of her kitchen cupboard: 'If it is to be, it's up to me.'"

Work and play defined Dorothy's early years. When the U.S. government needed an alternative to kapok, the naturally buoyant cotton fiber then used to fill life jackets but in short supply, it asked children to gather milkweed. The children of Windsor #3 wanted to do their part for the war effort. Dorothy recalled bundling up and walking the roads around the school with her teacher and a dozen children from grades K-8 to pick the pods from milkweed plants growing abundantly in nearby ditches. Like school children throughout the country, they filled gunny sacks that adults took to town and added to dozens of sacks collected by other schools in the area. Dorothy noted, "We were proud to contribute to saving countless lives of sailors and downed flight crews. Today, my World War II buddies who flew B-17s tell me they are quite sure their life jackets were filled with the milkweed gathered by the students of Windsor #3."

Growing up on a farm prepared Dorothy to navigate the roads she would later follow. As a child, she liked being outdoors, playing Tarzan in the woods behind the farm, and building forts and tree houses. She liked being the leader of the pack. As she grew older, she enjoyed working outdoors in the fresh air, driving tractors and raking hay, disking the black Iowa soil, pulling wagons, and, most of all, joining her father on the threshing crews. Neighbors worked together with one big threshing machine, going from one farm to the next, each supplying wagons and tractors to bring the oat bundles to the machine (McIntyre, 2005, p. 140; D. McIntyre, personal communication, March 7, 2013[1]). "I loved the noon meals," Dorothy recalled, "when the women helped one another to put out tables laden with food. I could never understand why I was the only girl driving the tractors, horses, and sometimes mules out in the fields, gathering the oat bundles." It would be years before she understood the full force of traditional gender roles.

In the meantime, Dorothy refused to conform to gender codes that threatened her independence. One story, in particular, illustrates her determination:

> The boys were a pain in the neck. My straw hat usually disappeared over the noon break, sometimes sunk with rocks to the bottom of the horse tank or wedged near the top of the windmill. One day while everyone was standing around the barnyard after the noon meal, I decided to challenge a wiry troublemaker to stop his harassment. I was strong and planned a quick throw to the ground. Then I would hold him down until he publicly admitted defeat.
>
> I made a mistake. We didn't set any rules. Suddenly I was in a wrestling hold that he must have learned from his brothers, and I had to give up when I ran out of oxygen. My strength and indignation took second place to breathing. It was humiliating with my dad and all the men watching my public defeat. However, after that confrontation, the harassment stopped. The boys knew I was smarter and the next time I wouldn't fall for any unfair tactics. My battle in the barnyard was an important lesson for confrontations to come in my adult life. (McIntyre, 2005, p. 140; D. McIntyre, personal communication, March 7, 2013)

Nineteen forty-nine marked another transition for Dorothy as she left the comfort of her country school, with a class of six, to attend high school "in town." Hawkeye was five miles from the farm, a town of 525 friendly people, according to a sign on Highway 18. At age 13 she entered a ninth grade class of 13. The students' parents and other relatives had gone to school there as evidenced by Dorothy's father's initials carved into one of the cloakroom walls. Again the world seemed bigger but still familiar.

At Hawkeye High School, a two-story brick building with elementary grades on the first floor and the high school grades on the second floor, Dorothy became involved with team sports. Behind the school was a smaller brick gymnasium where girls' and boys' basketball teams played. Dorothy's aunts played on those teams in the 1930s, and she recalled their pictures proudly displayed on her grandmother's bureau. But she didn't follow in their tracks:

> I played softball during recess in grade school, but we didn't have any basketballs. One day in the gymnasium, I tried dribbling in for a layup shot and found my coordination lacking. I backed away from thinking I could be a player. Admittedly, the bare midriff shirts then popular for girls' basketball uniforms were also a bit intimidating. So I became the team's student manager. I loved cutting oranges, gathering up the towels, riding the bus to games, and cheering on the team.

The Iowa State Girls' Basketball Tournament in Des Moines was already legendary in 1949. Everyone not at the tournament milked their cows early and listened to the radio or, in later years, watched the games on television. The *Des Moines Register* printed the sports section on peach-colored paper, and girls' basketball scores and pictures filled the pages for weeks before, during, and after the tournament. Stars of tournament games became local heroes (McIntyre, 2005, p. 141; D. McIntyre, personal communication, March 7, 2013).

Dorothy admitted to having "major regrets" that she didn't play basketball in Iowa when it was "the biggest show in town." Now, when asked if she played basketball in that era, she wishes that she could say she was an outstanding guard when the Iowa girls' six-on-six game was the love of the state. Although a one-time opportunity slipped away, she resolved never to let that happen again. So what if she took a risk and failed? So what if someone disliked what she said or wrote or stood for? She resolved to "get off the bench and into the game."

College and Vocation

During the spring of their senior year of high school, Dorothy and three classmates traveled 30 miles from Hawkeye to Decorah to attend a college open house at Luther College. Until that day, Dorothy had not thought much about her life after graduation; Hawkeye High School had no guidance counselor to lead such exploration. Her mother suggested she might work in an office or as a cashier in a store, since she was a good typist. Dorothy welcomed the possibility of a college education and fell in love with Luther. She recalled,

> I looked in awe at the beautiful campus of this small, liberal arts college, proud of its Norwegian heritage, and nestled in what is known as the Little Switzerland of Iowa. It was clear what I wanted to do. When I ran through the door back home, I asked, "Do you think I might be able to go to Luther College?" And I held my breath.

Dorothy did, in fact, enroll in Luther College in the fall of 1953. Although she never knew how her parents made it happen, she has remained thankful for their support.

With little direction during her first semester, Dorothy gravitated toward a music major since she played the piano "a little" and the accordion "fairly well." After a brief experience in music theory class, which included writing a gavotte and resolving dominant sevenths, she realized her naïveté: "It was pure torture. I could carry a tune but not at a performance level. After my brief tryout for the Luther Choir, my name did not appear on the list of second auditions." Although Dorothy didn't pursue the major, her musical career didn't end entirely:

> Finally, after all of my unsuccessful attempts, I found my niche in music at Luther: I played the accordion for the Norwegian Independence Day parades through downtown Decorah. When I was about twelve years old, my first accordion teacher, who also ran a dance studio for young children, wanted me to learn how to tap dance and play the accordion *at the same time*.... I couldn't tap dance even without wearing an accordion. My second accordion teacher gave me the confidence to play for farmers' cooperative banquets and schoolhouse programs and to compete in local talent contests. I won three of them. As I played in Dec-

orah, the physical education majors club performed Norwegian folk dances. Once again, the accordion saved me from dancing.

Dorothy discovered her calling at the beginning of her junior year, after two years of dabbling in history, government, and business courses. She attended a meeting of the Women's Recreation Association with friends who were physical education majors. She then realized that she could become a teacher. She ran to the office of the head of the women's physical education department and made her announcement. The department head then calmly reminded her that it would be difficult to take all of the required courses in the remaining two years and complete student teaching. Dorothy was undeterred and graduated in 1957, just short of her 21st birthday, with a double major in health and physical education *and* social studies.

The Road to Minnesota

Drawn to rural areas and advised to go north, Dorothy began her first teaching position in 1957 at Ellendale-Geneva High School, in a southeastern Minnesota town that was about the size of Hawkeye. With a teaching salary of $2,950 plus an additional $50 for serving as the junior class advisor, Dorothy thought she was rich. She taught a variety of classes, including 7th and 8th grade general science, where the boys tested her authority:

> When the boys brought a jar of garter snakes while we were out in the woods on a field trip, my farm background and the antics of the threshing crew boys held me in good stead. I reached into the jar, lifted out a snake and showed the class the finer points of its anatomy. From that point on, I was in charge of the class.

Dorothy favored health and physical education classes for 7th through 10th grade girls because they had never had a teacher trained in those subjects. She was responsible for providing all young women in her school the opportunity to play for fun and social enjoyment. In addition to physical education classes and a variety of activities, she formed a Girls' Athletic Association (GAA) at Ellendale-Geneva High School. Through this organization, she was able to organize team competitions with other schools in the region. Minnesota state tournaments for girls, however, were still years into the future.

Dorothy would later learn that many of Ellendale's young women had mothers, grandmothers, and aunts who had played on basketball teams against other schools in the 1920s, during the first era of girls' basketball. The Ellendale newspaper reported about teams traveling in every kind of weather by Model T cars, sleigh, and train, sometimes staying overnight in the homes of the opposing team players. The girls played a three-court game, with two players from each team on each court. One Ellendale player, Helen Johnson, was featured in the rotogravure (photo) section of the *St. Paul Pioneer Press* for scoring 64 points in one game. Ellendale had enjoyed its girls' basketball teams, and Dorothy would puzzle for years over the teams' disappearance despite their popularity.

Dorothy McIntyre teaching Eden Prairie High School students how to prepare for the beginning of a track event. 1965. Eden Prairie High School.

In 1959, just two years after Dorothy had begun teaching at Ellendale-Geneva High School, a superintendent from a nearby school walked into one of her physical education classes and observed her for a few minutes. Shortly after, he invited her to join his staff at the small, suburban high school he was building near Minneapolis. Eden Prairie High School then became her home base for the next 11 years.

At Eden Prairie High School, Dorothy taught a variety of social studies classes. She infused American History class with lessons about women pioneers and heroes like Sacajawea and her favorite pilot Amelia Earhart. She joked that she was "head of a staff of *one* for the Girls' Physical Education Department." Those classes were held in a new gymnasium with outdoor fields and a track nearby. Meanwhile, Dorothy combined intramural activities and interscholastic competition under the umbrella of a new Girls' Athletic and Recreation Association (GARA) at Eden Prairie High School. Events filled the facilities with young women before, during, and after school, as well as on many weekends. Being "a staff of one" required Dorothy to be involved in all of the girls' athletics and recreation activities.

Dorothy taught a variety of activities from badminton, basketball, and field hockey to volleyball, cage ball, and archery. Her students provided halftime demonstrations at boys' basketball games, using hoops, balls, and ropes to perform tumbling and rhythmic gymnastics. They went bowling, took camping trips, and held an annual overnight party in the gymnasium. (McIntyre, 2005, p. 142; D. McIntyre, personal communication, March 7, 2013). And, she noted, she also supervised the cheerleading squads, which meant attending many boys' football and basketball games. "Even *my* energy reserves were being challenged," Dorothy admitted.

During this era of girls' sport, events took one of two forms: play days or sports days. On play days, girls from the same conference schools met on a Saturday at a host school to play different sports. Each school's participants were scattered onto different teams so that games wouldn't become "too competitive." Nametags and recognition awards were homemade, and the day concluded with punch and cookies. But the girls preferred sports days, which allowed schools to play as teams against one another in shortened games, usually volleyball or basketball. Dorothy heightened the competitive spirit as best she could: "For one track and field sports day, I created an Olympic torch using tin foil, a coffee can, and a paint brush. It made a nice torch."

Schools did not fund these activities for young women, and the teachers volunteered their time. Dorothy and parents taxied students to events in their cars. To pay for gasoline, the girls held bake sales and sold greeting cards.

Typically, however, the teachers paid the expenses from their own pockets for the reward of seeing excitement and joy on the young women's faces.

The girls were aware of the inequity. Dorothy recalled the day when a group of girls walked into her office and implored, "We want to play real games like the boys do." They wanted to keep score, to win or lose, and to learn more about a favorite sport. They wanted to see how well they could play, and they wanted coaching and instruction.

The students' dreams touched Dorothy's Iowa roots. She called physical education teachers in neighboring schools, and they agreed to play a series of games. Before long, she had scheduled informal games in a variety of sports with schools in the area. But there was one problem: her car could hold only a few students, and asking parents for help had become complicated. Dorothy then realized, "We needed a bus!" She explained to the principal that over 60 trips were planned. "Sorry, no," he said. "It's school policy." His patient look suggested that he had been through this before. He reminded Dorothy that she was in charge of a physical education department, not an athletic department. Even though the after-school GARA program was "very active," the school provided only one bus trip a year for each department. Dorothy recalled in vivid detail the exchange that followed:

> I could see this wasn't going anywhere, so I countered with "But the boys go to other schools to have scrimmages. Could we have a bus if it was called a scrimmage?"
>
> Again, the *look*. "No," he answered, "the reason the boys can have buses for scrimmages is that the coach drives the bus, and it doesn't cost the school to pay a driver."
>
> The light bulb nearly popped! My years of driving tractors were now invaluable. I asked, "You mean if I get a bus driver's license, I could have a bus too?"
>
> He smiled and said, "Yes."

The principal's simple "Yes" set off a chain of events that would change history.

Dorothy called Joe, head of the bus drivers and father of three daughters in sport activities. The next morning, she walked out the locker room door and saw "a big beautiful yellow school bus." For the next five days she drove while Joe sat in the seat behind her instructing her on the rules of the road for a school bus, especially how to back up and avoid hitting mailboxes or other objects. "It wasn't difficult," Dorothy explained. "The bus was about as long as two oat wagons." The following week, after taking her bus driver's test in Minneapolis, she walked into the principal's office, handed him her new license, and asked, "Now, may I have my bus?" True to his word, the principal gave her keys to the bus garage and the gas tank. From the moment she put her hands on the steering wheel, she was once again the pilot, leading young women into an untraveled world. (McIntyre, 2005, p. 143; D. McIntyre, personal communication, March 7, 2013).

Clearing the Road to Title IX

As Dorothy worked to expand opportunities for her students at Eden Prairie in 1960, television broadcast the Summer Olympics for the first time. Many Americans watched Tennessee's track and field star Wilma Rudolph break from the pack to win three gold medals for the United States. Now that television viewers could *see* female athletes competing, they began to ask why there were so few female athletes competing for the United States. (McIntyre, 2005, p. 145; D. McIntyre, personal communication, March 7, 2013). In the early 1900s, before medical professionals, scholars, politicians, and media collectively claimed that physical activity threatened women's health and reproductive capacity, women throughout the United States had played rigorous sports. Then the Women's Division of the National Amateur Athletic Federation (NAAF-WD), fueled by the national backlash against women's rights in 1923, recommended that schools drop organized competition for girls and women and institute play days and sport days. When Dorothy faced young women's pleas for the opportunity to compete in the 1960s, the NAAF-WD legacy of limited interscholastic competition still governed physical education and high school athletics.

The immediate challenge was to create a feasible structure to support competitive opportunities for girls and young women. How could interested leaders start a national movement to train teachers to be coaches who would then train young women to compete? How could they break the gendered practice that boys play while girls watch? As a first step, the U.S. Olympic Committee and the Division for Girls' and Women's Sports (DGWS) collaborated to organize national clinics and to invite individuals from every state to attend. Participants were trained to conduct clinics in their states so that teachers could learn how to coach their students. "It was like a bucket brigade," Dorothy explained, "passing a bucket of information from one to the next." The goal was to groom the first elite competitors on high school and college teams. Organizers believed they would emerge to represent the United States in international competition. The plan was ambitious, and Dorothy couldn't help but join the chorus asking, "Will it work?"

Minnesota did not hesitate. Two state representatives to the first institute held in Oklahoma in 1963 returned to form committees in track and field and gymnastics. Eleanor (Ellie) Rynda, University of Minnesota–Duluth, led track and field training clinics and invitational meets. And Patricia Lamb, Carleton College, asked Dorothy to join the Girls' Gymnastics Committee of the DGWS. After responding with an emphatic "Yes," Dorothy considered her qualifications.

> Of all sports, gymnastics? I had participated, more or less, in a tumbling class in college and barely held a headstand. But, I reasoned, I am a teacher. I can learn by watching and practicing and reading and watching films. Then I can teach it to my students and others. And we did! We conducted training clinics all over the state. The more we did, the more coaches and young women wanted!

One morning in 1964, clinic organizers at one clinic in northern Minnesota watched the sun rise while thermometers read minus 40 degrees, or minus 80 degrees if they factored in wind chill. They expected few would attend, so they ate breakfast and shivered their way to the school. "Buses were arriving from all over the Iron Range with more girls and teachers than we could have expected," Dorothy said. "They had come to learn gymnastics from those 'teachers from the Cities'" (McIntyre, 2005, p. 145; D. McIntyre, personal communication, March 7, 2013).

The gymnastics committee offered clinics on judging gymnastics routines, learned to conduct competitive meets, and organized a few small competitions before holding its first larger event. In 1966, Eden Prairie hosted the first statewide invitational girls' gymnastics meet. Dorothy admitted that the routines and equipment were primitive:

> The gymnasts all performed the same compulsory routine in each event: floor exercise, uneven parallel bars, balance beam, and vaulting. I wrote the compulsory routine for the uneven bars, with back hip circles, a scale performed while standing on the low bar, and underswing dismounts. Remember, in 1966, it was the beginning and it was exciting!

The first uneven bars at Eden Prairie were a sign of innovation. They were made of metal plumbing pipes, so the girls put sponges over their hip bones for protection. The beams were wooden, sometimes "homemade," with no leather covering or padding. Floor exercises were performed without mats on a bare gymnasium floor. "Our young women were pioneer athletes and very brave to put themselves into the hands of novice coaches," Dorothy remarked. "I simply said, 'Don't worry; I won't drop you,' and I never did."

Dorothy's leadership at Eden Prairie High School served her well when, in 1966, she was elected chair of the Minnesota Association for Health, Physical Education, Recreation and Dance Division for Girls' and Women's Sports. She represented a circle of trusted colleagues whose platform was to promote young women's opportunity to compete on teams and to help teachers in Minnesota learn how to train and coach their students. They asserted that competition was a healthy activity for young women and that it would not "shake things out of place."

Connecting with the Minnesota State High School League

"One of the benefits of being the chair of a state organization is that it spins off into other offices," Dorothy observed. In 1968 she was elected to be the AAHPERD Midwest Region DGWS representative for several Midwestern states and went to Washington, D.C., to serve on the national DGWS Executive Committee. There she met with DGWS constituents to discuss changing the paradigm for girls and women in sports across the United States. She recognized that she was entering a conversation among physical education authorities: "Around the table were women with their doctorate degrees who were authors of my college textbooks and heads of college and university departments."

Momentum grew within Minnesota's state physical education association. MAHPERD sent a recommendation to the Minnesota State High School League, whose membership included all Minnesota high schools, saying that the League should administer both girls' and boys' athletic programs. The group felt fortunate that, although he was a male, Executive Director Beverly H. Hill believed in sports programs for girls.

Dorothy worked specifically with a committee to draft bylaws for girls' athletics. By the fall of 1968, the committee presented its proposed bylaws to the League's Delegate Assembly, the voting arm of the League. While delegates returned to their area schools to meet and to discuss the proposal, Dorothy traveled with Executive Director Hill to speak on behalf of the proposal to add girls' athletics as a League-sponsored program.

The delegates returned to vote in the spring of 1969. As Dorothy noted, 32 men held the future of girls' athletics in their hands. The gendered hierarchy was obvious, Dorothy recalled:

> As I stood outside, preparing to go in for our final presentation before the vote, a man at the door, said, "Bet'cha a quarter it doesn't pass." He's lucky that I had enough restraint after all of our years of hard work to walk past him and into the room.

The vote was 32 in favor and 0 against. Girls' athletics in Minnesota were now a program sponsored by the Minnesota State High School League. (McIntyre, 2005, p. 148; D. McIntyre, personal communication, March 7, 2013). Dorothy never saw the man and his quarter again.

Riding the wave of victory, Dorothy and her peers believed that doors would open to the gym, the fields, and the pools. They believed they were beyond past inequities. "It was a naive assumption," Dorothy said in retrospect. "Our small group of thoughtful, committed citizens didn't realize that this was only the beginning of a long journey to change the face of sports."

Working at the League

During the 1969–70 school year, the Minnesota State High School League created a position on its executive staff for a woman who would assist schools in the development of their girls' interscholastic athletic programs. In December of 1969, several months after the call for applications, Executive Director Beverly Hill called Dorothy to ask about her interest in the position. She felt conflicted about the possibility of leaving her school, the young women she coached, and her bus. Hill wanted Dorothy to join his staff and offered her a week to decide. "I convened my circle of friends, those willing warriors who shed the blood, sweat, and tears to get us to this moment," Dorothy said. "Their response was 'You don't have a choice. You are going to apply for that position.'"

The words that Dorothy had read so many times in her mother's kitchen now rang in her ears: "If it is to be, it's up to me." So she applied, and the Board of Directors hired her. The opportunity felt almost unreal:

> Here I was, a kid from an Iowa farm, a teacher with no administrative experience, armed only with a passion for doing the right thing for young women, but fortified by my circle of friends who said they would have my back. Scared? You bet.

Dorothy recalled her first day at the League, where she would work for the next 32 years:

> On July 1, 1970, I walked in the door of the League Office, then located in the Plymouth Building in downtown Minneapolis. They pushed an empty desk into the middle of the secretary's area and told me to start by reading the Official Handbook of the League. I opened the Handbook to a new section called 'Bylaws for Girls' Athletics.' I believe my hands shook a little as the realization hit: that's my new responsibility!

The MSHSL Women's Advisory Committee included eight women from regions across Minnesota. From Dorothy's perspective, the Committee stood "holding an empty plate." The challenge was to catch the attention of schools

Dorothy McIntyre speaking for the Minnesota National Girls and Women in Sports Day. 2015. Photograph by Samuel X. Parent.

and the public and to demonstrate that competition for young women could be fun and not harmful to their health and welfare. Dorothy likened the group's moment of paralysis to "standing on the end of the diving board." But the Committee knew what it wanted.

Its first action was "a big leap." In 1971, the Committee asked the League Board to approve the first state tournament for girls in track and field. Committee members reasoned that facilities for track and field were available in most schools. Because physical education teachers taught a unit on track and field, girls were already learning how to run, throw, and jump. It was a logical sport for a big launch and could draw participants from all over the state. The Board approved, and the first MSHSL girls' state track and field meet was scheduled for the spring of 1972.

Months passed as schools organized into competitive regions and held qualifying meets. On the Sunday when Dorothy had to prepare the state program for the printer, a spring storm cut the League office's electricity. By the light of a window in her office, she typed in the heats and lane assignments on a manual typewriter, recalling with irony her mother's observation that she was a good typist.

Images of that first tournament have remained vivid in Dorothy's mind for four decades:

> Finally, all was ready. The officials were assigned, the equipment was double-checked and the big day arrived at St. Cloud Apollo High School. A line of yellow school buses bearing the names of schools from all over Minnesota began arriving. Out of them spilled hundreds of young women and coaches who were ready for a new experience. When the day drew to a close, every girl and relay team in every event had set a state record. It was the stuff dreams are made of!

She recalled, too, the tournament's impact on the athletes:

> At the close of this historical meet, the International Falls and White Bear Lake teams had tied for the team championship. The White Bear team preferred not to flip a coin, so it offered the trophy to the Falls team while another would be ordered. They knew the Falls team had traveled from far northern Minnesota and had faced the season with only the gravel road in front of the school and the parking lot for practice facilities. On the road, they ran dashes, relays and runs, and practiced their throws and jumps in the school parking lot. One Falls athlete recalled that the old wooden hurdles were the worst. Skinned knees with imbedded pieces of gravel should have been enough to discourage them, but not the Falls athletes. Their reward on the 250-mile ride home was a beautiful championship trophy and another historical first. One of their team members won the discus event held early in the day's schedule. She was awarded the first gold medal in the history of a statewide tournament for girls in Minnesota. To this day, Susan wears the medal on a chain around her neck.

As organizers waved goodbye to those pioneer athletes and coaches and their yellow school buses, they began to sing their revised version of "I am

Woman," Helen Reddy's now famous anthem of the 1970s women's movement. In their version, woman is not alone:

> We are women, hear us roar
> In numbers too big to ignore
> And we know too much to go back and pretend
> 'cause we've heard it all before
> And we've been down there on the floor
> No one's ever going to keep us down again.

Title IX of the Education Amendments of 1972

After such a transformative event, the Minnesota State High School League paused to consider the next step. Dorothy declared,

> There was no turning back now. This was no time to be wishy-washy, to worry ourselves into a state of inertia. It was time to make decisions based on our best instincts and do something. There would be time later to evaluate, make adjustments and do it again, even better the next time.

The League's momentum was crucial because challenges from schools were heating up. Following the first state tournament, the practical realities of adding so many girls' teams to the existing boys' program "hit like tsunami waves," Dorothy said. Schools resisted. Dorothy recalled typical questions she received over the telephone, through the mail, and at the office door that claimed gymnasiums, pools, and fields were full. Opposition claimed they wouldn't be able to fund girls' teams and find officials for their games. (McIntyre, 2005, p. 148; D. McIntyre, personal communication, March 7, 2013).

The League persisted above voices repeating, "No room.... No room." Dorothy explained,

> Women had heard it all before: no room on juries, in the voting booth, or in elected office. When Alice went to the tea party and heard the same response from the Mad Hatter, she said, "I didn't know it was YOUR table. It's laid for a great many more than three." She sat down, and so did we.

And then came Title IX.

Dorothy was quick to clarify that Title IX did not *create* changes that would provide competitive sports for girls and women; many coaches and physical educators were already organizing and administering competitive events for girls and women in the 1960s. Title IX, she emphasized, put the legitimacy and force of the federal government behind an existing movement.

But the transition was not easy. The passage of Title IX ushered in a long period of uncertainty, rumors, and confusion for Minnesota schools.

When Minnesota high schools learned about a new federal law requiring gender equity in sports, questions about requirements and compliance flooded the League office. Federal financial assistance could be withdrawn from schools that did not comply. No district wanted to lose funding or damage its public image.

During the years when the Department of Education's Office of Civil Rights was developing regulations and policy interpretations, Minnesota equity advocates and legislators decided to write the state's own version of what they believed gender equity in sports should be, set within the framework and intent of Title IX. In 1976, the state passed Minnesota Statute 126.21, spearheaded by State Representative Phyllis Kahn. During that same year, the Department of Health, Education and Welfare (HEW) issued federal interpretations and gave secondary schools until 1978 to bring their programs into compliance.

Support for these changes then came from a variety of sources. A forceful and vocal leader was State Commissioner of Education Howard Casmey, who emphasized that young women should have their fair share of sports facilities and finances. From 1969 to 1981, school administrators across the state heard his influential voice. The state school board association and the superintendent and principals associations likewise added their support.

At the same time, activists involved in civil rights and equal rights for women began to promote gender equity in sports. These activists, experienced in political advocacy, worked with organizations to develop state policies and regulations. Dorothy viewed the developments as "a framework being built over the foundation" that further stabilized the place of girls and women in high school and college athletics.

Increasing the number of tournaments required the League to keep several events in motion at the same time. Dorothy likened her work at the League to spinning plates and explained,

> In the early days of television, the *Ed Sullivan Show* featured individual acts to entertain the audience. One man would put a plate on the top of a pole and spin the plate, add another pole and spin another plate, one after the other. The challenge was to see how many plates he could keep spinning before one would inevitably begin to wobble, fall off, and shatter on the floor. Our entertainment was watching him run frantically from one pole to the other, giving each plate a spin as it began to wobble, trying to avert disaster.

As one tournament finished, others were whirling into action. Events required assigning officials, hiring tournament personnel, confirming sites, and managing other logistics. In the middle of one tournament, the League had to address questions about other events. "It was crucial," Dorothy emphasized, "that we kept all plates spinning."

Meanwhile, the daily work of running the League demanded Dorothy's attention. Committees visited the League office to plan meetings and conferences, to resolve issues, or to plan future statewide seasons. Correspondence and telephone messages requiring immediate attention lined up on Dorothy's desk. There were interviews and articles to write for League publications and other organizations. Describing how she accomplished all of the work, Dorothy confided, "The oil burned late into the night."

In addition to her work for the League, Dorothy frequently gave speeches to a variety of organizations and at athletic banquets. She felt a responsibility:

> I was frequently the first woman to be the main speaker, sometimes to the chagrin of someone. One athletic director told me that a member of the community, upon learning a woman was going to speak at the biggest banquet of the year, asked the athletic director if he needed more money so he could get a "good speaker." After I received a standing ovation from the audience, the athletic director and I both smiled.

With a pioneer's spirit, Dorothy traveled the state advocating for sport opportunities for girls and women:

> Before GPS systems, those faithful paper maps of Minnesota became wrinkled and torn as I explored freeways, highways, and county roads, through the sun, storms, ice, and snow. Sometimes I shared those byways with deer, elk, fox, coyotes and other creatures of the night. The moose and wolves likely watched the solitary headlights through the trees.

She was navigating a time of immense change in Minnesota and beyond. Nationally, between 1970 and 1974, the number of high school girls on teams increased from less than 300,000 to over one million. Growth has never yet matched expansion during this four-year period.

Girls' Basketball and the Challenge of Equity

As interest in girls' basketball surged in the 1970s, Dorothy learned the fate of the earlier era of competition. Girls' basketball was popular in Minnesota before 1923, the year that the Women's Division of the National Amateur Athletic Federation (NAAF-WD) recommended that schools drop competition that included uniforms and trophies. The NAAF-WD wanted to emphasize fun and enjoyment. By the late 1930s, girls' competitive basketball in Minnesota disappeared. Then, leveraged by leaders like Minnesota and Title IX, it re-emerged in the 1970s. Teams again played throughout the state, but one logistical problem prevented the League from scheduling a state tournament. The western half of the state played girls' basketball in the fall, when boys vacated gymnasiums to play football. Meanwhile, the eastern half of the state played volleyball in the fall and girls' and boys' basketball in the winter. Both sides argued for their schedule, stalling progress toward a state tournament.

During the 1974–75 school year, the Minnesota State High School League prompted the first step toward coordinating a single basketball tournament. The League conducted "season championships" that year, one for schools playing in the fall, and the other for schools playing in the winter. The League also studied the overall map of seasons for the variety of girls' and boys' sports. Following the season championships, the Board of Directors recommended scheduling girls' volleyball in the fall and girls' basketball in the winter because girls' volleyball was also growing as a team sport.

Dorothy went on the road to explain the League's rationale:

> What a furor it created! And that is an understatement if you had stood in my shoes and read the letters, newspaper columns, and editorials, listened to callers on the telephone for hours on end, or stood in the front of a room full of school administrators with their eyes narrowed and arms folded.

One administrator later wrote to Dorothy,

> I rode up in the elevator with you when you came to speak to our principals meeting and knew you were in for a tough meeting. Now, I feel that I must apologize for the way you were treated, but you stood your ground and had a lot of guts while we acted like jerks. You are one strong woman!

Not everyone agreed with that administrator's assessment. Some referred to Dorothy as "*that woman* at the League." Dorothy recalled in painful detail the attitude of a frustrated boys' basketball coach from western Minnesota who sent a venomous letter to newspapers around the state, accusing the League's Board of losing its backbone and being weakened by the "whims and wiles of this refugee from another state." In this tense climate of March 1975, the Board of Directors deliberated the details of a single season for girls' basketball. The discussion went back and forth until Superintendent Fred Marsden, who represented the smaller Class A schools in the heart of fall season girls' basketball, stood up. His constituents had directed him, in no uncertain terms, to vote for the fall girls' basketball season. He looked at the Board and said,

> Today I have to decide whether to be a politician or a statesman. I choose to be a statesman and do the right thing. Girls' basketball should be played in the winter, alongside the boys' basketball program. I will vote for the *winter* season for girls' basketball.

The vote was then called. The Board of Directors declared girls' basketball a winter season sport and approved the first state girls' basketball tournament to be held in March of 1976.

After the year of planning that followed, Dorothy stood ready to join in singing the *first* national anthem of the *first* MSHSL state girls' basketball tournament in the Met Center, Bloomington, in March of 1976. She looked up to see Fred Marsden, who had suffered a stroke shortly after his return to unhappy constituents, approaching in his wheelchair. She described tears welling as they sang together, with their hands over their hearts, "Oh, say can you see…?"

Maintaining Sport Opportunity through Title IX

Work at the League was so all-consuming that Dorothy reflected on the two decades following 1972 as a single unit of time. "Life was not easy in the trenches," she said. She relied on a familiar illustration to explain how to be fair when dividing a school's resources: "One piece of pie sits in the pie pan and two children in the family want it. The wise and fair parent gives one child a knife to cut the piece in half and gives the other child first choice." The days when boys' sports automatically received first choice and the prime piece of the athletic pie had to end. Ensuring fairness required dividing a school's resources in such a way that both girls and boys received equitable opportunity.

School superintendents and school boards were instrumental in creating change. Schools at the forefront of the movement began by asking young women what sports they wanted to play. They then provided girls' teams with comparable equipment, qualified coaches, uniforms, and practice times. This process of documenting and accommodating interest addressed one of Title IX's three compliance measures and could, by itself, constitute compliance (Carpenter & Acosta, 2005, p. 77). Just as important, these model schools made female athletes feel welcome in their schools' athletic facilities.

But not everyone embraced change. As resistance and apathy continued, Dorothy faced a full menu of excuses and questions:

> "But it took us twenty years to build that new football field and equip it with the scoreboards and stands, and now you expect us to let the girls play soccer on it?"
> "How can you expect us to divide our budgets so that we can add all the sports that the girls want to play and not damage the boys sports programs?"
> "We know you people don't understand that we have just one gymnasium and a limited budget. We just can't do everything overnight. Why can't you be patient?"

Despite resistance, Dorothy observed, "change was going to happen, and it helped to face it sooner rather than later."

Expanding Gender Equity in Sports

Years of trial and error taught the League that schools needed a system to help them efficiently evaluate their plans for gender equity in athletics. In 1990, the League established a Gender Equity Committee and, together with the Minnesota Department of Education (MDE), wrote *Gender Equity in Athletics Review Manual*. "It was a good partnership," Dorothy remarked. Schools could follow the manual's blueprint, conduct self-reviews, and prepare a compliance plan. The MDE then reviewed the compliance plans submitted by the schools and worked with districts to enforce equity laws within athletics.

Despite progress in many sports, girls still had limited opportunity to play ice hockey. Some schools surrounding the Twin Cities introduced ringettes, a Canadian ice sport played with a round ring and a stick used to propel the ring into a goal. Other community teams played traditional ice hockey. To determine what girls wanted to play, the League distributed a statewide student interest survey and learned that 8,000 girls wanted to play traditional ice hockey. The mandate was clear: Minnesota needed girls' ice hockey.

Schools again cried, "No room." Parents and citizen groups took up the cause and actively urged the state legislature to take action. In 1994, a new state law required all public ice arenas to guarantee equal access to female hockey teams by 1996–97. In addition, the legislature allocated state money to fund the construction of ice arenas in several communities.

Until facilities were available, schools needed to develop ways to share existing rinks and budgets, just as they had shared gymnasiums, pools, and fields. Dorothy recalled resistance:

> I attended a meeting in far northern Minnesota with administrators and hockey coaches to remind schools that girls' hockey was growing rapidly and there would be a League-sponsored state tournament coming soon. If they hadn't already done so, I said, it was time to get girls' hockey moving in their community. In the back of the room, two boys' hockey coaches stood with their arms folded. One leaned over and said to his buddy, "Over my dead body!" I could easily read his lips, so I raised my hand toward him to ensure I had his attention and said, "If that's your choice!"

That particular school did create a girls' ice hockey program. "I trust the coach is still alive and well," Dorothy concluded.

Minnesota is justifiably proud of its female skaters and their prowess on ice. Since the first MSHSL State Girls' Ice Hockey Tournament in 1995, Minnesota players have advanced to women's collegiate hockey teams as well as national, international, and Olympic teams. Of the 16 NCAA Women's Ice

Hockey National Championships since 2001, the University of Minnesota–Twin Cities has won six, and the University of Minnesota–Duluth has won five.

Regrets and Reflections

"Few people live their life and have no regrets," Dorothy reasoned. "I regret the pain that others endured when they fought for sports programs in their schools on behalf of their young women." She observed many women fighting silent, frequently lonely, battles. "They are the real heroes," Dorothy declared, "the trailblazers, those who struggled against the injustice and barriers every day. They truly felt the barbs and arrows of shabby treatment, and yet, they kept going."

In a letter written in the 1990s, one friend whom Dorothy described as "a model teacher, coach, and mentor to so many in her area," confided,

> I had to file a sex discrimination charge against my school with the Minnesota Department of Human Rights. After fourteen years, the school dissolved my job as Assistant Athletic Director for Girls' Athletics on the pretext that it would save money. The Athletic Director is paid $3,100 beyond his regular teaching salary and I have never received a salary for supervisory work done outside the school day. I was asking for $2,000. The superintendent told the athletic director that I was starting to ask for too much time and money. Now I must endure the reactions of my community. Some will support me and others won't. Why does it have to be so hard? [Anonymous, personal communication with D. McIntyre, n.d.].

This friend's experience was not an isolated incident. One woman coach shared the story of her girls' softball team, who played on fields that the maintenance person believed were for use by only boys' teams. When visiting girls' teams came to play, he turned on the sprinklers and went home. Although the coach learned how to turn them off, she felt unwelcome in her own school. Another friend revealed, "I had a Title IX file in my desk drawer at school labeled 'Sausage and Baloney.' I figured if someone snooped around to see what I was up to, he would think it was full of recipes. And it was: full of recipes for change in our school!"

Players, too, felt the anger and grief of women's history of inequity. A coach's daughter played on her mother's state championship basketball team. During a post-tournament interview, the daughter was amazed to learn that girls' sports teams didn't exist when her mother was in high school. The daughter became visibly upset when she learned that her own school, just ten years earlier, had provided only one set of uniforms to be shared by the girls' volleyball, basketball, and track and field teams. For many years, girls' teams received the least desirable practice times. When her mother told the reporter that many male coaches had threatened to quit if girls got equal gym time, the daughter asked, "They'd *say* that?" Her mother smiled, "Not anymore."

Like Ruth Schellberg, Celeste Ulrich, Fay Biles, Doris Corbett, Anita DeFrantz, and many other women leading changes in athletics during the decades surrounding the passage of Title IX, Dorothy recognized the high cost of change:

> I will forever regret the merging in the 1970s of the separate girls' and boys' physical education and athletic departments, into one department with one director. The result was the loss of hundreds of positions held by women as administrators, teachers, and coaches. Many young women will never experience playing on a team with a woman as their head coach.

But reflections yielded more than regrets as Dorothy identified the Minnesota State High School League's successes. Most importantly, the League acted; it didn't wait for a better time to start removing barriers. The League encouraged schools to avoid excuses that their teachers didn't know how to coach, that there weren't enough officials or money in the schools for girls' teams, or that others wouldn't like them if they moved into their territory. "We trusted that it was the right thing to do," Dorothy explained, "and kept moving."

The League also didn't let criticism deter it. When the League conducted the first girls' state basketball tournament in 1976, *Minneapolis Tribune* columnist Robert T. Smith reported that "watching skunk wrestling with loaded skunks would be more interesting" (1982, p. 2B). He hoped it was the first and last state tournament for girls. The League ignored him. Six years later, after attending the 1982 Girls' Basketball Tournament, he wrote a second, apologetic column: "Pardon me a second here while I put a little salt and pepper on my crow" (1982, p. 2B). He explained that his earlier column "wasn't very kind" and now proclaimed, "The girls have gotten good.... I saw some marvelous shooting, great passing, talented ball handling and defenses that were tight and effective" (1982, p. 2B). After clarifying that the girls were "not all good" and "not as good as the boys—yet," Smith conceded, "But you can't use the old line: They play well for girls. Now they just play well" (1982, p. 2B). The apology was "worth the wait," Dorothy said.

As she had so often, Dorothy returned to the importance of teamwork: "Like the V-formation of geese, we flew sharing the brunt of the wind, changing positions when the leader grew weary, and honking encouragement to the others to keep going and not to give up."

Dorothy's list of thanks is inclusive. She thanked all of the women who struggled bravely and took down barriers so that young women would have a fair and equitable opportunity to become athletes. "To my coterie of friends, you kept your word and were there throughout the journey," Dorothy said with gratitude. "You have changed the face of sports." She likewise recognized the men who helped to open doors and who gave willingly of their experience and support for the young women and their coaches. "You were the dads, brothers, fellow coaches, athletic directors, and school and community leaders who made all the difference in the world to the young women in your lives." Dorothy thanked the legislators and members of the judiciary who wrote, advocated, passed, and enforced laws that enabled fairness and equality for girls' and women's athletic programs. And she thanked the media who reported fairly, investigated situations, communicated information that shed light on inequity and unfairness, and shared photographs of girls and women displaying their athletic skills, personal courage, and determination. Ultimately, she recognized parents "who gave their daughters the wings to fly."

Creating, implementing, and enforcing sport opportunities for girls required hands-on work and vision that satisfied Dorothy. Nevertheless, she still had wishes:

> I wish I had been one of the women in the late 1800s who threw away their corsets and long dresses, wore bloomers for the first time, and rode away on their new bicycles. I wish I could have participated in the 1923 meeting of the National Amateur Athletic Federation—Women's Division when the platform calling for the dropping of all competitive sports was introduced. I wish I could have helped to find alternatives to correct abuses without eliminating the positive programs for young women. I wish I had been the navigator in 1937 for Amelia Earhart's final flight around the world. I wish families, teachers, and local and world leaders would make changes so that girls and women can safely go to sleep, go to school, and work in a world where there is no fear, war, harassment, or hunger. I wish everyone would choose to work *together* to develop a world where justice prevails and women have taken their rightful place at the table where decisions are made and their voices are heard.

Dorothy admits that wishing on a star is wonderful, but every individual must work until wishes become reality. In the pioneering days of girls' and women's sports, Dorothy and her peers wished and then worked for years to hear balls swoosh through hoops and feet beat upon the track, to see sports pages report news of female sports teams and their stars, and to feel the stands rocking with cheers and applause of family and fans.

The Next Chapter

By 2001, Dorothy had taught for 13 years and served as an associate director on the Minnesota State High School League executive staff for 32 years. She recognized the moment to move into the next chapter of her life and retired from the League.

As soon as Dorothy retired, she began looking for a new project. One of her associates, Marian Bemis Johnson, had invested years researching why her mother had played basketball in the 1920s yet there were no teams for Marian in the 1950s. Marian followed a trail of women across the state, interviewing them and gathering their stories, photos, and memorabilia. She searched files at the State Historical Society and Department of Education for missing information. Marian's map of Minnesota showed teams representing little towns and larger cities all over the state. An entire era of girls' sports had flourished between 1892 and 1942 and then disappeared. Marian promised the women that their stories would be preserved in a book.

This history of basketball was precisely the kind of project Dorothy had been searching for. She asked Marian if she might help bring her "tubs full of information" into a format that could be published. Soon, Dorothy was again at her desk, this time with a computer, entering Marian's research. Dorothy was quick to acknowledge that "the learning curve was terrific." Writing the book required two intense years of collaboration with people who had ventured into self-publishing. Meanwhile, faithful friends proofread drafts. When the book was ready for publication, Dorothy and Marian expedited the process by organizing McJohn Publishing, LLC, and self published *Daughters of the Game: The First Era of Minnesota Girls High School Basketball, 1891–1942*. The project felt reminiscent of their teaching years, when they had committed countless hours and personal money to developing educational resources. Weighing six pounds, the book's 396 pages include hundreds of photos of teams and personal stories that preserve a specific time and place in girls' sport history.

Dorothy and Marian knew the effort was worthwhile when they saw the looks on the faces of the women who opened the book and found their photos and stories. One woman said, "I never would have believed that my story would be in such a beautiful book. Thank you!"

Dorothy was once again on the road, this time to promote the book. By that time, in 2005, many of the women featured in the book were in their 80s and 90s, and they were still physically able to attend the programs. Dorothy relished meeting them:

> It appeared that playing basketball must contribute to longevity as evidenced by the women of this era. One woman walked into a meeting, after riding 90 miles from her home, handed her walking stick to her son to verify she didn't need assistance, and said, "I am 102 years of age and that uniform hanging there is just like what we wore!" She vividly described her team's experiences traveling by bobsled and train, sometimes staying overnight in a local hotel, eating fudge, and playing cards with the boys' team.

Women across the state shared school letters, uniforms, small medals, and scrapbooks that carefully protected newspaper clippings and memorabilia. One remarked with a smile, "My 'hope chest' never held doilies and sheets. It was full of my basketball memories!" At one reading, a man holding the book approached Dorothy. His hands were shaking and a tear rolled down his face as he pointed at a team photo. "That's my MOTHER," he said. "We never knew she played basketball!"

Dorothy relayed a particularly vivid memory of a woman named Marie from Belle Plaine, "a great storyteller and spokesperson for her era." Marie's mother had told her that she was disgracing the family and making a spectacle of herself by wearing bloomers in public. Marie told her mother she was sorry she felt that way, but Marie was determined to play basketball. "All right," her mother declared, "but I'm not coming to your games!" And she never did. In 1990, when Marie and other pioneer players were honored at the girls' state basketball tournament, Marie held her plaque up high and said, "Mother, I hope you're watching!"

The success of *Daughters of the Game* inspired Dorothy and Marian to write a second book. In 2012 they published *Two Rings: A Legacy of Hope*, an historical novel told from the perspective of a contemporary young woman athlete. Sarah, the hero, receives a school assignment to find a female ancestor whose life left a legacy for her. Sarah's search uncovers a girls' sports history that spans four generations of her family. The novel becomes a call to action for Sarah's generation to confront the discrimination and unfair practices that still exist. Sarah realizes that she must step up, get into the game, and pay it forward. Readers who know Dorothy's life story will recognize a familiar spirit in Sarah's conviction to act.

If It Is to Be, It Is Up to You

Dorothy has lived according to her mother's words. And in facilitating changes for girls and women in sports, her work has empowered generations. "What women can do as strong, confident athletes," she observed, "confirms what women can do when they take their rightful place in a world that desperately needs their talents and leadership." Her "life lessons" draw from the language of competition: "Be willing to lose a battle if you want to win the war" and "When faced with a test of your mettle and resolve, confront your worst fears, earn the respect of your challengers, and then set rules to make it a fair fight." Her lessons reflect the real battles for gender equity that women experienced before, during, and after Title IX's enactment.

Dorothy has always worked for the good of the team, singing with her circle of friends "We Are Women" rather than "I Am Woman." At the end of her stories, Dorothy's advice was simple: "Don't take anything for granted. Find another woman's life story and share it through ancestry programs, social networking, and media. And this is very important: keep a journal of your life and pass it on." Like a relay runner playing for the team, Dorothy has always stood ready to accept challenge and to hand off accomplishments and challenges to the next runner.

6

Willye White
Competing for an Equal Chance in Life

In 1956, as Greenwood, Mississippi, erupted with racial tension, a parade gathered to celebrate Willye White's departure for the 1956 Olympic Games. The high school state champion long-jumper had much more at stake than winning a medal in Melbourne, Australia. At age 16, Willye was Mississippi's second female athlete and the state's first black female athlete to compete for the United States. "It was exciting to have someone from the Delta cotton fields make the Olympic team," she recalled.

Willye was a portrait of 1950s femininity with her hair secured beneath the white scarf she tucked into the jacket of her track uniform. In one photograph, her smile stretches almost as wide as the U S A logo on her jacket. Just one year earlier, the murder of Emmett Till had put Willye's birthplace, Money, Mississippi, on the map. The Olympic Games then complicated her worldview. As she said often during interviews, Willye stated, "Before my first Olympics, I thought the whole world consisted of cross burnings and lynchings. After 1956, I found there were two worlds, Mississippi and the rest of the world."[1]

At another time in history, Willye might have viewed her 1956 and 1964 silver medals as lifetime achievements. But standing in second place reinforced her social position as a black female athlete. Her participation in five consecutive Olympic Games (1956–72) began during the Civil Rights Movement and ended the year Title IX became law, blurring her athletic drive and her determination to overcome racism and gender bias. If Willye couldn't win a gold medal, she could still empower others through her work as a coach and community activist. She was a model of her often-repeated advice, "You determine your destiny."

Early Childhood

Willye B. White was born in Money, Mississippi, just before midnight on December 31, 1939, or just after 12 a.m. on January 1, 1940. Like so many moments in her later life, the exact number comes down to matter of minutes or seconds. For Willye, the bigger picture was more important. She was adopted by her grandparents in Greenwood, Mississippi, when she was three days old. "My father was dark, and my mother was light. He told my mother that I was not his because of my light skin," she explained. Because Willye's sister and two brothers were also dispersed to various family members, her only sense of family came from the grandparents whom she called her parents.

At some undefined moment when she was ten, Willye discovered running. Perhaps she began running to school, racing with the boys, or leaving a day's work in the cotton fields. She never said why she started to run. It seemed to be her intuitive response to the single message she heard at home and at school: you must beat the odds to succeed. "My grandfather showed me that there were many roads to travel. Then he put me at the fork in the road, and he introduced me to the worst of the roads: picking cotton." Willye recalled that the alternatives for blacks in the South were cleaning, childcare, and laundry. But Willye's grandfather didn't want his children working in white people's homes. Instead, he sent Willye to the cotton truck at four o'clock in the morning on weekends and during school vacations. She and the other workers travelled 40 to 50 miles to various plantations where they picked or chopped cotton all day for two dollars. Willye acknowledged, "It was the lowest job you could have. But he was trying to show me that if I didn't get a good education, I could spend the rest of my life in the cotton fields."

In almost every interview Willye gave as a celebrated athlete, she chanted, "I was going to use athletics as my flight to freedom. Freedom from the cotton fields, freedom from illiteracy, freedom from prejudice, freedom from segregation." But as an adolescent, she was searching for her place within the black community:

> We have a color caste system among blacks. If you have a light complexion with green eyes, like me, you must have the hair to go with it. I didn't have the hair. I was a tomboy in overalls and high top shoes. I had a head full of corn braids, which were not fashionable at the time. I was not chosen for a lot of singing and dancing programs, so I played with the boys. They accepted me.

Willye never went out in the evenings unless she was attending a school-related activity. Her grandparents created a college fund and expressed high expectations. They warned her that she would have to leave if, like so many young girls in the area, she became pregnant. Willye understood. She would get nowhere in life with a baby and no education. "We came out of a system of separate but equal. So the teachers taught us home economics, manners, and etiquette. When we went out, we had to represent our city and our people."

Early Competition and the Olympic Games

Willye began running competitively in fifth grade at McLaurin Grade School. "We had just *one* varsity track team," she explained, "and whoever was good enough got to be on it. It didn't matter what grade you were in. If you had talent, you were there." And Willye had talent.

She would reign as Mississippi's three-time high school state champion. Her break came in 1956, when Tennessee State University coach Ed Temple invited her to try out for the Tigerbelles, Tennessee State's track club. She accepted with great anticipation of spending the summer away from home and the cotton fields.

Sharing Willye's "flight to freedom" philosophy that summer was Wilma Rudolph, the future gold medalist she described as her teammate and friend. Wilma would shine in the 1960 Olympics with gold medals in the 100 meters, 200 meters, and 4 × 100-meter relay. "There was fierce competition when we got on the track," Willye admitted. So she practiced every day from five to seven in the morning, from mid-morning until noon, and then from four to six in the evening. "We had struggles," she said of that summer with Wilma. "We grew up through hard times together."

Following her summer of rigorous training, Willye competed at the 1956 Amateur Athletic Union (AAU) meet in Philadelphia. Her first long jump met the Olympic standard, and her second jump surpassed it. But Coach Temple

Willye White, Tennessee State University, 1959. Tennessee State University Archives.

did not immediately consent to take her to the Olympic trials in Washington, D.C. She explained, "I was jumping only seventeen or eighteen feet, and he had no knowledge that I could jump further. My performance prior to that national championship didn't indicate that I was Olympic material." But after Willye surpassed the Olympic standard again, on the second day of competition, Coach Temple knew she had a chance. Willye was on her way.

Despite her athletic gains, Willye faced familiar limits of segregation on her journey to the 1956 Olympic Games in Melbourne. She recalled traveling to the Olympic trials in Washington, D.C.:

> There were only certain places that blacks could eat. After leaving Nashville, our first stop was Cincinnati. We stopped to eat at a train station where blacks were allowed to gather. We had two drivers and traveled non-stop because blacks weren't allowed in hotels.

Later that summer, at the Olympic training camp in Emporia, Kansas, black athletes were segregated from white teammates and housed at Emporia State University. In retrospect, Willye indicted the United States Olympic Committee for choosing segregated cities to host events that included many black athletes.

Willye expected Australia to embody some of the same institutionalized racism that she faced in the United States, but the Olympic Games introduced a world far removed from Mississippi's Ku Klux Klan cross burnings and lynchings. The Olympic community in Melbourne transcended race in ways that she had never imagined possible. "That was the first time that I had been where blacks and whites ate together, played together, and became lovers. Until then, I thought the whole world was separate but equal."

In November 1956, Willye "had no idea what she was doing" on the track in Melbourne because she had never had a long-term coach. She prepared for events by imitating other athletes, and her performance surprised her:

> In fact, I didn't realize that I was jumping as well as I was. I was lying on the track reading a Bible when one of the officials came up and told me that I was in first place. The other girls had trained hard, and I had trained hard, and they were not going to beat me. The young lady who beat me had experience, and all I had was desire and determination.

Willye won a silver medal for her 19' 11¾" long jump, approximately nine inches behind Elzbieta Krzesinska's gold medal jump.

Track and field competition took Willye around the world. During the summer and fall of 1956 she travelled to California, Melbourne, Hawaii, and the Fiji islands. One year later, she was among the first American athletes allowed behind the Iron Curtain. "Moscow was a very depressing city," she recalled. "The sun didn't shine, and we discovered what it was like to be restricted. We couldn't talk to anyone, and we couldn't wander through the

Willye White, Tennessee State University, track event, 1959. Tennessee State University Archives.

city." From Russia, she traveled to Warsaw, Poland, which she described as "Heaven after being in Russia for eleven days." Even so, she said, "it looked as if it were the day after the war, and the only thing they had done was taken the people out of the street and removed the rubbish." She concluded, "During that year I decided that I was going to travel all over the world, and that's what I did for the next 20 years."

Education and Employment

As Willye trained for the 1960 Olympics, she realized that being an Olympic athlete required more than running, jumping, and fierce determination. She had entered Tennessee State University on a track and field scholarship after winning a gold medal at the 1959 Pan-American Games in Chicago. But people's expectations of her had changed now that she was an Olympic athlete. Her new status demanded that she be either a public persona who fulfilled people's expectations or a rebel who believed first in herself and her goals. She was not accustomed to new expectations that she associate only with people of "good character." "The socialites expected me to change," she explained. "But the derelicts and the city drunks treated me like I was a very special person. They embraced me because I belonged to them. I had to be able to relate to all of them, and I did."

Willye was still negotiating her identity when Coach Temple dismissed her from the team at the beginning of the winter quarter because of philosophical differences: "I was no longer sixteen years old. I was a young lady who knew what I wanted to do, and I knew what I had to do. And I was an individual. He just wasn't accustomed to that. I was ahead of my time." Coach Temple told Willye to go home for the winter and return for the spring quarter to prepare for the 1960 Olympics. But when she learned that she wouldn't return on scholarship, she contacted the coach of the Mayor Daley Youth Foundation Team in Chicago:

> They invited me to Chicago and gave me a job. They were the best team. Perhaps I could have gone to Tuskegee, which was rivaling Tennessee State at the time, but it wouldn't have been about college.... I needed to get in shape to make the Olympic team.

Like Willye's birth date, records regarding her performance at the 1960 Olympics in Rome are inconsistent. She may have finished eleventh, twelfth, or sixteenth in the long jump. Even she could not recall her exact finish: "I can remember if I got first or second, and I think the rest of them were eleventh or twelfth, all of them other than the '56 Olympics." Winning mattered, and when she didn't win, the details of her performance slipped away with time.

Most clear in Willye's life at that time was her need to combine athletic competition with other goals. Her grandparents' advice about education resonated with her. Willye had long since decided to become a nurse when she arrived in Chicago in 1960. She applied to Cook County Hospital's nursing program, passed the nursing league exam, but was denied admission. "I was black, and they took only one black per year," she explained. "They told me that I had to be number one in my high school, and I had not been number one."

Since nursing school applications were accepted only in September, Willye waited until the following year to apply to Michael Reese and Saint Joseph's, teaching hospitals that likewise admitted only one black student per year. After being denied admission to both programs, Willye worked as a nurse's aide at Provident Hospital, the first U.S. hospital owned and operated by blacks. When the nursing program denied her admission, the nursing director finally gave her a concrete reason. She said that Willye was too worldly and would be a bad influence on other students. The director suggested that Willye enter another field because she would never be accepted into a nursing program. Willye was devastated:

> The underlying message was that they didn't want me at that hospital because I had traveled all around the world, and they also thought that I was making a lot of money. And why would I want to give up my travel around the world to come to nursing school?

Willye proved the director wrong. In 1963, while preparing for the upcoming Tokyo Olympics, she completed the Chicago Board of Education's one-year practical nursing program. She then worked as a practical nurse in Cook County Hospital's delivery room for six months. When frequent travel and late night hours made the job difficult, she resigned without notice:

> I left because I'm not a night person, and I had to work late nights. At lunchtime, I chose not to eat; I chose to sleep. After one very hard night, the head nurse came and told me that I could not sleep in one of the beds and that I would have to go out to lunch. And so it dawned on me that I was only 23 years old, I had no children, no responsibility.

Feeling that she could do better for herself, she went to work for private physicians.

Willye reflected on the racism that hindered her career in the 1960s:

> I was later denied television jobs and told that because I was black I was not marketable. Athletes who have much less to offer are making a fortune. I could get a job as a public speaker. They pay white athletes three or four thousand dollars; they'll give me five hundred. But that's five hundred more than I had. And I can get more five-hundred-dollar speaking engagements than white athletes can get for their price.

Years later, after quitting competition, she would aspire to be a television commentator but never succeed because she didn't fit television's mold of the black spokeswoman. If she was going to represent black athletes, the media expected her to talk like a stereotypical black woman.

Despite such blatant racism, Willye remained positive:

> I love life. People are always trying to take away my smile, but it's mine and they can't have it. I do not allow people to get free rent in my head. I am my own person. And I found out a long time ago that if you're honest and sincere and if you don't do anything to hurt people, then good things will come to you.

Nineteen sixty-four progressed as Willye's glory year on the track. At the Tokyo Games, she won the second silver medal of her career, this time as a member of the 4 × 100-meter relay team. She placed twelfth in the long jump with a jump of 19'11". Later that year she broke Wilma Rudolph's indoor 60-yard dash record of 6.8 seconds by one tenth of a second.

Despite her athletic success, Willye returned from Tokyo to face familiar employment dilemmas. She considered leaving Chicago after working in a number of positions as a practical nurse. When Mayor Daley heard that she might leave, he contacted her to ask what it would take to keep her in Chicago. She knew what she needed:

> I needed a job that would allow me to run, to do the things that I wanted to do, and not be terminated for doing it. So he got me a job with the Department of Health. All that he asked of me was that when I stopped running I give back to Chicago what Chicago had given to me. And that's why I'm still in Chicago. He was a beautiful man. He wanted the best for Chicago. I was the best, so he welcomed me with open arms.

The security of her new job enabled Willye to focus on training. She finally found a daily rhythm of training and working.

> I trained from five to seven-thirty in the morning, came home, got dressed, went to work, and at lunchtime lifted weights or ran on the beach. Then I'd go practice at three o'clock, and I'd run until seven or eight, or however long it took until I was done. I did that twelve months of the year.

Willye competed successfully while training for the 1968 Olympics in Mexico City. In 1967, she won a bronze medal for the long jump in her third Pan-American Games in Winnipeg, Canada. Everything seemed to be working in her favor for the 1968 Olympics until she suffered an accident. While lying on a rubdown table two hours before her jump, Willye was struck by a falling heat lamp and received first-, second-, and third-degree burns on the calf of one leg. She was not allowed to take any pain medication because it would have altered her urinalysis. She competed in spite of the "severe pain" and placed eleventh in the long jump.

More important than winning in 1968, the Games deepened Willye's understanding of what it meant to be an Olympic team member. Runners Tommie Smith and John Carlos had told teammates that when they received their respective gold and bronze medals they would make a token gesture against race discrimination in America. Willye viewed their bowed heads and raised fists as gestures of strength and power that brought the track and field team together as *one* team, not a black team and a white team. But the U.S. Olympic Team, pressured by International Olympic Committee President Avery Brundage, responded by sending Smith and Carlos back to the United States after their silent demonstration at the medals ceremony.

For Willye, both messages went well beyond the gesture.

> All great minority Olympians prior to 1968 had been discriminated against: Jesse Owens, Jim Thorpe, Tommie Smith, Lee Evans, and John Carlos. Avery Brundage, president of the

International Olympic Committee, made racism blatant. Brundage used Carlos and others to show that he was the power. By suspending them, he basically showed them, "You can represent my country, but you cannot go against my beliefs because if you do I will strip away from you your little lousy medal."

Willye wondered if the team might have reacted differently if Brundage had not tried so openly to use Smith and Carlos as "a whipping post." "But," she concluded, "because of what Brundage did, all of the teams bonded. It became the first time that we were a true United States of America team."

Willye returned to Chicago with two goals: to win a gold medal in the 1972 Olympic Games and to finish her bachelor's degree. She landed short of her first goal, placing twelfth for her long jump of 20' 6 ¼". She had made five attempts for the gold medal, and her performance in Munich called into question her athletic goals. She was identified as "the best" throughout her career, yet she could not prove it by winning a gold medal. The question came down to whether or not that kind of proof was necessary. Meanwhile, she took courses at Kennedy-King College, Roosevelt University, Loop Junior College, and Chicago State University until, in 1976, at the age of 36, she received her degree in public health care administration from Chicago State University. All the while she struggled with the familiar question of life balance.

Tragedy at the 1972 Games compounded Willye's doubt about her future as an Olympic athlete. The Palestinian terrorist slaying of 11 Israeli athletes "changed the face of the Olympic movement's purity," Willye said. She continued,

> The Palestinians came in and invaded the only place on earth where there were no wars. When they invaded the Olympic Village, they killed members of my family. The nightmare of seeing the Olympic flag of peace flying at half-mast, of seeing the blood of my family members on the wall, and of watching my family members loaded into an airplane to be killed is still with me.

Haunted by the killings, Willye began to assess other personal costs of competition:

> It's very difficult to date someone when you run seven days a week. You're running in the morning, you're running at lunch time, you're running at night, you're going to the weight room, you don't party, and you don't hang out. It's very difficult to have a social life.

Willye's strength was intimidating at a level that fundamentally challenged gender roles of the 1970s:

> You can't be a wife, because as you excel in life guys become afraid of you. You've seen everything and you can discuss everything. They can't give you anything. You are visible, and you pay a big price. You live in a very lonely world. You leave home alone, come home alone, and you spend all of your time alone.

She added that many athletes get strung out on drugs or alcohol because of this isolation. Those individuals, she believed, must learn to accept their uniqueness or it will kill them.

These gender role conflicts also raised questions about an athlete's sexual orientation in a culture that viewed heterosexuality as the norm. Willye felt the tension:

> It wasn't politically correct to spend all of your time on the track because people would say you were a tomboy or gay. Or you had to constantly fight the stereotype of being gay because you wore sweat suits all the time. When you came off the athletic field, you had to make sure that you dressed as feminine as you possibly could.

Willye made light of the double standard, most likely because she knew it was inescapable. "It became fun to play a role, to be as masculine as I could be on the athletic field, and then to take a shower, wash it all away, and become ultimately feminine."

Willye trained for her sixth consecutive Olympic Games despite serious doubts about her goals and her drive. At the National Outdoor Track and Field Championships in July of 1976, while recovering from a pulled hamstring, she qualified for the 1976 Games with her second jump. Although a third jump was gratuitous, she jumped and re-injured her hamstring. One week later in Eugene, Oregon, she placed fifth in the Olympic trials and moved into fourth when the athlete who placed fourth was ruled out. She would have made the team if she placed third. "I missed by a half-inch," she said. She was an alternate jumper, but only the top three went to Montreal.

As an Olympic athlete in the early 1970s, Willye was removed from the tensions and celebrations surrounding Title IX that touched high school, college, and university coaches and athletes. She was among the class of female athletes who competed on AAU and Olympic teams and whose access to competition had not been interrupted in the 1920s when NAAF-WD halted interscholastic competition. But her gendered experiences as a world-class athlete were proof of problems that Title IX would begin to address through physical education and competitive athletics for girls and women.

Post-Competition

Willye stopped competing after jumping short of a spot on the 1976 Olympic team. She explained,

> I quit at 37 because I couldn't take steroids, and the only way for me to continue at the world class level was to take steroids. I quit without any pain. I woke up one morning and told myself that I wasn't going back anymore. I did not retire from track in 1976. I quit!

The bittersweet truth was that she loved competition, but its changing culture troubled her:

> I loved the adrenalin. I loved the unknown and the thrill of defeat and victory. Because then you can really judge yourself and find out what you're made of. I love competition when everyone is healthy. I started hating competition when athletes started cheating with steroids and drugs. Then it was not based upon the best athlete; it was based on who had the best access to a doctor and to drugs.

When Willye walked away from competition, she didn't walk away from sports. In Chicago in 1976, she saw many "fantastic" athletes who lacked coaching, so she started coaching. Her goal was to teach the basics so that athletes could perfect their skills. "I went around and I chose the best athletes from the Chicago metropolitan area and brought them into Chicago," she explained. "I coached children from all walks of life throughout the entire city: rich, poor, black, white, green, and yellow." Her philosophy was to develop the total person athletically, mentally, spiritually, and academically. She believed in these young athletes so much that she spent her own money to coach them. When people heard about her efforts, they donated money. Willye also organized fundraisers to help the Metropolitan Striders Track and Field Team, which she founded.

Like Olympic competition, coaching had its problems. Willye's coaching created tension with high school coaches whose athletes she worked with during the summers. When the athletes improved considerably under Willye's guidance, they began to question their school coach's methods. When they told their coaches, "Willye White told me to do this," friction created sparks between Willye and the coaches. Eventually, coaches went to watch her work with athletes, and she felt good when they attended her practices. Their observations signaled that she was a good coach.

Willye started a farm team with the understanding that other coaches would eventually take on her athletes. "That would give me an opportunity to measure my ability. If children weren't pulled before they were juniors or seniors, I was extremely upset." She likewise became upset when coaches pulled talented athletes from her guidance just when they were ready for national or international competition. But she accepted this process as part of coaching and concluded, "I never taught my athletes to be loyal to me; I just taught them to do their very best."

The issue of loyalty created a dilemma for Willye. She reasoned that she could not *make* her athletes stay with her:

> I demand respect, and I give respect. Loyalty is something that they must decide on, and it was not something that I should have to tell my children. I never did, so they left. But they all came back. They came back in either their junior year in college or their freshman year

in college, in fifteen minutes, or the next year. Then I would tell them to stay with their coaches. They could always call me, and I would tell them what they were doing wrong.

Ultimately, Willye loved the athletes and the challenge of coaching but felt used by the parents:

> I would make certain that the children went to school, and in return I would ask the parents to help me raise money. I felt it was not fair for lay citizens to continue to give me money for someone else's children. Many of these children then went to college on a full scholarship. I felt that their parents should make some kind of contribution.

Willye coached until 1984, when she grew disenchanted with parents and her work as a public health administrator made the time commitment to coaching impossible.

Willye left her administrative position with the Chicago Health Department in 1991 for work that combined her coaching, nursing, and administrative talents. In her new position as Director of Recreation Services for the Chicago Park District, she created sport opportunities for children through recreation programs. That same year, she established the Willye White Foundation to promote the total development of girls' minds, bodies, and spirits. The Foundation focused on girls because Willye believed that "if we turn them around, they will turn the boys around, and both will turn the parents around." Elaborating on the Foundation's goals, she said, "Athletics develop the body, the educational component develops the mind, and if you care for yourself, you develop your spirit. One thing that's wrong in our society's development of people is that we develop parts, not wholes."

Willye had joined the Board of Directors for the Fellowship of Christian Athletes in 1989 to nurture the spirit through sport. She admitted feeling conflicted about some of its programs. For instance, she viewed athletics, not specific kinds of prayer, as the answer to youth problems:

> It's very hard to tell a young man to pray and to believe in God when his sister has been raped and his mother has been killed, and his father has been assassinated. How can he see an out? The whole community is involved with drugs. If you put these children in a computer class or a sports camp and teach them how to throw and how to speak and to prepare themselves for tomorrow, then we'd see a difference.

Despite her caution with the organization, Willye didn't dismiss faith. She was deeply spiritual, even though she never claimed a particular denomination. In fact, she found more satisfaction in an empty church than a full one. "I feel that God is everywhere. He had his services on the rock, by the side of the road, on a mountain top. If you follow the Ten Commandments and help your brothers, then church isn't necessary."

As dedicated as she became to any new work, Willye admitted, "I do not want to commit to anything the way I did to track and field. Nothing will consume my life as track and field did." Personal balance again became a challenge. When Willye quit competing in 1976, she gave up running completely. Within a year she was burdened with medical problems. Surprised to learn that she was addicted to physical exercise, she resumed regular workouts, which she continued as long as her health allowed.

In September of 1993, Willye's position as Director of Recreation Services was phased out. At 53, she reeled with anxiety and depression, eventually hitting her lowest point. But the problem, she realized, was not entirely her own. Lack of communication among women about health had created confusion and fear. "You have to talk to several women to get the true understanding of what you're seeking," Willye said. "So I started talking and found out that I wasn't losing my mind."

The following year, health complications and surgery forced her to reassess her life again:

> The body basically shuts down after surgery. As a nurse, I could tell you those things, but I could not relate to them. Now I can't do three-quarters of the things that I used to do. I work out, and then I come home and go to bed. And I don't work out the next day.

Her awareness of self-limitations prompted her to withdraw from several of the many boards on which she served. "I've taken time off to learn about myself, to get a true introduction to Willye White. And I've decided that I can't do everything and be all things to all people."

Philosophy and Reflections

Willye White still holds the record as the only American woman on the U.S. Track and Field Team to compete in five consecutive Olympics. She personally embraced the honor of being an Olympic athlete:

> I reached the ultimate dream of going to the championships of amateur athletics. Winning the silver meant that I was the very best that America had and the second best in the world. It was a measure of what I could accomplish alone because I did not have a coach to push me further.

She attributed her success to the self-motivation that her grandfather had instilled in her.

Despite personal fulfillment as a measure of success, she never considered herself an American celebrity. In 1993, the *New York Times* confirmed, "while White is well-known in national sports circles as a lively, generous resource, her public voice is less well-known" (Lipsyte, 1993, p. 27). Willye attributed this imbalance to two significant factors:

> I am black and I am a silver medalist. I am an American, and being black I just don't get the same kind of exposure and opportunities. Being a silver medalist has no bearing because it's not number one. It doesn't matter that you're competing against seven or eight thousand people, that you're lucky enough to be one, two, three, four, even in the top six, because if it's not gold, it has no bearing. And if people do not recognize your accomplishments and abilities, then you do not get the exposure.

Her experience characterized a trend she observed about the Olympics:

> The Olympic Games belong to the corporate world, because they spend trillions of dollars. We competed before radio and with very little television and newspaper coverage. So we actually competed. Now it's just a great big glamorous showcase, and it's one of the greatest festivals every four years. But some of the athletes are getting money. It's no longer the glory of competing; it's how many medals you win. If you don't win any medals, then you're nothing and you're cast aside.

Although Willye critiqued the Olympics, she was quick to declare,

> Athletics made me better in the business world. I worked with a lot of employees of different ethnic and cultural backgrounds. Having traveled to Asia where the customs are different, I was not disturbed when I worked with a man who had a problem taking instructions and guidance from a woman, because I knew that women were not leading citizens in his country. I knew how to deal with it. Athletics taught me to take chances. I'm not afraid to make decisions. And through athletics I know who I am. I feel that I've taken what I've learned from athletics and applied it to my work ethic. If a decision has to be made, I will make it. If it's a wrong decision, it will not destroy me. I'll go back to the drawing board and find out what I did wrong, and I'll try to correct it and not make that same mistake again. I grow from each mistake, as I grew from each defeat in athletics.

The greatest skill that Willye developed through athletic competition was her ability to read people. "When I come into a situation, I have to be able to know your strong points and your weak points," she said. "I had to know the weak and strong points of my opponents. I can tell basically what people are going to do before they do it."

Willye's athletic accomplishments and generous community work attracted many honors. She received the President's Council on Physical Fitness and Health National Honor Award (1984), The Chicago Multiple Sclerosis Society Lifetime Achievement Award (1987), and other awards for outstanding athletic achievement. She was inducted into the National Sports Track and Field Hall of Fame, the Helms Sports Hall of Fame, the Chicago Sports Hall of Fame, the Women's Sports Foundation International Hall of Fame, Tennessee State University Hall of Fame, and the Black Sports Hall of Fame, among the most notable. In 1991, she received both the Sojourner Truth Sports Award and the Clairol Personal Best Award.

Willye's most revered honor was her induction into the Mississippi Hall of Fame in 1981. For the occasion, Mississippi Governor Winter invited her to be a guest at the Governor's mansion in Jackson. She recalled,

That was the greatest honor in the world for me because I had not been allowed even to go to the mansion or to the capitol as a child. But then the governor gave me a personal call and invited me to be a guest in his home. That is the highest honor I've ever received.

After leaving her job with the Chicago Parks District, Willye stayed on Chicago's South Side because she didn't want the city's youth to think that she had deserted them. She often ran through the South Side, talking with young girls along the way. She wanted to instill in them the same motivation that her grandfather taught her, to know that they control their destinies and that they can escape drugs and pregnancy if they learn to love themselves. But she was well aware of the clash of dreams and politics:

We all have our dreams, and America is not geared to the dreams of our children. Of all the things President Carter could have done to the Russians for invading Afghanistan, why did he decide to take away the dreams of 5,000 athletes by telling them they couldn't go to the 1980 Olympics? Had it not been for the Olympic Games, there would not have been a Willye White, a Mohammed Ali, a Wilma Rudolph, or a Mary Lou Retton. Why would the president of the United States take away the dreams of young adults? No one would do that with professional athletes because there is money involved.

Willye knew that she could not singlehandedly change America's attitude, but she offered this advice: "Children are our future. If you have a child, you should make a commitment to spend time with that child for the next 30 years, to teach that child values, to try to develop a whole child, to listen to the child." She followed her own advice with Chicago's youth. She listened to their dreams and to their frustrations. Meanwhile, she hoped that people would begin to understand the changes America faces with its youth:

We must bring back the family concept. A family is not a mother and father and child; a family is a group of people working for the same common cause, for the development and growth of America. We must be sensitive to the needs of other people and teach our children to be sensitive to the cultures and ethnic backgrounds of other people.

Asked to complete the sentence "I believe Willye White was put on this earth to…," Willye did not hesitate: "To make people laugh." She laughed and continued, "I ask myself that same question. I was sitting there thinking last night what I would like to have written on my tombstone. I'd like something like, 'Every day is a holiday, one great big party.'"

Willye then explained that a party does not mean just drinking; a party means having a good time, with no pain, no troubles, no problems, and a lot of laughs. Although life certainly was never one big party for Willye, she found laughter despite loss and believed in her destiny. Willye died in 2007 at the age of 67. Throughout her life, she let no one take her smile.

7

Doris Corbett
Promoting Human Rights through Sport

As a child living in the segregated South during the 1950s, Doris Corbett knew there were places she could not safely go. Signs designating "colored only" and "white only" divided the bus station where her family went to enjoy ice cream on Saturday mornings. While she recognized injustice, she also understood the danger of challenging the law and deeply embedded social norms.

Her parents, Henry and Isadora Corbett, encouraged Doris and her siblings to exceed expectations. In church and in school, Doris pushed. And she hasn't stopped. Doris began her career as a faculty member, coach, and administrator at Howard University in 1972, the year that Title IX became law. In 2012, she moved into her current position as director of the School of Health, Physical Education, and Leisure Studies at the University of Northern Iowa, where she teaches, mentors students, and conducts research on race and gender in sport. Throughout her career, she has been an active member of national and international physical education and sport organizations working for social justice through sport.

Despite the many changes she has witnessed, Doris sees ongoing barriers for women in sport. "They may not exist in ways they did in the 1980s," she asserted. "They exist more in certain parts of the country," she added, alluding to under-resourced institutions that enroll primarily African American students. She emphasized the importance of recognizing the intersection of race and gender when working for social justice. Given that intersection, civil rights and women's rights work in tandem:

> To breathe every day as a person of color, you are an advocate of civil rights. The extent to which one is an advocate and seeks to take a position on issues of supporting, enforcing Title IX legislation, you're also enforcing, supporting civil rights [D. Corbett, personal communication, March 4, 2016].

With this worldview, cultivated through experience and family, and later by mentors, Doris continues the work of Title IX by promoting physical education, sport, and fair play as human rights.

Family and Early Education

Doris and her identical twin sister, Barbara, were born at the Corbetts' home on June 9, 1947, in Elizabethtown, North Carolina. Until she and Barbara went to college, they dressed alike, and people often couldn't tell the two apart. The confusion had its benefits and challenges:

> I remember walking to neighbors' homes annually collecting dimes on behalf of the March of Dimes. My twin sister would start at one end of the road, and I would start at the other end. Each of us would do each side twice, because people could not tell us apart, and there was no need for us to walk to the other side.
>
> When I think about all of the things we did as children, much of it had to do with people not being able to tell us apart. We were accused of taking tests and exams for each another when we did not.... Our grades were pretty much the same, and we tended to miss the same questions on exams, because we learned the same information the same way [D. Corbett, personal communication, June 13, 2008)].

The Corbett family was respected in Elizabethtown for living their values of hard work and religion. Doris's mother, Isadora cooked in the school cafeteria, her father, Henry worked in a sawmill, and her two older brothers helped care for the twins. The Corbetts greeted each morning with prayer:

> Our lives were spent in the church, and anyone who knew us knew that we were either at church or at home.... That is just how we lived, and to my knowledge that is how everyone in the community lived. I did not know anyone who did not go to church on Sunday, and I did not know anyone who did not go to work during the week. I did not know anyone who was on welfare. I did not know anyone who had children out of wedlock. Now I am certain that those things happened, but we were not aware of those things [D. Corbett, personal communication, June 13, 2008].

Religion was a family legacy and has remained a part of Doris's life:

> My grandfather was the Reverend Al Herbert Beatty, a Methodist minister, and we were the children of the Corbett family, a family that was prominent in the church. We had church in my hometown, Elizabethtown, on the second and fourth Sundays, and church at my daddy's hometown, Ivanhoe, which was about 40 miles away from Elizabethtown, on the first and third Sundays. So all four of us children went to our church on every second and fourth Sunday, and we drove to my Daddy's hometown and went to his church on the first and third Sundays of the month. We were always in church. We were at church all day on Sundays, we sang in the choir, and we were in Baptist Student Union. When we were old enough to drive, we drove my grandfather to various churches [D. Corbett, personal communication, June 13, 2008].

Church became a place of social as well as spiritual development as Doris and her sister learned to be Sunday school teachers, to read announcements in different churches, and to read at funerals.

Typical for the 1950s, Henry and Isadora Corbett wanted to give their children more educational opportunity than they had. Henry had a third-grade education, and Isadora finished the eleventh grade before marrying Henry. They modeled a work ethic and expected their children to work as tirelessly as they did. Because Elizabethtown was racially segregated, Doris completed grades one through 12 at the town's school where African American teachers taught African American children. Teachers commonly lived with respected families during the 1950s, so the Corbetts often opened their home to teachers (D. Corbett, personal communication, June 13, 2008).

Doris measured her family's middle class prosperity in terms of health, the property they inherited from her grandparents, and an ability to provide for family:

> I have spoken to my sister and brothers about this over the years, and we cannot remember a day that my father and mother did not go to work. I don't ever remember a day that they were even ill. We owned our home; we owned property (land). We had three freezers at the smokehouse (an indoor facility we had outside).... We were considered middle class, because we owned our home, and my parents had several vehicles. I can remember my mother from time to time saying, "We do not owe anyone." We were a very proud family, because we had the best that anyone had [D. Corbett, personal communication, June 13, 2008].

The importance of owing no one reminded Doris of a story that further illustrated the family's self-sufficiency:

> I recall that one time we had an English paper due, and we borrowed a friend's typewriter to type the paper. My father was very, very upset. We did not borrow things. You worked, earned, and acquired for yourself the things you needed. You took care of yourself and never disrespected the family. So borrowing a typewriter from a neighbor was just not a good thing. Shortly after that, daddy went out and worked some extra hours on the weekend to earn money to purchase us a typewriter. He cut yards and worked as a gardener for other people at big houses owned by those who ran the sawmill [D. Corbett, personal communication, June 13, 2008].

Henry Corbett imprinted his work habits on Doris, who would apply this ethic in school, teaching, research, administration, and ultimately in her work for social justice through physical education and sport.

In their small town where "everyone knew everyone," word traveled quickly when Doris struggled in a sociology class:

> I remember on one occasion that a teacher, a counselor at the school, Mrs. Shields, said to my mother in the cafeteria (because my mother worked there) that I was not doing as well in my sociology class as I did in the previous six weeks' grading period in school. Before I got home and barely put my foot across the screen door, mama was telling me that I was failing. Now, I earned a "B" in the sociology class that particular six weeks, but according

to my mother, I was failing. Our parents expected us to always be the best. "Anyone can be at the bottom," I remember mama saying. We were expected to be at the top of whatever it was we were doing. That was the expectation [D. Corbett, personal communication, June 13, 2008].

Despite the family's self-sufficiency and middle-class affluence, they experienced racial inequality of the 1950s. "On Saturdays," Doris recalled, "my father would take us to the bus station and buy us a banana split or a milk shake, whichever one we wanted, but we always entered the 'colored only' section" (D. Corbett, personal communication, June 13, 2008).

Residents of Elizabethtown didn't dare challenge signs dictating "colored only" and "white only" because, as Doris explained, they lived in Bladen County, on whose border stood a sign that said, "Welcome to Ku Klux Klan Town." "We knew our place," she stated. "We learned it very early, so one did not live without knowing and experiencing discrimination as a child growing up" (D. Corbett, personal communication, June 13, 2008). Doris was 15 or 16 years old by the time the town began to remove signs that dictated segregation.

Although the Corbett family obeyed the signs, they were not tacitly compliant. Doris and Barbara participated in the young people's NAACP:

> On one occasion we attempted to sit down and place an order at our local drug store. We were told that if we did not leave, we would be arrested. As I reflect back on that period, we engaged in what were minor abuses to the law of the day [D. Corbett, personal communication, June 13, 2008].

While their civil rights activism challenged the law with only "minor abuses," the town sawmill fired her father as a result. He then commuted 50 miles to work in Wilmington. "So there were those life examples that were not unique for that day and time," Doris concluded. "They were common, and it was the life that we lived" (D. Corbett, personal communication, June 13, 2008).

Gender likewise defined Doris's early experiences. Sport experiences for girls in the 1950s emphasized non-competitive play. Doris noted, "I remember having play days where one class played another class in volleyball or basketball in seventh, eighth, or ninth grade" (D. Corbett, personal communication, June 13, 2008). Before President Dwight Eisenhower established the President's Council on Youth Fitness in 1956, schools commonly did not offer physical education instruction in elementary grades; physical activity was limited to recess play. Physical education instruction with trained teachers began in high school, where Doris was a cheerleader and played on the girls' intramural basketball team.

In the early 1960s, when Doris was in high school, play days moved beyond individual schools but still emphasized participation and play. Groups from area high schools traveled to a host school where they created teams comprising students from different schools, to avoid competition. Doris recalled "wrapping the Maypole, playing tag, and engaging in relay games" (D. Corbett, personal communication, June 13, 2008). But beyond those recreational activities, girls had no options for competitive play.

College and Physical Education

Doris and her siblings fulfilled their parents' dream of higher education. Both Doris and Barbara earned doctorates, one brother became a practical nurse, and the other was a certified auto mechanic. The journey then, more than the arrival, was unpredictable.

Doris did not intend to major in health and physical education. In 1965, she and Barbara enrolled in North Carolina College (renamed North Carolina Central University in 1969, the year Doris graduated). The college, which offered strong teacher preparation, was the first liberal arts college supported by the state for black students (North Carolina Central University). Because Doris had excelled at history and English in high school, she surprised and possibly disappointed her former teachers when she declared a health and physical education major at North Carolina College. The decision "evolved," according to Doris:

> My choosing physical education as a major came about in part because I had a Spanish teacher in college who felt that my identical twin sister and I were too dependent on each other, and she suggested that we should not be in the same major. At that time my sister and I were history majors. My sister chose business, and I chose physical education. My sister ended up with nearly a physical education minor, and I ended up with nearly a business minor [D. Corbett, personal communication, June 13, 2008].

Doris wasn't sure what motivated her teacher's advice or how much it resonated. She changed her major because she enjoyed physical activity. Because play days were the norm, varsity programs for women didn't yet exist at North Carolina College. Competition was local. For instance, sororities formed intramural basketball teams and competed against each other. Doris played intramural basketball and attended a few play days at North Carolina College, but she redirected her focus toward professional activities after declaring a health and physical education major.

Within her new major, Doris grew to admire professors LeRoy Walker and Lavonia Allison. Both were nationally recognized figures in physical education and sport. Walker, who chaired the physical education department when Doris was an undergraduate, created the track and field program at

North Carolina College and, in 1976, became the first African American to coach the U.S. Olympic Track and Field Team. According to Doris, the health and physical education major's strong professional emphasis reflected his belief that undergraduates should be involved professionally:

> What I remember most about my undergraduate program is that we were required to attend our physical education meetings, and we were required to go to at least one, if not two, professional conferences, whether state, district, or national. That was a part of the undergraduate expectation in order to graduate [D. Corbett, personal communication, June 13, 2008].

Walker lived the professional involvement he encouraged in students. "Dr. Walker was someone who was professionally engaged," Doris observed. "That was what I wanted to do. I realized that he was someone who moved in the direction that I felt was important. Without being all that conscious of it, I think I tried to model his professional involvement" (D. Corbett, personal communication, June 13, 2008).

Even more directly, Walker influenced Doris's first professional role. He told Doris, "'You are going to Duke University and work in this program, and this is what you are going to do'" (D. Corbett, personal communication, June 13, 2008). He then selected her to work as a counselor-in-service for a speech camp at Duke during the summer following her graduation. She noted, "I was their first person of color to be a part of the youth speech camp program that they had in place" (D. Corbett, personal communication, June 13, 2008).

After LeRoy Walker's death in 2012, Doris's memoriam in the *Journal of Health, Physical Education, Recreation & Dance* (2012) paid tribute to his leadership: "He had the vision of a giraffe and the quiet roar of a gentle lion" (9). She had earlier expressed gratitude toward her former mentor through her 1990 AAHPERD presidential theme, "Committed to Excellence—A Shared Responsibility." Her theme riffed on "Excellence Without Excuse: A Shared Responsibility," Walker's emphasis during his time as chancellor at North Carolina Central University (Corbett, 2012 "In Memoriam," p. 10). Walker's influence has resonated throughout her career as she has resisted limits that racism and sexism create.

Like Walker, Lavonia Allison taught in the department of physical education and recreation and modeled professional engagement. Doris explained,

> Although we were not close, her style, passion and commitment to professionalism and service impressed and struck me. I took note of that, not in a very conscious way, but upon reflection I realize that at the time I was an undergraduate student, I came to respect her. Dr. Allison, I believe and I don't think I'm mistaken, was one of the persons on the national convention floor in the nomination of Kennedy. She was very involved in the Civil Rights movement and the political scene during that time [D. Corbett, personal communication, June 13, 2008].

These early role models cultivated in Doris a sense of responsibility to the profession. Whether traveling with students to a conference or holding office in an international organization, Doris has continued to impress on others the importance of professional engagement.

Doris completed her bachelor's degree in health and physical education in 1969, three years before Title IX became law. North Carolina College maintained single-sex physical education departments, women led women's departments, and athletic competition for high school girls and college women was limited to play days and intramural sports. When Title IX became law, and its impact on high school and college athletics unfolded, many physical educators and athletic directors of her generation then faced a particular challenge. How would they construct a new model of equity in athletics while trying to preserve the values and power generated by women who built the existing programs? Doris's undergraduate professional involvement was vital training for her later work for equity in sports for women.

Early Teaching Career and Graduate School

Doris broke social barriers in 1969 when she became the first African American physical education teacher at Camp Curtin Junior High School. She repeated this first in 1970 as a new teacher at John Harris High School. Both schools, located in Harrisburg, Pennsylvania, enrolled a majority of white students with "a sprinkling of black kids," according to Doris. Her duties reflected the breadth of expectations of a physical education teacher. She taught health and physical education, coordinated the intramural program, directed an African Dance Company, and supervised junior varsity and varsity cheerleaders.

Just before she left John Harris High School in 1971, Doris wrote a proposal to create varsity women's basketball. She wasn't yet involved with conversations related to Title IX and women's sport but recognized girls' need for opportunity in athletics. Although she left before she had the opportunity to coach the varsity team, it would be part of her footprint at the school.

In the fall of 1971, Doris took a leave of absence from teaching high school to pursue her master's degree at North Carolina Central University. "I was determined to do it in a year and a summer," she explained, "because I had only saved enough money for being in school for that period of time" (D. Corbett, personal communication, June 13, 2008). John Harris High School expected her to return after she completed her degree. What happened next has grown murky over time, but it put in motion her next professional step. Doris explained,

While I was at the AAHPERD [American Alliance for Health, Physical Education, Recreation, and Dance] convention that particular spring, I was recruited by both Howard [University] and Michigan State. I did not go to interview booths, and I did not seek the positions. People came to me from Howard and Michigan State. I don't know why and how that evolved, but I was asked to take a position at both of those institutions. I finally chose Howard, because my sister was in the area [D. Corbett, personal communication, June 13, 2008].

Since John Harris High School wasn't funding her master's degree, she wasn't obligated to return. She resigned and in the fall of 1972 became a physical education instructor at Howard University.

A few months earlier, on June 23, 1972, President Richard Nixon had signed Title IX, enabling unpredictable changes for women in education and sport. "Discussions centered on the need for equity for women as it related to sport," Doris clarified. She continued,

In 1972, upon my arrival at the university, there were no varsity sport programs for women. In my second year at Howard University, I chaired a committee that drafted a proposal to initiate the women's athletic program, which was ultimately approved by the Board of Trustees. I coached the first Howard University women's basketball team [D. Corbett, personal communication, March 4, 2016].

Responses to the committee and its proposal varied. "I largely put together the members of that committee," Doris said. Some of the women she invited declined. According to Doris, "They were not feminists, not pro-women in sport." In fact, one of her colleagues who said she had no interest in women's sport later became the women's athletic director. Not all women were proactive about women being in sport at Howard University. Some labeled Doris and another female colleague feminists, which they were. "It was not a supportive environment for putting forth a proposal for varsity sport," Doris concluded. "The proposal moved forward because of Title IX, not because of an avalanche of support" (D. Corbett, personal communication, March 4, 2016).

For two years, Doris taught primarily activity courses as she prepared for the next step in her education. In the fall of 1974, she entered the doctoral program in sociology of sport at the University of Maryland, College Park. The program required her to be a full-time student, so for seven years she taught full time at Howard University while completing full-time coursework and her dissertation. Her motivation was practical:

Outside of my residency I could not afford to go to graduate school full time. No one advised me about scholarship funding. I think that is why I give and have given so much attention to young people, college students, in trying to advise, direct, and assist them in terms of their matriculation—matriculation in terms of graduate school but also assistance in handling their career choices. I really didn't get any assistance in that regard. I would have liked to have earned my doctorate by going to school full time throughout the time I worked on the degree, but because of expenses, I did it as best I could while working full time.... It was crazy, insane, and very challenging, but I did it [D. Corbett, personal communication, June 13, 2008].

As Doris recalled, the schedule left little time for eating and sleeping:

> A typical day began at about 5:00 or 5:30 a.m., a quick breakfast, an hour's drive into the university. I taught from 8:00 a.m. to 2:00 or 3:00 p.m. daily and then headed to the University of Maryland, College Park, for classes. I attended classes at least twice a week and was actively engaged in Howard faculty activities (student advising, various committee assignments, and coordinator of the Student Physical Education Majors Club [D. Corbett, personal communication, March 4, 2016].

Doris's goal was to earn a degree despite the practical challenges. She admitted that if she knew what she knows how, she might have been fearful or not sure she could reach the goal. But preparation for higher education began a long time before she went to college, when her mother insisted that to earn a B was to fail. "You don't expend energy lamenting that you have to do all of this," Doris said. "Sometimes it's good not to know the future" (D. Corbett, personal communication, March 4, 2016).

The discipline now known as sociology of sport didn't yet exist at the University of Maryland when Doris declared her doctoral focus in that area. Her dissertation, too, was cutting edge in the early 1980s, as Second Wave feminism and the sexual revolution offered new arenas and emerging language for articulating gender, sexuality, and sexual orientation. Doris's dissertation, "The Relationship Between Androgyny, Self-Concept and Social Status Among Minority Female Athletes and Nonathletes," reported her findings about issues of sexual orientation and androgyny, social and economic class, and the correlation between social standing, economic class, self-esteem and sexual orientation and the selection of sport participation. This early research established her interest in and methods for ongoing study and publications about the intersecting impacts of race, ethnicity, and gender on women's sport participation.

Doris characterized her experience at the University of Maryland as "unforgettable," largely because of support from her advisor Dr. Anne Gayle Ingram. "She was from Georgia—a wonderful person, a strong professional, a researcher, and a feminist," Doris recalled. "Working with her was a good fit for me." Ingram, a faculty member in the physical education department from 1962–1988, was particularly interested in women's rights, the women's movement at the University of Maryland, and the Association for Intercollegiate Athletics for Women (AIAW) (University Libraries Digital Collections). Doris confided,

> Had it not been for her, I would not have remained at the University of Maryland, College Park. I would have taken the advice given to me by many to select a different kind of insti-

tution. I have been told that I was the first person of color to earn a degree from their program [D. Corbett, personal communication, June 13, 2008].

Like her advisor, Doris identified as a feminist and has lived according to feminist practice. "I have always been an activist," she explained. "As a product of the 1960s, I hold strong beliefs about equity and fair play in general" (D. Corbett, personal communication, March 4, 2016). She noted, however, that barriers for women in sport still exist, not as they did in the 1980s, but "in certain parts of the country, in dollars and cents," because of inequitable distribution of resources (D. Corbett, personal communication, March 4, 2016).

Title IX, Tension and Developing Leadership

As civil rights and feminist movements challenged barriers to women's equality, physical education and sport would not be left behind. Title IX enabled discussion and action in these arenas. Doris's interest in race and gender in sport intersected with these larger movements. When she completed her Ph.D., she taught fewer activities courses and more social science of sport, including History and Philosophy of Sport, the Role of Women in Sport, and Sociology of Sport. Her teaching and research examined not only the differences between women and men, as traditional feminist scholarship had done; it addressed race and class differences among women that would be crucial to equitable implementation of Title IX. "My goals aligned with those of leaders of Title IX's implementation," she noted (D. Corbett, personal communication, March 4, 2016).

Doris's constellation of interest and experience situated her for leadership both at Howard University and in professional organizations. In 1983, she became coordinator of department and division curriculum and activities at Howard. Although deliberations that led to the merger of women's and men's physical education departments took place before Doris arrived at Howard in 1972, she experienced transitions typical for many institutions in the wake of Title IX:

> When I came to the university, there were separate physical education departments for men and women. I was the first female to have an office and teach classes in the men's gym. It was men's physical education and women's physical education. I taught coeducational classes, and I was one of the first to do that. In the early 70s, the department merged into the Department of Physical Education and Recreation and was inclusive of both men and women. Today [2008] we are a Department of Health, Human Performance and Leisure Studies [D. Corbett, personal communication, June 13, 2008].

Merged departments and co-educational classes addressed curricular sex divisions, but they also raised new questions about who would teach, administer, and coach in these new departments.

Doris didn't wait for an invitation. She circumvented the athletic director's lack of support for women's athletics when she organized and coached Howard's first women's basketball team in 1974. She scheduled competition with AIAW teams in and around Washington, D.C. (Carter-Francique and Richardson, 2015, pp. 71–72). The team, however, faced two common problems for new women's athletic teams: inadequate practice facilities and no budget for uniforms and transportation. A. Carter-Francique and F.M. Richardson learned from Linda Spencer, a member of that first team, "Corbett's team was not allowed to use the main gym, so they either practiced in the basement gym at whatever time made available to them, or the team utilized gyms that were located off campus" (p. 72). Common territory battles such as this one revealed the challenge of translating Title IX's federal legal power into local practice.

Supplying uniforms and getting to games were no less a challenge. According to Carter-Francique and Richardson, Spencer describes how offended the women were when the athletic director offered the team the men's old intramural uniforms. Doris then stepped in and "managed to get her team shorts, t-shirts, Chuck Taylor Converse All-Stars" (p. 72). Her efforts modeled the importance of gender and economic equity within athletics and made a significant impression on Spencer, who later coached women's basketball and volleyball at Howard. Doris also recalled that team members drove their own vehicles and paid for gas (D. Corbett, personal communication, March 4, 2016). That was the price of participation. Spencer then paid forward the lesson of Doris's leadership by supplying her teams with adequate shoes and uniforms. She explained, "'I didn't want any of my girls to feel different. I wanted them all to have the same, thus no one would be able to identify socio-economic status. They would just be a team'" (as cited in Carter-Francique & Richardson, 2015, p. 72).

After coordinating curriculum and activities, Doris twice chaired Howard's Department of Health, Human Performance, and Leisure Studies. Reflecting on her first term as chair, in 1989–90, Doris acknowledged being spread too thin: "At that time I was too involved in leadership roles both nationally and internationally, so I left the chairmanship for a period of time" (D. Corbett, personal communication, June 13, 2008). She would resume the position as department chair from 2006 to 2012.

In addition to department leadership, Doris's role in national organizations in the early 1980s situated her at the core of Title IX changes. At that time, two national associations within the American Alliance for Health, Physical Education, Recreation, and Dance (AAHPERD) governed women's athletics: the Association for Intercollegiate Athletics for Women (AIAW) and the National Association for Girls and Women in Sport (NAGWS). AIAW emphasized, organized, and supervised intercollegiate competition among women, and its members were institutions. NAGWS, in contrast, favored participation over competition. It established rules for women's athletics, published them through a series of guides, and maintained individual memberships (Carpenter & Acosta, 2005, p. 104). Doris served both associations at a critical point in the history of women in sport. She was a member of the AIAW executive board from 1979 through 1981. At the same time, she served NAGWS as president elect (1979–80), president (1980–81), and past president 1981–82).

Leaders of girls' and women's athletics faced ambiguity at this junction. Would they maintain the philosophy of broad participation that had shaped girls' and women's sport before Title IX, or would expanded opportunity bring with it the men's sport paradigm of competition among elite athletes? These questions led to conflicts over governance of women's athletics, and the tension divided AAHPERD. As AIAW supported an increasing number of women's athletic championships, it pursued independence from AAHPERD. This conflict reunited Doris and LeRoy Walker, no longer student and teacher but now professional colleagues. Walker had been AAHPERD president in 1977–78 and, with past president Celeste Ulrich, advised AIAW to remain within AAPHERD governance. Although AIAW separated from AAHPERD in 1979, the cleaving didn't destroy AIAW as Walker believed it would. The separation did, however, cause growing pains for women's athletics and everyone involved. In 1982, AIAW officially dissolved and the NCAA gained governance control of women's collegiate athletics (Ware, 2007, p. 170).

According to Doris, governance change threatened the authority of NAGWS guides. This series of sport-specific guides presented skills drills and rules that had shaped women's sport since the publication of *Standards in Athletics for Girls and Women* in 1937 (Carpenter & Acosta, 2005, p. 95). "We dealt with the NCAA attempting to take over the writing of the rules— the guidebooks for girls and women in sport," she explained (D. Corbett, personal communication, June 13, 2008). On one occasion, she met with the high school federation leaders in Indiana to discuss the NAGWS guides and rulebooks. She also spoke in defense of Title IX at forums associated with AAHPERD:

> Too often the climate was not positive. I was a guest on a local television show during the time I coached the first Howard University women's basketball team, and the moderator asked me "if all my girls' were women." I responded, "Would you ask that question of a male coach?" On another occasion, during a university symposium panel discussion, the moderator informed the audience that women's sport took money and resources from the men's program [D. Corbett, personal communication, March 4, 2016].

Doris didn't dwell on these tensions during her NAGWS presidency. She turned, instead, to concerns regarding ongoing guidance for girls' and women's sport and athletics. A particular goal was to maintain the publication and quality of NAGWS guides. Doris exclaimed,

> The guides were outstanding; it was who we were! We provided a much-needed service to girls' and women's sports programs throughout the country. We lost some of our strength in that regard when sport pulled away from NAGWS and the focus became that of competition. The guides were one of the things that we did very well, and they were the central identity for the National Association for Girls and Women in Sport. Certainly we were trying to define who we were and what we wished our goals and purpose to be once that divide occurred. It affected all of us [D. Corbett, personal communication, June 13, 2008].

No matter how successful the guides were, the merging of women's and men's physical education departments and athletics, as well as NCAA governance of women's intercollegiate athletics, made them obsolete. In 2010, NAGWS would join the University of North Carolina at Greensboro Center for Women's Health and Wellness and became part of the new *Program for the Advancement of Girls and Women in Sport and Physical Activity*.

While NAGWS supported sport and athletics participation for girls and women, as well as professional organizations for those who taught in, coached, and administered programs, its name was misleading, Doris insisted. First, it was not a gender exclusive organization, Doris emphasized:

> Men are a part of that Association. During one of my three years in office for NAGWS we had a man on the Board.... My husband was and will always be a member of NAGWS.... I don't think we could exist even today without the support of male professionals.... I would feel that we were promoting an ideology that I could not embrace if we were excluding the participation of men [D. Corbett, personal communication, June 13, 2008].

In addition to being gender inclusive, NAGWS efforts to provide access to physical education and involve women in leadership went beyond Title IX and the United States. NAGWS contributed to international programs and devoted significant energy to providing workshops and seminars in Central and South America and the Caribbean. "We pulled together groups of professional women to go to those countries to be instrumental in developing women leaders of sport and in developing physical education programs in those areas of the world" (D. Corbett, personal communication, June 13, 2008).

The organization's attention to gender equity could not, however, mask ongoing racial inequity. Personal experience and research expertise made Doris acutely aware of discrimination. She recalled one NAGWS meeting that exposed the problem:

> Once we were trying to determine what clinicians we would select to go to Central and South America to do a series of workshops for NAGWS. As we sat around the conference table making suggestions and reviewing the credentials of those professional colleagues that had been proposed and recommended for consideration, I noted that for each professional person of color that was suggested there was much query and discussion about the individual's capability. During one of our breaks I said to the individual who was primarily the lead person in that kind of deliberation, "Are you aware of the nature of the questions that are proposed when certain names vs. the names of others are presented?" The individual recognized that she was not conscious of her behavior. She was very unaware. I showed her the statements and questions that I had written down, and the comments and nature of the discussion that ensued as a result. So they began to recognize the variations in their responses to the candidates under consideration [D. Corbett, personal communication, June 13, 2008].

This intervention had both short-term and long-term effects. Doris added that, during a conference presentation several years later, the individual from NAGWS shared her past behavior as an example of subtle discrimination. "I think many people are unaware of the oppression they put forth on others and of how others have to learn to handle such behavior," Doris concluded. "People expect people of color to ignore it, not acknowledge it, and/or pretend it does not exist, because we don't like to have real discussions about such issues" (D. Corbett, personal communication, June 13, 2008).

Reflecting on this critical moment of Title IX's implementation, Doris emphasized its complexity:

> It was the law, and it was the right thing to do. Did I envision the level of participation? Probably not. Keep in mind that as a person of color I had hope. We had come a long way in terms of civil rights, so naturally with a focus on women and Title IX, I believed we would have results. I wasn't as pessimistic as others. Largely Title IX focused on people, not people of color.

So, while Doris was hopeful about the impacts of Title IX, her experience confirmed that its impact on under-resourced historically black colleges and universities would be less than its impact on well-resourced institutions. "Men's sports want to be winners, so to share limited resources with women's sports is difficult," she explained. "We find ways to negotiate our responsiveness to the letter of the law" (D. Corbett, personal communication, March 4, 2016).

Life wasn't all work for Doris at this time. In 1982 she married William Johnson, who taught anatomy and kinesiology in Howard University's department of physical education. "I married late," she stated. At 35, she considered herself past her prime age for bearing children. She would, nevertheless, be a mother. She explained,

> My husband was previously married and brought to our union a daughter whom I consider to be my daughter. Because my sister and I were identical twins and an egg divides to make two, half of her is me and half of me is her, and my sister and her husband's son is also my son. Therefore, I have a daughter and a son. Although others might define them as a stepdaughter and nephew, I define them as daughter and son [D. Corbett, personal communication, June 13, 2008].

International Voice and Vision

Reflecting on her work in the mid–1980s, Doris characterized herself as a "young thing" who wanted to be more deeply engaged professionally. Participating in her first international conference in 1985 had involved a leap of faith:

> When conference abstracts were called for, I submitted an abstract and went to my first international conference in London. I presented my paper and met an array of people. I did not know a single soul; I simply submitted the abstract and went! [D. Corbett, personal communication, June 13, 2008.

At the 1985 World Congress of the International Council for Health, Physical Education and Recreation, Doris presented her dissertation research to demonstrate the intersecting impacts of socio-economic class, race, and fitness education on ethnic minority women. Interested colleagues then invited her to conduct a three-day workshop, in Concepcion, Chile, on the sociology of sport. She observed "an old-boy network" shaping the culture of the early ICHPER-SD conferences she attended. "I think it was a surprise to them that I took an interest in the programs and continued to attend the various conferences whereby I submitted abstracts, received approval, and presented papers," she confided (D. Corbett, personal communication, June 13, 2008).

As a result of her experiences in England and Chile, Doris became more involved in the International Council of Health, Physical Education, Recreation, Sport and Dance (ICHPER-SD). In 1988, elected to serve as international vice president of ICHPER-SD, she was the first American, first female, and first African American to hold the position.

Meanwhile, there was work to be done in the United States to promote equity and fairness in sport. Doris continued as international vice president of ICHPER-SD while serving as president of the American Alliance for Health, Physical Education, Recreation and Dance for the 1990–91 term. AAHPERD membership in 1990 was approximately 26,000 teachers, coaches, students, and administrators, and the national convention drew one of the largest groups ever to attend. "Those were strong years for us," Doris noted, "not only in terms of membership but in terms of the financial stability of the organization" (D. Corbett, personal communication, June 13, 2008). In 2015 membership in the organization, renamed SHAPE America in 2013, was 20,000 (SHAPE America National Convention and Expo).

"I must tell you an interesting story," Doris said as she reflected on the process of becoming president-elect in 1989:

> JoAnne Owens-Nauslar, who is not just a colleague but also a friend, was the other candidate. The two of us ran against each other. Although we were running for the same position, we would get up early every morning (and you know how grueling the campaign trail is for a president-elect candidate) and walk two miles together.... Every morning we walked the halls. We found a floor level that gave us a great deal of privacy for our morning constitution. We worked out together during that entire conference.... It was a wonderful bonding for us. People thought we were so strange to spend time together in that way. I think the early morning exercise we engaged in together was good for both of us [D. Corbett, personal communication, June 13, 2008].

This story typifies the way Doris prioritized people and relationships in all of her roles.

Instead of setting her own agenda as president of AAHPERD, Doris responded to current issues facing the organization. One particular effort was to develop a more collegial relationship with the President's Council on Physical Fitness and Sports (renamed President's Council on Fitness, Sports & Nutrition in 2010). Doris recalled working specifically with two programs. Physical Best, an AAHPERD program, designed physical education curriculum and fitness tests that emphasized lifelong activity. The other, Fitnessgram, was a fitness assessment program developed by the Presidential Youth Fitness Program.

Doris described the work as "very political" and "very scientific":

> Our concerns were marketing who we were, getting the Physical Best product in place, and going through the various guidelines associated with that program. We had sub-groups, ad hoc committees, that dealt with the issues of Physical Best.... We had different groups working to try to bring bi-partisan groups and issues together to unify the Alliance around the question of Physical Best [D. Corbett, personal communication, June 13, 2008].

To stabilize Physical Best, organization leaders identified prominent stakeholders whose support would reassure AAHPERD members of the program's quality. Doris invited Arnold Schwarzenegger, chair of the President's Council on Physical Fitness and Sports from 1990 to 1993, to give a plenary address at AAHPERD's annual conference. Her strategy worked. Both Physical Best and Fitnessgram found niches among new fitness and measurement programs. Physical Best still exists as a SHAPE America program, but its visibility and implementation have decreased. Doris's leadership on behalf of these programs contributed to a national emphasis on lifelong fitness that remains at the core of SHAPE America's standards for physical education (SHAPE America, National Standards).

Still balancing multiple service roles with her full-time position at Howard University, Doris advanced from the office of vice-president to president of ICHPER-SD in 1991. She was, again, the first woman elected and the first African American to serve in that role since ICHPER-SD was founded in 1958. The first woman to lead the organization, before governance included the election of a president, was founding member Dorothy Ainsworth. Doris described Ainsworth as "a visionary and someone who recognized the importance of physical education, education of the physical from a global perspective, and who sought to bring harmony to the world through physical education and the discipline areas related to physical education." She added, "It was historically such a male's preserve in the early days, so for Dorothy Ainsworth to have been one of the founders is tremendous" (D. Corbett, personal communication, June 13, 2008).

Doris acted as both an administrator and a visionary while president of ICHPER-SD from 1991 through 1999. She deepened existing alliances and established ties to other international organizations invested in education, sports, and human rights, such as the United Nations Educational, Scientific, and Cultural Organization (UNESCO) and the International Olympic Committee (IOC). At the same time, she continued the work she had prioritized as president of AAHPERD, this time observing and addressing the quality of physical education in government-supported schools around the world. Doris emphasized the intersection of sport and human rights:

> My work in the various countries looked at issues of quality physical education and issues of ethical conduct in sport, because my research and scholarly writing focused largely on human rights issues relating to race and gender issues in sport. I see the lack of quality in physical education and sport programming and instruction as a human rights issue, and I see the wide array of abuses in sport as a human rights issue [D. Corbett, personal communication, June 13, 2008].

By the time Doris began traveling the world with this message, Anita DeFrantz, another prominent advocate for human rights through sport, was becoming an outspoken member of the IOC Executive Board. Multiple voices joining a chorus meant each had a greater chance of being heard.

Leadership has taken Doris to more than 30 countries including Hong Kong, Japan, Jordan, South Africa, and Australia, and all over Europe, Asia, and South America, to lecture on ethics and social issues. To demonstrate her appreciation for cultural difference in each location, she offered her opening remarks in the language of the host country. She explained her preparation:

> I took the time to find someone who spoke the language and had that person or persons work with me to phonetically write my opening remarks in the language of the country.

Then I would spend hours and/or days practicing and rehearsing the speaking of a specific language.

I recall that on one occasion when I was in China and made my opening remarks in Chinese, I was interrupted at least five times with a standing ovation from the audience. This was an audience of people who were present for the Asian Games Scientific Conference that convened prior to the Asian Games leading up to the Olympic Games of that particular year. I was overwhelmed, moved by the fact that they so embraced in a positive way that type of presentation. It was a moving experience to the extent that each time they interrupted me to applaud, I started my opening remarks over again, because I was so taken aback by the whole experience that I didn't even know where I was in my text [D. Corbett, personal communication, June 13, 2008].

With each step outside her comfort zone, Doris modeled the cultural exchange that she advocated through teaching and leadership.

New Directions in Teaching, International Service and Research

Although Title IX required that all U.S. schools receiving federal funding comply by 1978, (Carpenter & Acosta, 2005, p. 8), lagging implementation stalled progress. Then, in 1992, a landmark Supreme Court decision yielded a significant gain. Until that point, the Office of Civil Rights (OCR) handled cases related to Title IX. The results were often empty promises of compliance; schools never actually faced funding cuts as a result of non-compliance (Carpenter & Acosta, 2005, p. 24). In the case of *Franklin v Gwinnett County Public Schools*, however, the Court ruled in favor of a female student who filed a lawsuit seeking financial redress, following an unsatisfying OCR decision. Prior to this decision, Carpenter and Acosta (2005) explained, "the difference in the potential outcome of an OCR complaint and a lawsuit was negligible; neither could result in monetary damages but only in a promise from the institution to 'go forth and sin no more'" (p. 24). Now, the Court had set precedent for monetary awards in lawsuits that determined violation of Title IX (Carpenter & Acosta, 2005, p. 124).

With increasing tools for ensuring girls' and women's access to sport and athletics in the United States, leaders of Doris's generation increasingly cultivated international networks and emphasized human rights. Questions of governance and competition structures no longer demanded the bulk of leadership energy. By the early 1990s, the logic for equity reasoned that health, fitness, and physical education enhance the quality of life, and quality of life is a human right. Therefore, everyone has the right to health, fitness, and physical education. Doris reflected on her contribution to this effort:

> When I have had the opportunity to speak to Olympic CEOs, whether in Greece, Australia, Japan or Hong Kong, Belgium, the Netherlands, Barcelona, Malaysia, Singapore, or the Philippines, I have tried, from an academic perspective, to get the academic and sport community of professional groups to see the relationship between health and fitness and education of the physical to the quality of life that the citizenry of their country can enjoy as a result of quality health and physical education programs [D. Corbett, personal communication, June 13, 2008].

Her connection between physical education and citizens' quality of life made her point, and it would soon take her beyond sport audiences toward unpredicted opportunity.

One such opportunity led Doris into the halls of Congress, where she worked as a Congressional Research Fellow during her 1993–94 sabbatical from Howard University. She was recommended by Dr. Carl Troester, one of ICHPER-SD's founders and a strong supporter of her research career and international leadership. Doris explained,

> The United States Capitol Historical Society, which is an arm of Congress, was beginning to invite scholars to write a series of books that reflected different discipline areas, whether agriculture, food or engineering. For whatever reason, there was interest in looking at Congressional members and their relationship with sport. My name came up at the behest of Dr. Troester. I was one of many who responded to a request by submitting an application, was interviewed, and subsequently prepared and submitted several proposals that would indicate what type of book I might write concerning congressional members and their relationship to sport [D. Corbett, personal communication, June 13, 2008].

The resulting book, *Outstanding Athletes of Congress*, presents profiles of 12 Congressmen, including Jack Kemp, Ralph Metcalfe, Tom McMillen Morris K. Udall, and former U.S. presidents George Herbert W. Bush and Gerald R. Ford.

Doris worked with an advisory committee of "distinguished" and "wonderful" people to select the final 12 Congressional members profiled in the book. "It had to be a bipartisan publication," she explained. "Therefore, I personally interviewed six democrats and six republicans" (D. Corbett, personal communication, June 13, 2008). One interview stood out in her mind:

> Probably the most unique experience I had with this particular piece of research was my phone interview with former President George Bush, Sr. It was unique because his secretary was supposed to get back to me in advance of when we were going to conduct his oral interview. Of course, I had my protocol prepared in advance. My questions and my tape recorder were typically set up in advance, and I knew what I was going to do in terms of setting everything up. When the United States Capitol Historical Society secretary called my office, she said, "Dr. Corbett, President Bush is on the line." I thought she said President Bush's secretary is on the phone, to schedule the interview. But, oh no, that was not the case; President Bush himself was on the phone! [D. Corbett, personal communication, June 13, 2008].

Although George Bush, Sr., was no longer president, Doris used the title of respect. She was flustered because she wasn't ready to interview him:

So I said, "Mr. President, would you give me a moment; I was actually prepared to hear from your secretary at this time, but not you." In the process I disconnected us. Oh, was I embarrassed. But I did that not once, but twice! That was very memorable to say the least [D. Corbett, personal communication, June 13, 2008].

The book's title reflects the male norm of athletics before the impact of Title IX. *Outstanding Athletes of Congress* was the second book of the Outstanding Members of Congress series. The first book in the series (1995) is *Outstanding Women Members of Congress*. The third book (1998) is *Outstanding African Americans of Congress*. Although all of the athletes featured in *Outstanding Athletes of Congress* are male, "men" doesn't appear as an identity category in the title as do "women" and "African Americans" in the other titles. Most likely, few if any of the female Congressional members as of 1993, when Doris conducted research for the book, had the opportunity to become "outstanding" in the ways their male colleagues did.

Immediately after Doris completed her year as a Congressional research fellow, the chair of the physical education department at the United States Military Academy, West Point, offered Doris a position as a distinguished visiting professor for the 1994–95 academic year. Moving five hours north of her home in Washington, D.C., she settled into her new role as a program reviewer. She clarified,

> I did not teach. I did a series of lectures on topics related to sociology of sport. My primary role there was to serve as a reviewer of their program, so I spent a year understanding the West Point culture. I wrote about their culture from the point of view of analyzing the quality of what they attempted to do in physical education and evaluating their structure in terms of the kinds of personnel they used to educate the cadets in the curricular discipline area of physical education pedagogy. I looked at their program in terms of being an external evaluator, who served as an internal evaluator, at that point [D. Corbett, personal communication, June 13, 2008].

While Doris was academically suited to study West Point culture, the position was also part of a legacy. LeRoy Walker had previously been a distinguished professor at West Point. Doris said, "I felt privileged to walk the halls in an area that he had also served" (D. Corbett, personal communication, June 13, 2008).

Doris thrived. Each visiting appointment yielded invitations for other distinguished teaching positions and lectures. From West Point, she traveled to Singapore in 1996, where she spent the academic year as an invited scholar and distinguished professor in the School of Physical Education at Nanyang Technological University. She taught a comparative, international physical education course at the university, but for the majority of the year she traveled throughout Southeast Asia and the world lecturing on ethics, moral reasoning, and moral conduct in sport. Through live lectures, television, and radio, she addressed scholars and faculty in both education and physical education. She also spoke to the Singapore Olympic Committee and the International Olympic Committee (IOC), opening new pathways for gender equity in sport.

The IOC selected Doris to represent the United States at the 1st IOC Conference on Women in Sport in Lausanne, Switzerland, in 1996. This Conference marks an historic moment for girls and women in sport. Anita DeFrantz, IOC executive board member, former IOC vice president, and founding member of the IOC Women and Sport Commission, emphasized that Title IX is a U.S. law. But despite its limited legal power, its cultural impact was moving beyond U.S. borders.

One resolution that emerged from the 1st IOC World Conference on Women and Sport was "that all women in sport be provided equal opportunities for professional and personal advancement, whether as athletes, coaches or administrators" (International Olympic Committee, Resolution). The resolution set a quantifiable measure of progress, calling for at least 10 percent representation of women on International Federation and National Olympic Committee working groups to create practical plans and goals for increasing women's participation in sport (International Olympic Committee, Resolution).

Following the conference, Doris continued her IOC work as a member of the IOC Sport for All Commission from 1997 to 2002. She was one of two Commission members who were not IOC members. The Commission determined how much money individual countries received to support and promote Olympic projects, some of which included physical activity and physical education. "The projects had to be inclusive, non-discriminating in any form, reach certain age groups, and had to address certain criteria in order to be acceptable to receive the patronage, that is, financial support from the IOC," Doris explained (D. Corbett, personal communication, June 13, 2008). Doris's research on discrimination in sport equipped her with all of the right tools to serve the IOC in this capacity.

Reflecting on professional activities that launched her voice in international conversations about girls and women in sports, Doris described her presentation at the International Conference on Sport and Human Rights in 1999, just prior to the Olympic Games in Australia, as "one of the most impacting":

> The International Sport and Human Rights body that sponsored the conference in Sydney, Australia, invited me to give one of the main addresses, and I spoke about ethical conduct in sport, basically looking at the politics of race in sport and its connection to the promotion of human rights. The presentation was very well received. At the same time, I was invited

to do a television show on *Lateline*, which in the United States is referred to as *Nightline* [D. Corbett, personal communication, June 13, 2008].

Her presentation and television appearance were, in her words, "a powerful moment" in terms of how people received and acted on her ideas about sport and human rights.

It's difficult to imagine how Doris tended her personal life and ongoing research while traveling, conducting program reviews, and giving presentations. But she did. Her husband often traveled with her and spent part of the year with her in Singapore. "He has gone on many of the trips with me," she explained, "so that has been a very supportive benefit to me, a good thing for us, and it has allowed us to spend time together in different countries" (D. Corbett, personal communication, June 13, 2008). After four years of visiting appointments, Doris returned to her full time position at Howard University in 1997, resumed her position as Coordinator of Sport Studies Division, and refocused her energies on teaching and research.

Throughout her visiting appointments, Doris had remained active in youth fitness program development. To her surprise, in 2002, she was invited to join The President's Council on Physical Fitness and Sports Science Board. The invitation to join the "very august group" surprised her, and she spoke humbly of the experience:

> The people on the PCPFS Science Board are just dynamic! They are the leading scholars in exercise science, physical education, pedagogy, and social science of sport. It was a tremendous honor to work with them—to be a part of that very serious, deliberate body that does the critical and massive amount of research literature in this area of the field [D. Corbett, personal communication, June 13, 2008].

One of the Board's primary activities was to make recommendations to the Council based on the Board's current research. Doris's contribution to the Board from 2002 to 2007 brought together her key interests in physical education, sociology of sport, and equal access to education, sport, and health.

During this time, studies published updated correlations between race and health disparities. Doris responded by expanding her previous study of obesity among African American girls and women in sport. She was particularly curious about the impact of technology habits on this population. She noted, in 2008, that National Center for Health Statistics data had reported at least 77 percent of African American women from ages 20 to 74 were overweight. "More than 77 percent! Lack of physical activity is a significant problem that African American girls and women face," Doris exclaimed, revealing her concern about a widespread problem (D. Corbett, personal communication, June 13, 2008).

Doris contrasted her college experience with contemporary habits to illustrate how cultural changes and technological advances contribute to the problem of excess weight and obesity:

> I reflect back on the time at which I grew up and when I was in college. We did not have fast food places. We ate in the college dining hall, and it closed at a certain hour. We were there for breakfast, lunch, and dinner, and we did not eat after 6:00 o'clock, because the dining hall was closed. We didn't eat junk food, because there was no place to get it. We did not eat at late hours, and we did not have money to buy things we should not have been eating. That type of lifestyle is not the case today. Also we did not have the modes of transportation that we have today, so we walked wherever we needed to go. We are just not engaged in physical activity, and that has taken a terrible toll on the quality of life, particularly for the African American community and for girls and women [D. Corbett, personal communication, June 13, 2008].

She further observed, while traveling, how different parts of the world emphasize healthy lifestyles. "That has always been a good thing for me," Doris pointed out, "and I walk a lot more and eat more fruits and vegetables" (D. Corbett, personal communication, June 13, 2008).

Doris aligned her ongoing research about physical activity and women of color in sport culture with her service to the Women's Sports Foundation. As a member of the advisory board from 1984 through 1989, she contributed research to "Title IX and Race in Intercollegiate Sport" (2003), a Foundation report that examined participation and scholarship opportunities and graduation rates among NCAA athletes of color. This report slices available data in several ways. It compares participation, scholarships, and graduation rates of female and male athletes of color. The analysis also compares experiences of female athletes of color and white female athletes. The report relies heavily on data from two sources—NCAA participation and graduation rates between 1971 and 2000 and U.S. Census Bureau statistics—and acknowledges limited availability of information about collegiate athletes of color following Title IX's implementation (Women's Sports Foundation, p. 5). Although Title IX encouraged close scrutiny of female participation and representation, scholarship access, and graduation rates, it initially didn't recognize differences among women that impacted their participation in sport. The report also examines the NCAA sport experiences of female athletes of color and recommends actions to address problems.

The Report documents Title IX's contribution to gains in gender equity and recognizes its limitations regarding representation of female athletes of color. For example, participation of female athletes of color in NCAA sports increased 955 percent between 1971 and 2000, from 2,137 to 22,541 (Women's Sports Foundation, 2003, p. 5). Despite the increase, female athletes of color were still underrepresented among the total number of women of color attending NCAA colleges and universities. The same was true for all female athletes. And while the graduation rate of female athletes of color who received scholarships was higher than the overall female graduation rate, as a group, athletes of color had lower graduation rates than white athletes (Women's Sports Foundation, 2003, p. 6). One conclusion emphasizes the importance of recognizing the impact of racism on experiences of female athletes of color who participate in NCAA sports: "If female athletes of color were only experiencing discrimination based on their gender, their participation rate would be 19.2% instead of 14.8%" (Women's Sports Foundation, 2003, p. 19). The report confirms that to capture the full scope of changes for women during Title IX's implementation, researchers must investigate women's intersecting experiences of race and gender.

Doris's research on racial ideology, racism, and sexism in sport has filled gaps in the historical narrative of women in sport. Synthesis of her research interests over time illustrates the fusion of her personal values and professional work. She recalled, in particular, presenting "Sport, Gender and Ethnicity: Inclusion and Exclusion" at the 2008 International Olympic Committee (IOC) 4th World Conference on Women and Sport, in Amman, Jordan:

> As a result of my extensive preparation for that presentation, I saw the relationship between my work on human rights and race and gender issues in sport as a direct parallel. Working on that particular research paper allowed me insight and understanding that I had not had about Middle-Eastern women. I think that when we allow ourselves to reach beyond who we are, as we see ourselves into arenas that we are less comfortable with, we are most challenged and we grow [D. Corbett, personal communication, June 13, 2008].

Doris was by then fully in the ranks of professional peers, including Anita DeFrantz, who recognized the power of world organizations to transform the lives of girls and women through sport.

Honors and Awards

The distinguished professorships Doris held and her catalog of invited lectures demonstrate the respect she commands in the field of physical education and sociology of sport. She also has received several of the profession's highest awards, including the Luther Halsey Gulick Award in 1997. Given annually by SHAPE America (formerly AAHPERD), the Gulick Award is "the highest honor SHAPE America bestows in recognition of long and distinguished service to one or more of the professions represented in the Association" (SHAPE America, Recognition Awards). Doris confided,

> In all honesty I felt that I was not deserving of the Gulick Award. I have been told when I said that to family and friends that I should not say that, but it's true. I always thought that individuals who received the Gulick Award were far more senior than I [D. Corbett, personal communication, June 13, 2008].

When Doris received the award at age 50, she was in fact younger than many past recipients. Her mentor LeRoy Walker, for example, received the Gulick Award at age 64. But the award honors service and leadership, which she began earlier in her career than many professionals.

AAHPERD had previously awarded Doris the Charles D. Henry Award (1992) for distinguished service to ethnic minorities in AAPHERD and the R. Tait McKenzie Award (1989) for influence beyond the profession (SHAPE Award Recipients). Doris explained why she was surprised to receive the Charles D. Henry Award: "Sometimes when you are busy doing the things you are doing, you are doing them because you feel that they are what you should be doing. Therefore, you don't expect to be acknowledged for doing those things" (D. Corbett, personal communication, June 13, 2008).

Doris was equally humbled to receive awards from organizations beyond AAHPERD. Notably, in 1995 she received the Civilian Medal of Honor from West Point for extraordinary civilian service to the United States Army. In 1997, receiving the National Association for Girls and Women in Sport Honor Award was less surprising because she had served as the NAGWS president. "It wasn't as much a surprise as some of the other awards," she admitted, "but at the same time the timing of the awards was such that I often thought of other people being so much more deserving of the awards" (D. Corbett, personal communication, June 13, 2008). Of particular significance to Doris was the Black Women in Sport Foundation Award:

> I felt very good about that, because it was a group with whom I had not been particularly close to with respect to my interactions and conference participation. I was very surprised and honored to receive acknowledgement from the Black Women in Sport Foundation [D. Corbett, personal communication, June 13, 2008].

These awards are only a few of many that have honored Doris's professional contributions. They recognize a particular leadership style, which Doris characterized with four adjectives: respectful, competent, responsive, and collaborative (D. Corbett, personal correspondence, 2016).

Life Balance and Reflection

After serving Howard University in almost every imaginable capacity, from facilitating the appointment, tenure, and promotion committee to directing the graduate program in Health, Physical Education and Leisure Studies, Doris served as the Department Head from 2006 to 2012. She continued teaching, conducting research, publishing, and traveling to give keynote addresses and consult with groups about equity in sport and athletics. The pace of her days made staying physically active a challenge. "When I am active," she noted, "it is tennis, swimming and cycling" (D. Corbett, personal communication, June 13, 2008). But, in 2008, she noted a decline in her activities:

> I really have a passion for tennis, and I still have my name on the tennis roster for two USTA Adult & Senior League teams. Three or four years ago I typically played on four teams at one time year-round. Now I am just on two teams. People continue to ask me if I am coming to practice on Mondays and Fridays, and I still find myself at the university when I really want to be on the tennis court [D. Corbett, personal communication, June 13, 2008].

To help balance the compromise of working long hours and being less physically active, she is committed to good nutrition and stress management, as well as working with a personal trainer. She admitted that is was nevertheless a compromise: "I want physical activity to be my number one priority and to become more fit than I have ever been in my life" (Corbett 63).

While Doris hasn't been slowing down professionally, she shared glimpses of her retirement dream. This vision included playing tennis and bridge "on a regular basis" (D. Corbett, personal communication, June 13, 2008). She added, "I look forward to having the time to read more than three books a month; to move up to what I used to do in 'the old days' whereby I read six or seven books a month" (D. Corbett, personal communication, June 13, 2008). Doris's fitness priorities for retirement reflect her understanding of physical activity as essential to the whole person:

> Whenever I retire, if the body is willing and the good Lord is willing, I will become more fit than I ever have been.... My friends who are retired, given what little time I have to see and spend time with them, are all very active. There are those who are very active in the church and there are those with whom I play tennis. They play tennis every single day! That's the world I used to be a part of, and I think I will indeed go back to playing probably not five or seven times a week, but I will probably play a minimum of three times a week [D. Corbett, personal communication, June 13, 2008].

Her vision for retirement was clear, but her career was still going strong.

Rather than slowing down, Doris accelerated. In 2012, she moved to Cedar Falls, Iowa, where she became the Director of the School of Health, Physical Education, and Leisure Services at University of Northern Iowa. "I like the challenges that come with changes," she said (D. Corbett, personal communication, March 4, 2016). Through her new position, she continues to work for access, opportunity, and equity.

Doris would most like her work to leave a legacy of change. "I would like to think people would see me as someone who really cared about trying to make a difference to effect a positive change," she said, "and that I was instrumental in helping particularly African American graduates move forward in their careers, go into doctoral programs, and be successful in their profession" (D. Corbett, personal communication, June 13, 2008). She hopes to be remembered for mentoring, coaching, teaching, and leadership that contributed to inclusive curricula and equity-based policy.

LeRoy Walker's mentoring style left a significant impression on Doris. Students must be "good citizens" of the profession if they want to work with her. "Don't waste my time otherwise," she stated. Her mentoring style values relationship:

Dr. Doris Corbett, Professor and Director, School of Health, Physical Education and Leisure Services, University of Northern Iowa. Courtesy Doris Corbett.

> I invest time and typically engage in providing guidance and support regarding professional career, and personal life. Strategically, there are certain defined expectations that I have for those I mentor. For example, professional engagement, development of a publication record, personal decorum, and a demonstration of a respect for the profession and our students. I often meet with protégés, they spend time with me in the work place, and we communicate electronically [D. Corbett, personal communication, March 4, 2016].

How much of her own mentoring reflects Walker's philosophy? "I think everything," she said (D. Corbett, personal communication, March 4, 2016).

In her tribute to Leroy Walker, Doris observed, "Dr. Walker held the viewpoint that 'you teach as you've been taught'" (D. Corbett, 2012, p. 10). Like her mentor, Doris has modeled professional engagement and demonstrated the importance of crossing borders to form networks. "I could never have imagined that I would spend time in Egypt, Ireland, or Israel because of my profession," she remarked (D. Corbett, personal communication, June 13, 2008). Although her extensive resume challenges anyone to imagine what

Dr. Doris Corbett, Professor and Director, School of Health, Physical Education and Leisure Services, University of Northern Iowa, speaking at the VII International Congress on "Health, People and Sport" in St. Petersburg, Russia. October 2015. Courtesy Doris Corbett.

more she could do, Doris felt disappointed that she has not achieved as much in her career as she would have liked to. But her reach has been ambitious and her sense of ethics uncompromising:

> You can't be in sport and have fair play without honoring human rights. Fair play by definition is about the right to participate. More than a privilege, it's a right. To violate that opportunity is unethical. Cheating is not strategy. It's not fair play. It's against the rules. How can we celebrate that as a win? We must have a conscience in sport [D. Corbett, personal communication, March 4, 2016].

Doris's life story reflects the impact of Title IX on social change and conjures hope that the students she has mentored are going forward to teach as they've been taught.

8

Anita DeFrantz
Making the World More Like an Olympic Village

Before her retirement in 2015, a typical day for Anita DeFrantz began with early morning exercise before she went to her office at the LA84 Foundation, a nonprofit organization that manages the 1984 Olympic endowment. As president of LA84 from 1987 to 2015, Anita oversaw daily operations. She is also an International Olympic Committee (IOC) Executive Board member and an irrepressible advocate for youth sport opportunities. Because of her range of responsibility, few days were typical:

> One of the interesting or challenging things is that each day is a little bit different. For example, this morning I had a 6:00 conference call, which meant I couldn't go rowing because I couldn't get there and back in time. But it was for the Juvenile Law Center Board. The Juvenile Law Center was my very first job as an attorney. That was 9:00 Philadelphia time. So that was interesting. 6:00 is not that harsh of a time, but it disrupted the normal day [A. DeFrantz, personal communication, March 5, 2012].

What drives this depth of commitment to equal opportunity, particularly through sport? Anita has been historically first on several occasions. She was a member of the first U.S. Olympic Women's Rowing Team, the first African American elected to the International Olympic Committee (IOC), and the IOC's first female vice president. But her ambition, she explained, took root long before her career began:

> When I was about eight or nine I remember asking my mom why Grandma Lucas didn't have a better job. I said, "Why doesn't Grandma Lucas have a better job? She works for other people, cleaning houses, washing clothes, but she's so smart. I talk to her about lots of things."
> My mom looked at me and said, "You ask her."
> So I did. "Grandma, why don't you have a better job?"
> She looked at me and said, "Well, sweetheart, I wanted to be a nurse so I could help people. But, when I was little, colored girls didn't do that. Things have changed now. You can do whatever you want to do. You just have to be very good in school and continue your education. You promise me that you will do whatever you want."

I said, "Yes, Ma'am. Yes, Ma'am, I will." I was just a little kid, but I think I saw a tear in her eye. I'll never forget that moment [DeFrantz, 2001, pp. 5–6].

For Anita, doing what she wants means working with many different groups to create opportunity through sport. During her long tenure as president of LA84 Foundation and as an IOC member and leader, she drew insight from her experiences as a former Olympic athlete and as a practicing attorney. Her international perspective has shaped her view of Title IX as an essential but distinctly American law. The Olympic Movement's embrace of diverse cultures and its response to world issues inspire her international vision of equity and empowerment through sport.

Childhood and Early Influence

Anita's first lessons in the art of negotiating were within her family. Born in Philadelphia in 1952, she was the second eldest and only girl of four children and, in her words, "the peacemaker."

A rich family history of social justice work shaped her parents' lives and would later influence Anita's personal and professional vision. Anita Page and Robert DeFrantz met in the late 1940s at Indiana University, where Anita was a sophomore and Robert was a campus activist studying for his master's in sociology. Robert, then president of the university's NAACP (National Association for the Advancement of Colored People) chapter, was working to integrate student housing. Women's housing was the first to be integrated, and Anita Page was one of the first five to seven women to live in integrated student housing at Indiana University (DeFrantz, 2001, p. 8).

"My father was a proud man," Anita explained (DeFrantz, 2001, p. 15). Robert DeFrantz modeled determination. He abandoned his master's thesis about NAACP activity at Indiana University when his advisor told him to rewrite it entirely. Instead, her father shifted his goal, returned to school, and earned his master's in social work when she was approximately seven years old. She recalled, "After seeing how hard he worked, I vowed at that time to be sure to finish all of my education before I married and had a family" (DeFrantz, 2001, p. 15).

Anita's mother was another source of inspiration. As a child, Anita marveled at her mother who worked while studying for her master's degree. Anita Page DeFrantz later earned a Ph.D. in Communication from the University of Pittsburgh and became a professor, all while Anita was at Connecticut College. Anita elaborated on her mother's determination:

> This meant that her youngest was still in grade school, and her second youngest was in high school. She left Dad at home with the two boys. She had trust in her husband and felt certain that he was taking care of those two. I honor my mother and my father for doing that. He had a lot of pride in her achievements [DeFrantz, 2001, p. 15].

Because every woman in Anita's family and community always worked, she has felt disconnected when women of her era talk about their mothers' difficult decisions to work or not to work. She confided, "It was very strange for me to hear their angst. And now, people are talking about how the children today are running into trouble because of having no one at home.... They're blaming it on having no parents at home" (DeFrantz, 2001, p. 15).

In fact, Anita's mother was her greatest role model:

> First of all, she gave me her name, which meant to me that she trusted me and wanted me to be able to do all the things that she did.... I always introduce her as the "original" Anita DeFrantz. I am a mere imitation, trying my best to keep up with the legacy that she has given me [DeFrantz, 2001, pp. 15–16].

Anita's mother also instilled an immutable value in her children. She taught them at a very young age that there is only one race: the human race. "I learned that over and over again," Anita emphasized. "I learned to respect all people" (DeFrantz, 2001, p. 9).

Anita's parents moved the family from Philadelphia to Indianapolis in 1954, when Robert began work at the Senate Avenue YMCA. Anita explained,

> All the Y's for colored people had street names like Senate Avenue Y, never YMCA like the Y's for white people. Why? So that traveling folks could find them. They were the only place, other than people's homes, where traveling colored people could get housing. For a long time that continued, in fact, when I went to college [in the early 1970s] that was still true [DeFrantz, 2001 p. 7].

Robert's work at the YMCA was rooted in a history of family activism. Her paternal great-grandfather, Alonzo David DeFrantz, and his wife, who was Creek Indian, settled in Kansas after traveling there as part of the "Pap" Singleton Movement of emancipated people. Alonzo was, at one time, both president and secretary-treasurer of the "Pap" Singleton Movement. Contrary to social norms for African American men in the late 19th century, Alonzo was educated. His father's father, Charles DeFrantz, who held enslaved people in Natchez, Mississippi, had said to his son, "'If you wish, I'm going to make sure that you are educated because I really love your mother who I have held in slavery. But you can go and you will own land'" (DeFrantz, 2001, p. 6).

"This long history of standing up for people plays a significant role in our family," Anita emphasized. Her grandfather, known to his community as Big Chief but to Anita as Pappy, organized Monster Meetings at the YMCA in Indianapolis. Monster Meetings, named for the size of the crowds they drew, hosted African American leaders to give lectures and answer questions. Anita recalled,

> I thought that was such a funny name as a child. I guess it could be dangerous to bring that many people together at one time to hear these leaders. The speakers would usually stay at my grandparents' house so my father had the opportunity to meet these great people: artists, architects, scientists and others. Some of the speakers included W.E.B. DuBois, Langston Hughes, Paul Robeson, artist Hale Woodruff, and others [DeFrantz, 2001, p. 8].

Anita witnessed both the power and inspiration of leadership:

> These people said to our people that they could achieve, they could stand up and say "yes, I am who I am, and I can do these things." They said don't be trodden, you can be educated and you can do what you want to do, just like my great-grandmother said to me. You can do this. Set your own goals. Even George Washington Carver, who had lots of fights back and forth, offered a sense of pride and hope to the people at these meetings [DeFrantz, 2001, p. 8].

Pappy's vision for equality may have been shaped by earlier discrimination. Anita recounted,

> As a student at Kansas University, he played on the football team until the time his helmet came off. The other team realized he was colored, as they said then, and that was the end of his playing on that football team. I have another picture of him playing on a football team of all colored guys. I don't know who they played, but he was determined to keep playing football because he was quite good. He had made the varsity team at Kansas University [DeFrantz, 2001, p. 7].

While being a role model of activism, Pappy also set a family standard for higher education. He attended two years of medical school at Kansas University and earned good grades. But Jim Crow laws prohibited him from taking an internship that would require him to touch white patients. These restrictions would require him to travel almost 200 miles to intern at "the colored hospital" (DeFrantz, 2001, p. 7). He dropped out of medical school, returned to college, and, in 1910 or 1912, earned a master's degree in social sciences related to social work or sociology. He then took the job with the Christian Street YMCA in Indianapolis.

Because her great-grandfather, grandfather, and father had worked for the YMCA, physical activity was a family norm. Anita learned to swim when she was four years old. Swimming then became her primary sport experience during elementary school in the early 1960s, a decade before the enactment and implementation of Title IX. At age 8, she joined a local swim team and began competing against other public park teams and Amateur Athletic Union (AAU) club teams. Racially segregated swim practice and competition took place at the Frederick Douglass Public Park Pool, the facility for African Americans in Bloomington, Indiana. Anita remembers it vividly:

> It was an enormous pool—this huge oval. I think it was more than fifty meters. The women's dressing room was very dark and had stalactites and stalagmites everywhere. I was usually the only one in there and my dad would wait outside to make sure I got out. He couldn't go in there with me, being a dad and all, but he'd wait. Every once in a while there was another girl there who was a much better swimmer than I, but she didn't come that often. It was a very old facility, probably named something before it was named Frederick Douglass. The scariest part was the dressing room [DeFrantz, 2001, p. 11].

Competition presented Anita with her first ethical challenge in sports. During her second season, her coach awarded her the high point medal award for girls. This award troubled her. "I don't think I can accept this," she told him. She then told her father that the award worried her:

> He said, "Well, did you do the work?"
> I said, "Yes, I worked very hard."
> He asked if anybody else worked harder, and I said, "No."
> "Were you there every time supporting your team?"
> I said, "Yes. But I feel badly because of my brother and the other guys on the team. They worked hard, too" [DeFrantz, 2001, p. 12].

Anita's parents told her to reflect on the award, insisting that she decide. She was swimming at her best, had won two bronze medals in two races during each of the past two seasons, and had, in fact, earned the most points. Meanwhile, her brother had won two silver medals. "The guys were pretty good," she concluded, "but I was younger and not as good a swimmer" (DeFrantz, 2001, p. 12).

Anita accepted the high point medal for girls with reservations:

> Now what was the problem? I was the only girl on the team. Of course I was the high point girl; I was the only girl. It was impossible for anybody else to be the high point. It just didn't feel right. They also gave a high point award to the guys, and there were about eight guys on the team. Even today it doesn't seem right [DeFrantz, 2001, p. 12].

Robert DeFrantz wanted his only daughter and one of his sons, also a swimmer, to become the first African Americans on the United States Olympic swim team, an opportunity denied to African Americans at that time. Although Anita loved to swim, she didn't know much about the Olympic Games. According to Anita, her father wanted his children to think outside the box and said, "'Let's do it kids.'" She added, "My family was about opportunity. I'm about opportunity" (DeFrantz, 2001, p. 11). But inequitable training between her team and others impacted her performance:

> The kids weren't always particularly nice to me, a little chunky kid who didn't have all the fancy stuff. Some of them were okay, but we didn't get a chance to really know them. They had all their "rah rah" parents, and they had access to year round training. We had an outdoor pool that was only open during the summer [DeFrantz, 2001, p. 13].

Anita was not yet a teen when the DeFrantz family moved from Bloomington back to Indianapolis, where Anita completed elementary school at

James Whitcomb Riley P.S. 43. She earned awards for excellence in every subject in eighth grade. The following year, at Shortridge High School, Anita expanded her extracurricular activities and deepened relationships:

> Shortridge High School was designated as a magnet school. It was just wonderful. Everyone was there because they wanted to be. I could go there automatically because I was in the region, but if you lived outside the region you had to apply to go there. If you were not African American, you got in, pretty much. We had such an eclectic group there. It was wonderful; I still have friends from high school that I communicate with [DeFrantz, 2001, pp. 12–13].

Anita joked about specializing in extracurricular activities. She sang and traveled frequently with the elite Madrigal choir, played the clarinet in marching band and the bassoon in orchestra, and participated in Thespians and in Quill and Scroll. Although she couldn't remember spending much time in class, she applauded her teachers and peers, saying, "I was majoring in fun and learning from my classmates" (DeFrantz, 2001, p. 14).

In retrospect, Anita would advise young people differently:

> I had gone through school believing that you're supposed to learn everything you need to learn in class. I remember being shocked during my senior year in high school when an exchange student from Northern India who was staying with us said to me, "Aren't you going to study for your exam?" You could push and do your homework, but that wasn't the same as studying for your exam. It was a miracle. I studied for that physics exam, and I got 18 out of 20 correct. That was the first time I had studied. But I always did my homework, stuff that we had to do, but that was not the same as studying [A. DeFrantz, personal communication, March 5, 2012].

The fun was tempered by racial tensions as Shortridge High School was being desegregated. Anita's parents attended school board meetings, and her father was elected to the school board. Anita described it as a difficult time. She wasn't aware that her father voted, without telling her, to close the school. His silence on the issue led to lengthy discussions after the fact, but Anita looked back on the closing as "part of what needed to be done in order to finish desegregating all of the high schools in the district" (DeFrantz, 2001, p. 14). Although Shortridge High School closed in 1981, after Anita had graduated, it re-opened several years later.

A Student-Athlete with an Olympic Dream

For the DeFrantz children, attending college was always a question of where, not if or why. Anita discovered Connecticut College through a school peer who attended and praised the school, and through her mother's friend, an alum. Anita applied to Connecticut College, Radcliffe, and Yale, and she likes to say, "Connecticut College chose me" (DeFrantz, 2001, p. 12). Her decision to attend Connecticut College, a former women's college that became coeducational in 1969, clashed with her mother's hope that she would attend Sarah Lawrence or Barnard. "She wanted me to go to a women's college because she felt this was another area in which African American women were denied access," Anita explained. "Her wish was for me to go to one of the Eastern women's colleges. In her time, that was not allowed" (DeFrantz, 2001, p. 15).

Anita assumed she would be anonymous at a school 900 miles from Indiana. But one day as she walked through the administration hall where she was petitioning the first-year dean to enroll in and earn credit for classes at Wesleyan and Yale, the dean of the college approached her and asked, "Are you a DeFrantz?" The dean, who knew of her father and uncle, suggested that Anita visit for a longer conversation. Anita surmised that Dean Cobb had met her family at Idlewild, a popular resort in Michigan where African Americans could vacation and buy property when, prior to the Civil Rights Act of 1964, segregation denied these rights in much of the United States.

Anita entered her sophomore year in 1971, a pivotal moment for women's collegiate athletics. As advocates for women's athletics advanced high school and collegiate competition and questioned new governance structures, leaders of the existing Division for Girls' and Women's Sports (DGWS) rejected the NCAA's culture of competition. They favored equal play and broad sport experiences for women. In 1966, the DGWS had formed the Commission on Intercollegiate Athletics for Women (CIAW) for Women to explore governance of girls' and women's athletics. As competition developed, however, these two groups no longer agreed on a mission. Meanwhile, the NCAA sought to govern women's athletics. In response, the CIAW formed the Association of Intercollegiate Athletics for Women (AIAW), an independent organization that initially would challenge the NCAA for the right to shape and govern women's intercollegiate athletics (Carpenter & Acosta, 2005, pp. 102–04). These changes meant that many colleges and universities were then scrambling to organize women's athletic teams.

Was this turmoil apparent to athletes such as Anita? For most, the answer was no. A commonly-documented story conveys Anita's initial distance from the politics of athletics. One afternoon, as the story goes, Anita almost tripped over a rowing shell on the sidewalk outside the student union building. This moment set in motion her Olympic career and, ultimately, her life's work. Anita clarified,

> I wasn't looking for anything else to do; I was already on the women's basketball team. But I had certainly heard of rowing ... and wanted to be a rower. Bart Gullong [Connecticut

College head rowing coach] said, "It's for rowing, and you'd be perfect at it...." He could see that I was tall but couldn't tell that most of my height was in my legs. When I sit in a boat, I look short. Having long legs is very good, but it would be better if my upper body was in proportion because the body also has to leverage. I do have long arms, which is fine.... Still, I thought that was quite a line because I'd never been perfect for anything, but I did want to do this. I said, "I know how to swim, so tell me what to do" [DeFrantz, 2001, p. 17].

For the remainder of her college career, Anita both rowed and played basketball. She downplayed her involvement with humor: "We were not a particular force in athletics at the time. In fact, our mascot was the camel: We could go for a long, long time or a long dry spell without a lot of winning" (DeFrantz, 2001, p. 17).

"We were making intercollegiate sport happen," Anita said of the historical moment (DeFrantz, 2001, p. 18). As Title IX was slowly making its way through Congress to President Richard Nixon's desk, women's intercol-

Anita DeFrantz and Connecticut College women's crew team, 1974. Courtesy Linda Lear Center for Special Collections and Archives, Connecticut College.

legiate competition was defining itself without a clear model. For example, when Anita joined the Connecticut College women's rowing team, it often rowed against Princeton and other teams that had long-established rowing programs. "We were just beginning," she explained, "so when you compared personnel and the size of the schools, we were way outclassed. Long after I left, they moved into Division III, but when I was there, they were in Division I, and that was painful to admit" (DeFrantz, 2001, p. 15). Title IX regulations would offer institutions the tools to define their programs, levels of competition, and other essential elements of intercollegiate sports equity.

Amid the excitement of her athletic experiences, Anita stitched her past, present, and future philosophies into a coherent senior thesis entitled "The Philosophical Value in the Plurality of Ideas." She explained,

> During my junior year, the college decided that there could be something called Student Designed Interdisciplinary Majors. Prior to that I had been a music major, although I also loved philosophy and government. By the end of my junior year, I had enough credits in all of those departments to persuade the faculty that I was qualified to spend by senior year working in the interdisciplinary area of political philosophy. Even the music credits and the history of music were just perfect for this political philosophy interdisciplinary work [DeFrantz, 2001, p. 4].

Her thesis, specifically, argued that individual decisions contribute to a civil society and define one's place in society. This early exploration of the rights and responsibilities of the individual as part of a larger society echoed in later work, particularly as she defended athletes' rights.

More immediately, Anita faced difficult personal decisions. Senior-year pressures redefined her athletic and educational goals. She described the difficulty:

> Two years after rowing on the varsity team, I was demoted to junior varsity.... There was a new coach in town who made us do a lot of land training, which was important. I was a senior, I was a house-fellow, and I had a dormitory to run. This new coach had all these physical things we had to do, and I hadn't connected with the program properly. So I got demoted [DeFrantz, 2001 p. 18].

Head rowing coach Bart Gullong saw that the demotion troubled Anita, even as she remained a valuable team member. The junior varsity team needed her in order to have four in a boat for the four race, and she was loyal to the younger athletes who needed the experience. Despite the demotion, the coach suggested that if she trained she could make the Olympic team. Women's rowing would be part of the Olympic Games for the first time in Montreal in 1976. Anita's response was disbelief: "'Bart, Bart, Bart—come on'" (DeFrantz, 2001, p. 18). She thanked him politely, but he insisted that he was sincere.

Anita's choices were exciting though difficult. A family tradition of social activism coupled with her own pursuit of social justice drew Anita toward a law career. She had adopted the DeFrantz tradition of "standing up for things that needed to be done" (DeFrantz, 2001, p. 19). For example, when she recognized that Connecticut College had no Bill of Student Rights, she wrote one and moved it through the proper channels to be passed. Still planning to apply to law school, she now had the 1976 Olympic Games in mind. She thought, "Well you know, maybe I can. I should do this" (DeFrantz, 2001, p. 19).

So she did. Anita applied strategically to only one law school: Penn State.

Her parents, who had roots in Philadelphia, would be proud. Once accepted, she could train with the well-respected and successful Vesper Rowing Club located in the same city. "I wanted to be able to learn the language of power," she explained. "Truly that's what I wanted to be able to do. I also wanted to see if I could be an Olympian" (DeFrantz , 2001, p. 20).

Being a law student and an athlete training for the Olympic Games was expensive and time consuming. U.S. team members contributed to airfare, uniforms, and other incidental costs. Because Anita trained and competed in Europe during the summer, she couldn't, like her peers, work at a high paying law firm to finance the next year in law school. She instead worked and saved during the academic year. She described one particularly demanding but valuable job:

> I finally found a job working nights, the graveyard shift. First two nights, then three, and sometimes five nights a week, I worked at the police headquarters in Philadelphia at a place they called the Roundhouse. This was where defendants were taken and held before their bail hearings. We interviewed those defendants, asking very personal questions, which taught me a lot about dealing with people. It varied. Some were very tense situations. We interviewed what we came to call "pilots," drunk drivers who were the worst type of person to interview, because of the aroma and their difficulty in coming up with answers. We interviewed people who had murdered or were about to be charged with murder, to people from the MOVE group who, when asked their mother's name, would say the "moon," their father's name, they'd say the "sun," and things like that [DeFrantz, 2001 p. 21].

Anita worked around the clock to balance school and training:

> I would arrive at police headquarters at 10 p.m., do my interviews, finish my shift and maybe have time to go to my house, oftentimes not, and arrive at the boat house at 5:30 a.m. and prepare for my practice. Practice for me was always a great release—to go to the boathouse and row. I finished practice about 7 or 7:30 a.m., changed, and went off to law school. During the middle of the day, because I had the credentials as a Penn law student, I would go the gymnasium and do my weight work out, or "stadiums." In the wintertime I would do stairs in one of the tall dormitories, and then change and go back to class. After class I went back to the boathouse for our evening workout. After that I'd go home. All of this was probably on my bicycle. If I was scheduled to work that night, I'd show up at the Roundhouse. If not, I would study, or sleep. That basically was my schedule for two of my three years in law school [DeFrantz, 2001, p. 21].

Anita became somewhat disenchanted with Penn State when she realized that most of her classmates were there to learn just enough to make a lot of money. She recalled taking a class with Professor Ed Spare, "a wonderful man" who told students to look around and understand that every one of them would make $50,000 or more in the first year after graduating. His point, Anita explained, was about outrageous inequity. While some people had little or no income, these law students would earn an enormous salary because they had education. As she looked around, Anita thought, "No, I won't. I'll be in public interest law." Her prediction came true with a starting salary of $14,000 at the Juvenile Law Center of Philadelphia (DeFrantz, 2001, p. 20).

Only 10–12 of approximately 175 law students at Penn State in the mid-1970s were African American. Just over a decade had passed since the Civil Rights Act of 1964 made illegal the segregation within higher education that her parents had worked to abolish. But law could not eliminate deeper social tensions. "The undergraduate students were attacking the few African American students in law school," Anita recalled. She explained,

> They were saying how unfit we were to take up space at the law school.... Every day it seemed, in the student newspaper, maybe it wasn't that often but it felt so, there was another horrible attack on us saying we were unfit and talking about the special admittance process. Well, if you looked at our LSAT scores, they were really good scores. My colleagues had come from UCLA, University of Michigan, Princeton, Yale, Harvard, and Amherst. We were clearly qualified. The law school administration never once defended us [DeFrantz, 2001, p. 20].

In this atmosphere, Anita persisted in both her education and Olympic training.

National Rowing Team and the 1976 Olympic Games

In the fall of 1975, Anita competed for a coveted spot on the Vesper Boat Club's women's team with her sights on the Olympics. She earned a place in the first boat for both the pair and the four, race titles referring to the number of rowers in their respective boats. The Vesper team won the four at the National Championships. With hopes of rowing in the 1976 Olympic Games, they soon learned that they would not compete as a team in an upcoming Olympic trial. Historically, teams or clubs competed in an Olympic trial, and the winning entry became the U.S. team for a particular event. But USRowing, the sport's national governing body, eliminated this process in 1975 and established the National Selection Camp. Coaches nominated athletes, based on performance, to attend the camp.

Anita knew immediately that the working women on the Vesper Team would have difficulty traveling to the camp and to a trial. Defending the athletes' right to compete, the American Arbitration Association filed an arbitration against USRowing. Anita explained, "The outcome of the arbitration was that if Vesper won the National Championships in the eight, then they would have the right to go to the World Championships. If Vesper didn't win, however, athletes would be selected at the camp" (DeFrantz, 2001, p. 22).

Anita played a significant role in the arbitration:

> There was a lot of pressure because we were competing in several boats at the National Championships, and not everyone fully understood what was up. I later learned that people considered me a natural leader, I guess because I was in law school. All I was doing then was going to law school, doing my best to make the first boat at Vesper, and hoping to make the national team. But there I was at this arbitration, speaking on behalf of Vesper knowing a bit about the situation having read the constitution of the USOC, and reading all I could while going to this fancy law school. I was doing all I could to stay in law school, too. I was doing a lot [DeFrantz, 2001, p. 22].

The new selection process raised an ethical question. After Vesper members won in the four at the National Championships, a coach offered Anita and another team member a place on the national eights team if the two agreed to attend the National Selection Camp on weekends. Anita said in retrospect,

> I know an offer like that would probably not hold. They would have to see us in that environment, and of course we'd have to pay to go up there every weekend. But this would break up the four, which had won the right to go to the world championships; and it would make it impossible for the two other women, the coxswain from Vesper, and the coach to have that opportunity [DeFrantz, 2001, p. 22].

Since Anita was in her first year with the team, and she had strong loyalties, she stayed with the Vespers team. Meanwhile, the 1975 U.S. national team won a silver medal and placed fifth at the world championships in Nottingham, England. "People still believe I was in that eight," Anita remarked. "They can't imagine me not having done that, but I was loyal to my team" (DeFrantz, 2001, p. 23).

The following year, Anita was again invited to the National Selection Camp. She and approximately a hundred athletes arrived in Boston in June, one month before the Montreal Olympic games. Harvard's highly esteemed varsity rowing coach Harry Parker coached the women's national team. Anita explained,

> The camp couldn't start before Harry, Coach Parker, finished his responsibilities at Harvard. Of course, the Harvard-Yale race ended his responsibilities. The selection camp lasted about four weeks. We did a lot of seat racing. As it became clear that you were not going to be selected, you sort of packed up and went home [DeFrantz, 2001 p. 24].

Seat racing would enable Anita to win her spot in a boat at the 1976 Olympic Games. In seat racing, two boats race for three minutes. Rowers alternate seats in the two boats, such as the rower in seat seven in boat A moves to seat seven in boat B, to determine who has the highest positive impact on the team's performance.

According to Anita, the six weeks at camp were demanding:

> People were falling apart. There are lots of people involved, there are so many mind games, there is so much happening, but rowing is a mental sport as well as a physical sport. When you're sitting on the line at the Olympic Games you've got to be totally together, mind and body. By the time you get to the Olympic Games, there's nothing more to do for your body. Except, you know, certain people have different jellybeans than we have, but there's really nothing to do for the body. It's all up there in your mind. That's why it's a sport for older people, older meaning in your 20s [DeFrantz, 2001, p. 24].

After the eight rowers for the women's eight were selected, they trained as a team for seven to ten days at Dartmouth College. Then they continued on to Plattsburgh, New York, to get uniforms and other gear for the Olympic Games.

"Here is where history takes a turn for me," Anita declared. In Plattsburgh, three days before the Olympic Games opened, the team discovered that there were not enough uniforms that said *United States Olympic Team*. The men's and women's rowing teams were the last to go through processing, and the men received uniforms. Since Anita had been elected team captain, she believed she was responsible for getting uniforms for her team. She noted, "They were going to see a lot of me throughout the Games because my crusade was to get the uniforms for the women's rowing team.... I was not going to stop until everyone had every piece, including the rain suits, warm-ups, all the stuff that says United States Olympic Team" (DeFrantz, 2001 p 25). Within a year, every team member had a full uniform.

Anita's tenacity impressed some and annoyed others. She found the USOC office in Montreal and visited every day until someone agreed to talk with her. When she asked about the uniforms, USOC officials told her that Adidas just didn't care about the U.S. team. Anita added, "A lot has changed now, but at that time, the United States team wasn't important to them. Isn't that stunning?" (DeFrantz, 2001, p. 25).

Humor has softened the memory over time, particularly Anita's recollection of the women's opening ceremony uniforms.

> We had dresses, which I believe were designed by Ralph Lauren. I think he thought athletic women should be covered up; the less we see of them, the better. Our dresses were these long blue uniforms. When three of us stood together, people thought we were from the Salvation Army [DeFrantz, 2001, p. 27].

The USOC women's team leader recommended that the women wear, instead, blue pants and white jackets, which they referred to as "marshmallow jackets." According to Anita, their choice upset the Canadians, who had intended to be the first team to march in wearing slacks. They had no intention of offending the host team but, she emphasized, "our dresses were so ugly, we were told to use the slacks instead" (DeFrantz, 2001, p. 27).

The drama of gathering suitable uniforms was no match for the thrill of the competition. "Our first race at the Olympic Games was the first race that we ever had as a boat," Anita explained (DeFrantz, 2001, p 25). According to the former selection process, a team had a history of competing as a team. No wonder, Anita later realized, people were shocked the women's eight won a Bronze medal in the 1976 Olympic Games.

The first race yielded a new lesson in working physically and respectfully as a team. Anita recalled the U.S. women's eight team leading at the 500-meter mark. At 250 meters, as the German Democratic Republic team closed the gap, the U.S. coxswain called for a sprint. Anita felt as if the boat had stopped. The coxswain again called for a sprint, and Anita thought, "'All right, I'm going to pull this boat across that finish line'" (DeFrantz, 2001, p. 25). As the seventh seat rower, behind the seat setting the stroke, Anita couldn't see what was happening in the back of the boat:

> Suddenly, I see, out of the corner of my eye, an oar floating past. We get to the finish line, amazingly second, which is good.... As it turns out, our bow person had caught a boat-stopping crab. In the Olympic Games, that is a rookie thing to do.... I don't know how she survived. The pressure that we have at that level could have killed her or thrown her out of the boat.... It's called catching a crab to suggest that something under the water has grabbed your oar.... Probably the pressure against the oarlock finally pulled it out; then she let go and the oar went into the water. I give her all honor. We said nothing, maybe the coach did, but we had to prepare for another race in two days. No one said anything, but I'm sure she knew what we were thinking [DeFrantz, 2001, p. 26].

The next two races presented more tensions. According to Anita, the second race, two days later, was a "do or die" race. They had to win to proceed to the finals. They won and moved on. Anita best remembers the finals through a photograph that appears in the USOC yearbook: "We are just staring at the waves" (DeFrantz, 2001, p. 26). She described water conditions as "ocean" and "glass." That day, she recalls, the water was "ocean" with whitecaps:

> It was so bad that day that they moved the course over a lane. And yet lane one was "glass" for the last hundred meters, which is what you want to race on. We had the "ocean" the whole way: lane six. Amazingly enough, every U.S. finalist had lane six. It was just a fluke. And, just to finish the story, every Canadian finalist had lane one. We have a saying; "Someday you'll get lane one." ... We looked like a cement mixer coming down the course, and we got a bronze medal [DeFrantz, 2001, p. 26].

The 1976 Olympic Games seeded memories that Anita would carry and draw from in her later IOC work. First, living in the Olympic Village made her realize the deep connection between residence at the Games, teamwork, and performance. Anita shared a two-room apartment with 12 other athletes. They joked about a rule: "'No fewer than three people in the bathroom at any one time'" (DeFrantz, 2001, p. 26). Despite cramped quarters, the experience changed her life:

> At the Games, when I entered the village, that's what changed my life. Coming to this village and to this community where everyone was successful, and going to the dining hall where you could sit with anyone and speak the language of the Olympic Movement and share this "spiritual" experience. Spiritual is and is not the right word, but I don't have the right word yet [DeFrantz, 2001, p. 27].

Years after first reflecting on her experience in the village, Anita said "transformational" is a more accurate descriptor (A. DeFrantz, personal communication, March 5, 2012). Her experience would shape her future IOC work to integrate the village and strengthen the Olympic spirit through shared living.

At the same time, Anita observed the clash between sport and politics as she witnessed her first Olympic boycott. At the village gate with the U.S. teams, waiting for credentials, Anita introduced herself to a delegation from Africa. When she asked if they were excited about the Games, they said no, they were going home. The team was boycotting the Games because the IOC refused to penalize New Zealand for playing a rugby match with South Africa, the first nation expelled from the Olympic Movement for its support of apartheid and racially segregated sport competition.

Anita told one of the African team members, "'I am so sad for you. I'm going to learn more about this. I know that doesn't help you, but I will commit to learning all I can. I want to help to make sure this will never happen again.'" He responded, "'Thank you, sister'" (DeFrantz, 2001, p. 28). Anita added in retrospect, "Little did we know then about what would happen in 1980" (DeFrantz, 2001, p. 28).

1980s Olympic Boycott and Early Career Advocacy for Athletes' Rights

After the 1976 Olympic Games, Anita asked her coach if she had potential to win a gold medal. He thought for a moment, then said, "Yes." That was all Anita needed to imagine the next four years. She would continue training, graduate from law school, pass the bar, and pursue Olympic gold. Her vision was practical, as she told her coach, "After that I have to go on to my law career. I will have this education, and there will be people who I must use this career in law for. I'll give it four more years and then I'm finished" (DeFrantz, 2001, p. 29).

As a new staff attorney at the Juvenile Law Center of Philadelphia in 1977, Anita's salary was well below the earnings for new graduates that her law professor had predicted. But the minors she represented were important to her. One federal case stood out in her mind because she enabled the emancipation of a 16-year-old girl:

> She had gotten herself out of a terrible home situation. She actually had found a place to live and found a job, but she could not find a way to get back into school. An adult was required to sign her into school, and she wanted to finish high school. So I plead her case before the Eastern District of Pennsylvania federal judge and was successful in getting her emancipated. Yea! [DeFrantz, 2001, p. 30].

The sport world soon recognized Anita's power to speak on behalf of others. On two occasions, as a young professional, she offered expert testimony. In 1977, she met with Senators Ted Stevens, Richard Stone, and John Culver, who would propose the Amateur Sports Act of 1978. The following year, her second on the U.S. Olympic Committee Athletes Advisory Council, she testified in Congress in favor of the proposed Act, which President Jimmy Carter then signed into law. The Act's purpose is "to promote and coordinate amateur athletic activity in the United States, to recognize certain rights for United States amateur athletes, to provide for the resolution of disputes involving national governing bodies, and for other purposes" (Office of the Law Revision Counsel). In short, the law gives the United States Olympic Committee oversight of the Athletes Advisory Council. In his "Statement on Signing S 2727 Into Law," President Carter wrote, "This legislation, based on the recommendations of the President's Commission on Olympic Sports, establishes procedures and guidelines to resolve disputes without placing the Federal Government in control of amateur sports." Anita, who had been elected to the USOC Executive Board in 1976, occupied the unique role of both athlete and administrator.

Members of the Senate posed difficult questions during Anita's testimony. She emphasized the relationship between responsibilities and rights. When a senator asked why athletes should have rights, Anita responded,

> Because athletes are decision-makers. When they compete, they make hundreds and thousands of decisions during their competitions. That's what athletes are, they are decision-makers. Of course, they should have rights. All of us are not children. There are a few who are very young who compete at the Games, but more and more athletes are adults who had made the decision to compete, life changing decisions. Therefore, we must have rights [DeFrantz, 2001, p. 29].

Later that year, at a USOC meeting in Orlando, Florida, Anita addressed the USOC as an Athletes Advisory Council representative, elected by the U.S. Women's Rowing Team. The Council had asked Anita to make a speech that would unite the USOC on the issue of athletes' rights. By the time the Amateur Sports Act passed in 1978, it no longer had an Athletes' Bill of Rights. According to Anita,

> The USOC may or may not have been concerned, but the athletes were very concerned. Indeed, the problem with the NCAA [National Collegiate Athletic Association] and the AAU [Amateur Athletic Union] was that neither of them seemed to care much about athletes' rights. The battle between them was who had the right to sanction races or meets. In the meantime, athletes were being used as pawns. We were saying, "Wait, this is about us" [DeFrantz, 2001, p. 30].

With 45 minutes to compose the speech, Anita wrote it in the ladies room where she could concentrate. She consulted other members of the Athletes Advisory Council as well as USOC board of directors members who were recent competitors or Olympians to be sure they agreed with her main points. "Then it was show time," she said. "It was now up to the USOC constitution to include words about athletes' rights" (DeFrantz, 2001, p. 29).

During the next two years, as Anita prepared for the 1980 Olympic Games, politics pulled her even more deeply into disputes over the athletes' rights. She took a leave of absence from the Juvenile Law Center in 1979 and moved to Princeton to train for the pair with a rower who was an engineering graduate student. The U.S. Olympic team's head coach, also Princeton's coach, would be there throughout the year. "I moved," Anita said, "and essentially made life-decisions" (DeFrantz, 2001, p. 31). She worked as Princeton's pre-law advisor, in addition to doing other administrative duties, in exchange for room and board. "The only thing we didn't get was any coaching by the coach," she noted (DeFrantz, 2001, p. 31). She has remained nevertheless grateful to Princeton for its support as she trained and became a vocal opponent of the U.S. boycott of the 1980 Winter Olympic Games in Moscow.

A time-lapsed chronology highlights the complex political situation that erupted around the 1980 Games. In late December 1979, the Soviet Union invaded Afghanistan to support its communist government against insurgent anticommunist forces. In early January 1980, President Jimmy Carter hinted on television that the United States might boycott the Summer Games if Soviet troops didn't leave Afghanistan. According to Anita, he said the U.S. wouldn't send spectators to the Olympic Games. Anita thought, "'If he thinks we send spectators, we have a problem. Our President doesn't know anything about the Olympic Games. Not only that, doesn't he know that we are hosting the Olympic Winter Games next month?" (DeFrantz, 2001, p. 31). She saw the potential for both short- and long-term damage if the United States carried out the boycott.

Calling on connections she'd made as a law student while working in Washington, D.C., during the fall semester of 1976, Anita sprung into action:

> I did whatever I could. I would drive to Washington. I would make phone calls. I figured out how I could pay my bills and still do my training. Again, thank goodness for Princeton. I did my best to explain to the U.S. what the Games were about, and how this had nothing to do with the Cold War between the United States and the Soviet Union [DeFrantz, 2001, p. 32].

The major turning point was a phone call from a journalist who informed Anita that President Carter had said, "'We won't be going to Moscow'" (DeFrantz, 2001, p. 32). Anita's uncensored reaction is often quoted when she talks about the boycott:

> I shot back, "We? What do you mean we? Where was 'we' when I was training all year in the cold and freezing my butt off?" I went on to say, "There's not one penny of federal money that goes into training. It is a private enterprise and I, as a private citizen, have the right to decide" [DeFrantz, 2001, p. 32].

The individual's right to decide was at the heart of her passion, as it had been and would continue to be. "Most athletes follow their coach, they follow their leader," Anita reasoned, "and for the President of the United States to say, 'We're not going,' I understood their concern. I basically said it was our decision to make" (DeFrantz, 2001, p. 32).

Anita remained in Princeton throughout the difficult months:

> I had no place else. I had abandoned my home, my stuff was at my coach's house, what stuff I had at that point, and I was still training. I had very little. The only food I had came from eating in the student housing at Princeton, and I had so little money. Also, in 1979, my father had had a massive heart attack, and that was a real strain on our family. My oldest brother had finished college and had his own family. My younger brother had just graduated from Dartmouth, and my youngest brother was still at University High School in San Francisco, a private high school. My parents had to figure out how they could get him through high school. Times were tough. Certainly, I was independent and very involved in all that I was doing, but I told my parents that I had to fight this battle, and I hoped they understood [DeFrantz, 2001, p. 32].

Her parents said, "Absolutely, absolutely," and this family support buoyed Anita.

Meanwhile, the attorney, former Princeton javelin thrower and Olympic supporter Robert Zagoria encouraged Anita to file a lawsuit. Anita explained that she couldn't file until the USOC had voted to boycott the Games. At the same time, she was doing her best to persuade the USOC not to boycott. She was also working with athletes from other national Olympic committees to support their participation in the Games. In short, she said, "I was doing a lot.... There was a lot of stress at that time in my life, but courage kept me moving onward" (DeFrantz, 2001, p. 33).

On Saturday, April 12, 1980, in Colorado Springs, Colorado, the USOC voted against sending U.S. teams to the 1980 Summer Olympic Games. Anita had done her best to persuade members otherwise:

> In my speech, I paraphrased Ben Franklin. It was something to the effect of those who would sacrifice liberty for temporary security deserve neither security nor liberty. That's what it was about. The USOC was afraid of what the President said he would do. It's our liberty to make decisions. He said a few other things, but to me that was the most important message I was given [DeFrantz, 2001, p. 34].

The final vote was 2:1, or, as Anita preferred, 2/3 to 1/3. "A lot of people believed we should have the right to make the decision," she said. "Many of those people have since said I was right" (DeFrantz, 2001, p. 34).

After the vote, Anita returned to Princeton, met with attorney Zagoria, and rallied co-plaintiffs for a lawsuit. The American Civil Liberties Union (ACLU), the law firm of Covington and Burling, and Robert Zagoria agreed to take the case pro bono. "I filed suit against the United States Olympic Committee," Anita explained, "which was almost immediately joined by the Attorney General of the Justice Department. This meant that by then I was essentially suing the White House" (DeFrantz, 2001, p. 35).

The boycott and the lawsuit did not deter Anita's training. She earned her place on the U.S. Women's Rowing Team. Her goal, since co-plaintiffs had committed, was to save the U.S. team and protect the USOC. She elaborated,

> I mean I was taking the risk to make sure that we could go. But meanwhile, for those who I knew might not have the courage or the wish to go anyway, because you know, it's easy to say, "I was on the team, but we never got to go, I could have been a gold medalist," I wanted to protect them.... I'm looking down the road at the future of the Olympic Games. I wanted to protect the USOC, too [DeFrantz, 2001, p. 34].

Just days after the May 13, 1980, court date, United States District Judge John Pratt denied the athletes' request for an injunction of USOC action, and the case was settled: the United States would not send athletes to the 1980 Summer Olympic Games.

Defending athletes, the USOC, and the Olympic Games took its toll on Anita. In mid-June, the team was in Rottenburg, Germany, training for their next race in Amsterdam. It would be their last race as a team. Anita said she "was really a mess" and "had just run out of gas completely" when "the most beautiful thing happened":

> A team meeting was called. I had no idea what it was about. I was just going through the motions in everything, brushing my teeth in the morning, whatever.... I was there, and I can't even remember all of the things that happened, usually I'm very aware of all that is going on around me, but as I said I was just trashed [DeFrantz, 2001, p. 36].

At the meeting, a teammate said to Anita, "'We want to thank you for all that you have done. We all signed this'" (DeFrantz, 2001, p. 36). She presented Anita with a certificate signed by all of the coaches and members of the women's team. Although Anita has forgotten the exact words of thanks, she remembers crying. "They also had all chipped in to buy me a pair of lederhosen. I'd been looking for a pair, and they obviously had all chipped in to buy them for me. I still have them" (DeFrantz, 2001, p. 36).

The team's return to the United States was less celebratory. In July, the USOC held a White House reception for the 1980 United States Summer Olympic team. Critics said that Anita capitulated because she attended. But as Anita viewed it, the reception was her parents' opportunity to visit the White House and to meet the Olympians. She also wanted to be there to support her team, who recognized another chance to respond to the boycott:

> Our team had shirts made up that said "US Rowing Team" on the front, and on the back, "Threat to National Security." We wore those shirts during that weekend, and by then, no one messed with us. One of our team members … had stickers made up. A lot of us wore those stickers on our caps or hats or other places while we were on the bus or at the White House. The sticker said, "We're here to make sure this will never happen again" [DeFrantz, 2001, p. 35].

Although Anita did not attend the 1980 Summer Olympic Games in Moscow, the International Olympic Committee awarded her the Bronze Medal of the Olympic Order to recognize her courageous commitment to the Olympic Movement. She was the only American awarded a medal in Moscow and accepted it the following year at a meeting in Baden-Baden, Germany. "And although I would have preferred to win a medal for rowing in Moscow," Anita said in retrospect, "the IOC Bronze Medal of the Olympic Order was a great honor" (DeFrantz, 2001, p. 37).

From Athlete to Administrator: LA84 and the IOC

The four years that Anita had given herself to reach for Olympic gold were now behind her. The stress of the lawsuit was over, and it was time to move on with her career.

In 1981, while serving as a member of the USOC executive board, she joined approximately 30 staff members on the Los Angeles Olympic Organizing Committee (LAOOC). Los Angeles became the only viable bid for the 1984 Games after Teheran withdrew amid political change. Awarded the Games, Los Angeles faced the challenge of citizen support. "Now we knew the 1984 Games will be in Los Angeles," Anita explained, "but that got a little scary because the taxpayers of Los Angeles, especially in the [San Fernando] Valley, just did not want to have more traffic coming over the Sepulveda Pass" (DeFrantz, 2001, p. 39). More specifically, the voters didn't want to be financially responsible.

In response, the LAOOC engineered an agreement that made the USOC financially responsible for the Games. This fiscal responsibility wasn't easy for the USOC, but Los Angeles could then host the games without burdening its local government. Anita emphasized the importance of this shift of financial responsibility, because it marked the first privately funded Olympic Games and led to a surplus endowment. Forty percent of that surplus has since supported youth sport in Southern California through LA84 Foundation. Anita's role in the LAOOC would gradually unfold after its executive vice president Harry Usher asked her to define her role. She returned to the transformational experience of the Olympic village and defined her ideal work:

> I'm very interested in international things, but the village is the heart of the Games. I wanted to make sure the village was right. First, I read all of the final reports and especially the sections on the village. Then, I talked to as many Olympians as I could to find out which village was the very best village they experienced. At the same time, I went to the two places, USC [University of Southern California] and UCLA [University of California Los Angeles] that had been contracted to be the village. I looked at the footprint and said, "Houston, we have a problem. This is not going to work." I knew that we would have to do some negotiating. I then began that process [DeFrantz, 2001, p. 39].

Gender-segregated housing during the 1976 Montréal Games left a deep impression on Anita: "I didn't know which guys were on my team when I was in Montréal, because you don't always wear your uniform. You don't always see a sign that you're a U.S. team member" (A. DeFrantz, personal communication, March 5, 2012). "That had to go," she declared (DeFrantz, 2001, p. 39). In addition to keeping teams together, gender integration would enable women to be *chef de mission*, leader of the entire team, rather than designating separate leaders for women and men on a single team. When Anita proposed changes to the IOC board of directors, one member exclaimed, "'Extraordinary! Remarkable!'" (DeFrantz, 2001, p. 40). The IOC viewed her proposal as such a good idea that it didn't wait for the Summer Olympics; it housed teams in gender-integrated housing during the 1984 Sarajevo Winter Games and in every Olympic village since. This change was a victory for teams, athletes, and women.

Although Anita wanted "to get away from sports" after the 1984 Los Angeles Olympic Games, she felt called back to that work (DeFrantz, 2001, p. 41). A consulting job with the Amateur Athletic Foundation of Los Angeles (AAF), renamed LA84 Foundation in 2007, led her into a staff position in

1985. Two years later, she became president of AAF, a position she would hold for the next 28 years.

Using endowment funds generated by the 1984 Los Angeles Olympic Games surplus, LA84 supports sport-centered programming in three areas: it funds sports programs for athletes and coaches, supports sport research, and maintains a vast print and digital sports library.

"The AAF is a wonderful place," Anita emphasized. "If I had had the imagination to create my ideal job, it would have been my work with the AAF" (DeFrantz, 2001, p. 42). Anita was directly involved in programming. For example, as a staff member, she created a coaching program. She explained,

Anita DeFrantz during her time as President of LA84 Foundation. Courtesy LA84 Foundation. Copyright 1984 LA84.

> After a one-year stint as a novice rowing coach at Princeton in 1981, I realized how much power a coach had over the lives of the athletes. While I had been an athlete at the highest level in rowing, I realized that I had never been trained as a coach. The athletes would do anything I asked them to do. I enjoyed the coaching, but realized that coaches needed training. When I had the opportunity, I designed the program for AAF. To this day it is one of our best programs at the AAF. We have had great success and national governing bodies have even adopted some of our programs [DeFrantz, 2001, p. 41].

The research support is equally ambitious. Grants enable researchers to incubate and sustain, for instance, a longitudinal study of concussions in young soccer players and ACL-injury prevention common among girl athletes. The third area of programming, the library, houses and shares expansive historical documents of the Olympic Games and is, in Anita's opinion, "the best sports library in the world" (DeFrantz, 2001, p. 44)

To illustrate further the impact of one program, Summer Swim, Anita told a story that likewise revealed her personal involvement in LA84 programming:

> At one of the Summer Swim program meets, I noticed a very worried-looking girl standing in the marshaling area. I said to her, "You look very worried, are you ok?" She looked a lot like I did when I was that age, a little pudgy. She said, "I am. I'm afraid I'm going to run out of steam."

> This is a 50-meter pool. Thinking I could help ease her anxiety, I tried out my sports psychology skills and asked, "What's your very favorite thing in the world to do?"
> She said, "Swim."
> I said, "Well, that's great because that's just what you're about to do."
> She said, "I know, but I'm just so worried I'm going to run out of steam."
> I said, "I will be at the other end of the pool waiting for you, ok?"
> She said, "Ok, ok."
> As promised I was at the other end of the pool. She had a beautiful stroke, but as she feared, she did run out of steam in the last 15 meters. But she made it. She got out of the pool and said, "How'd I do, how'd I do?"
> "Oh," I said, "I was looking at you, I wasn't looking at the other kids."
> She said, "Oh no, I really wanted to qualify for the next race."
> I said, "That's all right, the best I ever did was a bronze medal."
> She looked up at me, hugged me, and said, "That's all right, you did your best."
> Here she was comforting me. That was just a wonderful experience; I was trying to help her and she was comforting me. It actually was true, the best I'd done was a bronze medal, of course it was at the Olympic Games, but she was so quick to hug me, to comfort me [DeFrantz, 2001, p. 44].

In 1986, at age 34, Anita was among the youngest members ever elected to the IOC. She described her dual roles at LA84 [then AAF] and for the IOC as work on a continuum:

> The work I do [at LA84] for children is a continuation of my life experiences. I want to make sure the children have opportunities to experience sport and that adults have opportunities to help children. At the IOC level, it's the same thing. There's no division. Certainly living in Los Angeles is parallel to the international and intercultural work I do with the IOC. The song "We Are the World" immediately comes to mind [DeFrantz, 2001, p. 43].

Election to the IOC bridged Anita's past, present, and future advocacy for athletes' rights. During her first session, she established her reputation of being a member who speaks up:

> I began to ask questions and make suggestions. For example, when I found out there was no specific orientation, I would ask my colleagues, "What do I do?" They indicated that it was quite unusual for a member to speak up during her first session.... That's what we do in the United States; we are taught to speak up; it's part of our culture and our education. I didn't always speak, but I learned early on that if you didn't speak, a decision could be made without your input [DeFrantz, 2001, p. 49].

Reminiscent of her days at Frederick Douglass Public Pool, when she questioned the ethics of winning an award as the only girl competing, and her later institution of a Bill of Rights for students at Connecticut College, Anita's new role with the IOC suited her inclination to speak up for what she believed in.

Prior to her election to the IOC, Anita had chaired the USOC Eligibility Committee. One key accomplishment under Anita's guidance was the new ruling that United States athletes could receive funding as they were training. The amateur rule had been struck from the IOC charter in 1973, but, in 1985, it was still against the rules for athletes to receive funding from the USOC. Anita emphasized,

> I was determined, after the experiences that I had gone through in the-mid 70s, to get this passed. One thing I forgot to mention, the Vesper team, at one time, literally stood on a street corner with coffee cans, begging for funds. We didn't do that for long because it just didn't seem right. Here we were, representing the United States, begging for money. It just seemed too unseemly [DeFrantz, 2001, p. 47].

Noting Anita's efforts to secure athletes' rights, IOC President Juan Samaranch (1980–2001) appointed her to the Athletes' Commission. She said,

> That was a wonderful commission for me because I was essentially only six years away from being an athlete myself.... I felt that I could contribute a lot. I could talk about how athletes' commissions and councils were formed in the United States, and I could encourage them to develop rules for other commissions and federations and the NOCs of the world. I could help them work on athletes' rights issues, and also on the issue of how long they should serve on such a commission. All this was the groundwork for what eventually happened in the IOC: to have athletes, elected by their peers, serve on the IOC Athletes' Commission [DeFrantz, 2001, p. 56].

The Olympic Charter designates more than a dozen IOC responsibilities, from encouraging ethics in sports to promoting a positive legacy for host cities and countries ("The Organisation," IOC). Anita has engaged in all of the areas during her IOC membership. During her first Olympic Games as an IOC member, in Seoul, South Korea, in 1988, the IOC acted on its responsibility "to lead the fight against doping in sport" (IOC, About) when it disqualified Canadian sprinter Ben Johnson after he tested positive for a performance-enhancing drug.

"I spoke out on that," Anita confirmed. As she spoke, she thought, "'Oh my goodness, here I am speaking out again'" (DeFrantz, 2001, p. 49). But even as an IOC rookie, her voice resonated in the sport world. According to Anita, former competitive middle distance runner and NBC track and field commentator Craig Masback wanted her to speak on television. He recalled her bravery during the 1980 boycott, even though the two supported different sides of the issue.

When she spoke on television, she condemned athletes' drug use as cowardice. Many people supported her, but, she recalls, "It was difficult because never before had such a high profile athlete been stripped of a medal. The first headline in one newspaper was, "Canadian Wins Gold Medal in 100 Meter." Then after Ben Johnson was stripped of his gold medal, the headline was, "Jamaican Shamed by Positive Drug Test" (DeFrantz, 2001, p. 50). Johnson's use of "jellybeans," as Anita referred to performance-enhancing drugs, led to long IOC debates about doping. She concluded, "We are providing a lot of funds to help people, but to me it is terrible that so much money is spent on those who cheat. I am tired of people believing that all athletes cheat. I don't believe that" (DeFrantz, 2001, p. 51).

The doping scandal tested Anita's ability to speak out on her convictions. The relationship between ethics of fair competition and an athlete's right to compete moved her, in 1989, to propose that the doctors, coaches, and entourage of athletes found guilty of drug use also be banned or heavily sanctioned. During IOC debates, Anita attributed her weak responses to lack of orientation she had experienced as a new member. "I didn't know then what I know now," she declared. "And that is, I should have been writing down what each IOC member was saying so that I could respond.... I could have done a better job, but I hadn't taken any notes during the discussion" (DeFrantz, 2001, p. 50). Her reflection reveals the self-awareness that inspired her to develop training materials for new IOC members.

Advocating for Women: Title IX and IOC Initiatives for Women

Another issue of fairness occupied the IOC: equity and women's opportunity in the Olympic Games. Anita noted, for example, that both men's baseball and women's softball were supposed to become official Olympic sports in 1992. However, baseball, for men only, became a medal sport in 1992 while softball did not become an official Olympic sport until 1996. For over a decade, U.S. high school and college athletic programs had used Title IX to increase competitive sport opportunities for girls and women. But beyond educational institutions, Title IX had no legal power. The IOC would have to initiate that change, and Anita was prepared to speak up.

Once she became an IOC member, Anita studied the gender disparity and told IOC colleagues, "'Now, get this corrected. If we have baseball for men, we must have softball for women. It's a similar game, not exactly the same, but similar. Let's make this right'" (DeFrantz, 2001, p 51). She was then appointed to the Program Commission and brought up the issue at every meeting. "Finally," she recalled, "before I would even speak, the chairman would say, 'Okay, Anita, we know you are going to speak.' All I had to say was 'softball'" (DeFrantz, 2001, p. 51). In their timeline of significant women's sport events in the United States, J. O'Reilly and S. Cahn (2007) credit Anita for "playing a key role in getting women's soccer and softball added to the 1996 Atlanta Games" (p. xxix).

Anita viewed gender disparity as uncharacteristic of the Olympic Movement:

> In 1896, at the first modern Olympic Games, women had no opportunity, but since 1900, the Games have been there for women, and worldwide for women. I believe the Olympic Movement has done and will continue to do very good things for women. In the last quarter of the twentieth century, the Olympic Movement has done spectacular things [DeFrantz, 2001, p. 52].

The IOC established the Women and Sport Working Group in 1995 to address gender disparity and promote equality at all levels of sport participation in and policy making for the Olympic Games. Anita has chaired the group since its inception. In 2001, she explained its original identity as a working group, not a commission:

> Certainly, the IOC has acknowledged that women in sport are something that is important and has acted by increasing the numbers of women's sports on the program. This working group has the goal of working itself out of existence. The issue of women and sport should become a non-issue [DeFrantz, 2001, p. 53].

To view it another way, as long as gender disparity in sport persists, the group will exist.

Anita has not lost hope that the group will someday dissolve. In the meantime, it has expanded its boundaries exponentially through many different social and economic spheres of women and men and, in 2004, was renamed the IOC Women and Sport Commission (International Olympic Committee, Factsheet). She clarified, in 2012, why she consented to change its status from working group to commission:

> I did not realize that the status of being a commission made a difference for the staff and for the people who were working with me. Once I learned that that made a difference, I realized that we should become a commission and that we simply had to be very focused on getting the work accomplished so that eventually, or hopefully sooner than eventually, we could change the name or have the work done. The idea that the IOC would need a commission forever is still one that does not sit well with me. And the fact that we have had great success on the field of play makes me feel even more confident that before too long this commission will be a thing of the past [A. DeFrantz, personal communication, March 5, 2012].

The Commission's work is reinforced through the IOC World Conference on Women and Sport, held every four years to re-examine progress and prioritize goals (International Olympic Committee, Factsheet). Locations of the first five conferences reflect multi-national participation: Lausanne, Switzerland (1996); Paris, France (2000); Marrakesh, Morocco (2004); Dead Sea, Jordan (2008); Los Angeles, United States (2012). 2012 speakers represented the range of participating interests, including Marjon V. Kamara (Chair, U.N. Commission on the Status of Women), Nancy Hogshead-Makar (former U.S. Olympian and Title IX expert), Beng Choo Low (IOC Women and Sport Commission Member), Geena Davis (actress and gender rights advocate), and Diana Nyad (journalist and distance swimmer) (International Olympic Committee, 5th IOC Conference on Women and Sport). With more than 500 women leaders in sports attending in any given year, a consistent goal is to compose and present to the IOC, and by extension to the United Nations, resolutions to improve the lives of girls and women through sport. The Resolution of the 2nd World Conference on Women and Sport (2000), for example, includes a call to action with 12 priorities. Among the points of action were many of the values that Anita had been working for:

- a minimum of 10% representation of women in decision-making positions and governing bodies within the Olympic Movement and sport organizations worldwide by 2010, at which point, organizations would set new representation targets through 2020;
- an increase in IOC support for women leaders at all levels of sport through scholarship and training opportunities;
- an agreement that sports organizations worldwide would "use sport as an instrument to promote a culture of peace, understanding and the Olympic truce in areas of conflict."
- development and implementation of a sexual harassment policy and codes of conduct for all individuals involved in the Olympic Movement [International Olympic Committee, 2000].

Each Conference resolution includes recommendations that participants must take back to their governments to initiate action. Anita clarified that while the IOC agrees with the recommendations, they cannot mandate them. "They were beyond the scope of the IOC except that the IOC can report this and put it on our web site and hope that people will read it and take action" (DeFrantz, 2001, p. 54).

To date, the IOC World Conferences on Women and Sport have achieved progress while negotiating ongoing challenges. Anita offered rowing as a success story: "In the noblest of sports, women represent 30% of their executive positions [in 2001]. Our FISA [International Rowing Federation] council is well represented by women" (DeFrantz, 2001, p. 54). As of 2001, several organizations had reached or exceeded the target for representation of women. She was optimistic about continued growth:

> With more female athletes participating in the Olympic Games, we anticipate that former Olympians will in time fill more of these roles. Most of the men in positions within the Olympic Movement have come through sports, so we anticipate that women will also come through sports [DeFrantz, 2001, p. 54].

Conference resolutions embody the multi-national worldview of the IOC. From this perspective, Anita reiterated Title IX's important but limited reach:

> We often think that we are the center of the universe. The Olympic Movement has been the greatest source of opportunity in sport for women, worldwide. Title IX affected the United States, but that was only in the last quarter of the last century. What about the women's sports movement in the rest of the world? If it hadn't been for the Olympic Movement, and the efforts they have directed toward providing opportunity in sport for women throughout the world, we would not see the level of sports performance that we see today [DeFrantz, 2001, p. 52].

Title IX is one response to gender disparity in education and, because of the fusion of sports with educational institutions in the United States, it became a tool to address gender inequity in sport. More recent developments, such as the 2012 introduction of the U.S. Department of State's Empowering Women and Girls through Sports Initiative, embody a more direct and global effort toward gender equity (U.S. Department of State).

In all aspects of her work, Anita has emphasized the importance of collaboration among world governments to promote peace, health, and economic development through sport. She celebrated the day that the IOC gained United Nations Observer Status in 2009. This partnership strengthened the IOC's access to UN tools for human rights work, and, in 2010, this collaboration yielded "Contribution of Sport to the Millennium Development Goals." Ten years earlier, sport was not included in the eight Millennium Development Goals that have served to improve girls' and women's lives through basic human rights. The 2010 supplement now identifies how sport contributes to goals that "aim to eradicate or reduce poverty, hunger, child mortality and disease, and to promote education, maternal health, gender equality, environmental sustainability and global partnerships" (United Nations Office on Sport for Development and Peace).

Sport's inclusion in the Millennium Development Goals made Anita cautiously optimistic: "This movement for girls and women is very, very important. Sadly discrimination against girls and women is most certainly worldwide. The more opportunities that girls have to feel free through sports, the better the world will be" (A. DeFrantz, personal communication, March 5, 2012). She added that countries now may use UN tools and treaties, such as the Millennium Development Goals and also the Convention for the Elimination of All Forms of Discrimination Against Women (CEDAW). These UN initiatives act as levers to promote gender equity in and through sport. Notably, the United States is one of the outlying countries not to ratify CEDAW. Title IX remains a critical U.S. law for this reason.

Reflecting on changes since Title IX, Anita recognized the tensions that accompany power shifts:

> For many years in the United States, there's been the Women's Sports Foundation, which started in the late '70s. People ask, after they go to this annual glorious dinner that is a

major fundraising event, "Why isn't there a men's sports foundation?" I say, "You've got plenty. You have the NFL, the NBA and just lists of professional men's sports organizations, and they have annual events." I look forward to the day when we can recognize both sexes, as should be the case.... And the nice thing about the Olympic Movement as we move forward is that the field of play will be close to 50% in the next 10 years, or in my lifetime. I can say that [A. DeFrantz, personal communication, March 5, 2012].

According to the Los Angeles Declaration (2012), which presents resolutions from the 5th IOC World Conference on Women and Sport, Anita's prediction was correct: "The number of sports on the Olympic programme will have full male/female parity for the first time at the Games of the XXX Olympiad in London" (International Olympic Committee, 2012).

"To me it's not a zero sum game," Anita concluded, addressing a concern voiced by many supporters of Title IX. "Many men are worried: 'If you take this then I can't have it.' You're an IOC member. I'm not going to take that away from you. You have to make room for more. That's all we're saying" (A. DeFrantz, personal communication, March 5, 2012).

Peaks and Valleys of Late-Career Leadership

A topographical map of Anita's career would show more peaks and valleys than level terrain. She identified the 1980s Olympic boycott and lawsuit as a particularly devastating time. Perhaps her family history of resilience, her training as an athlete, or her sense of being called to serve in work has pushed her from valley to peak during challenges. As she entered late-career leadership, she continued to climb in the IOC. On this journey, she would again descend and rise, working through professional disappointment with personal integrity.

Since her election to the International Olympic Committee in 1986, Anita has served on 15 different commissions, two of which she has chaired. With emphases ranging from finances to sport and law, these commissions invited her to draw from her distinct experiences as an Olympic athlete, attorney, and advocate for human rights through sport. Anita first served on IOC Executive Board from 1992 to 2001 and was vice president from 1997 to 2001. During those years, the IOC Women and Sport Commission that she chaired made inroads toward gender equity, as well as economic and social reform. As vice president, she helped the IOC navigate a scandal involving the Salt Lake City Organizing Committee (SLOC) bid for the 2002 Winter Games. The scandal precipitated major changes in IOC oversight. Throughout investigations, Anita was a voice of reason and legal sense.

Drama erupted on November 24, 1998, when a Salt Lake City television station reported having evidence that SLOC had been paying college tuition for Sonia Essomba, daughter of then IOC member René Essomba, Cameroon (International Olympic Committee, Crisis and Reform Chronology; Mallon). From these allegations, a series of internal and external investigations, reports, and IOC reforms followed. Outcomes included the expulsion of six IOC members, warnings to 10 additional members, the resignation of four members, creation of the IOC Ethics Commission, and adoption of reforms that aim to prevent similar behaviors regarding the selection of Olympic Games host cities (International Olympic Committee, Crisis and Reform Chronology).

Details of the investigations are messy and complex, often contradictory in media accounts. Anita's memories from the center of the controversy illuminate the shift that was occurring within the IOC and the Olympic Movement at that moment in history. She began at the beginning, with her initial, absolute disbelief:

> I had been a member of the Board of Trustees at Connecticut College for such a long time. If anyone said to me that thus and so person was going to thus and so university and had received a scholarship, it would mean to me that the person had gone though proper processing to get a scholarship. It would never occur to me that the bid committee was paying money for someone's tuition. That was far beyond anything that I would ever experience. That reference specifically said, "The bid committee is funding their education." At that point I would have said, "No, you cannot do this. Stop. Cease and desist" [DeFrantz, 2001, p. 59].

But in February 1999, the Board of Ethics of the Salt Lake Organizing Committee for the Olympic Winter Games of 2002, following its investigation, reported other gifts to IOC members, including scholarships, living expenses, and, in one case, cosmetic surgery (Mallon).

Despite disbelief of the allegations of a bid committee's blatant attempt to buy an IOC member's vote, Anita couldn't ignore the past. Trouble began in 1986. She explained with deliberate detail:

> That was when the bid cities started lavishing, giving gifts to members and inviting them to come and visit. It had never happened before. All of the sites to host the Games were selected without visits and without gifts. It never happened before 1986. Never, never, never. All of the Games sites were selected without IOC members traveling only for that purpose, period. I had researched the bidding process as part of the reform commission work, and the first time the concept of visiting the candidate cities was mentioned was during the 1985 session in Berlin. A member asked if it would all right to make a visit to a candidate city, and the response was yes. So any IOC member who believed it was necessary to go and see the site years in advance to be able to decide how to vote is misguided.... The first time IOC members visited a bid city [was] for the 1992 Games. The last time IOC members visited bid cities were for the 2004 Games. For the 2006 Winter Games in Turin, there were no visits by IOC members because we [IOC] changed the rules for those Games. I want to get that on the record. Most people think that was always the case, that you had visits [DeFrantz, 2001, pp. 60–61].

Anita recognized, nevertheless, that IOC members inevitably will visit major cities for their work. How then, would the IOC distinguish between formal and informal visits by IOC members to bidding cities? Anita, for instance, always tried to imagine bid cities she visited as home of the Olympic Village. She wondered about technical issues and how the city would treat athletes. "I wanted to know how the Olympic Movement would be treated," she explained. "And then I wanted to know how it would affect the city" (DeFrantz, 2001, p. 61). These questions, more than social events and preferential treatment from city hosts, occupied her interests.

Investigations into IOC members' behaviors involved the distinction between gifts and bribes, which raised questions about Anita's integrity. At one point between February 1985 and October 1986, when she was a former member of the United States Olympic Committee Executive Board and Board of Directors, a volunteer with the Anchorage Bid Committee, and not yet an IOC member, Anita visited Anchorage. During her stay, the bid committee gave her a cloth jacket like those that members of the committee wore. The jacket became the source of accusations:

> Someone in the USOC later accused me of having a fur coat. It was a cloth coat that had a hood trimmed with coyote fur. Every volunteer was given this coat and the whole coat cost no more that $45. If they had bothered, in their investigation, to call the Bid Committee and talk with the director, he would have given them that number. Yet, they wrote in their investigative document that I had received this coat. This was the Mitchell Commission (USOC Special Bid Oversight Commission). They were doing an investigation of me without really following it up which, as you can tell, is causing me some irritation to this day [DeFrantz, 2001, p. 59].

Investigations declared Anita innocent of any wrongdoing.

Two major outcomes emerged from the scandal. First, the IOC 2000 Reforms Commission drafted standards that now govern IOC structures and procedures, including a code of ethics and recommendations for transparency of IOC financial activities. Reforms eliminated visits to bid cities and revised the selection process for host cities (Miller, 2012, 333). Anita coordinated the working group on designation of Olympic host cities, yet another example of how she puts ideas into action. Second, Anita explained, the IOC learned more about itself as a body:

> We've learned that we must be much more vigilant and we have done the things that my working group proposed, which are very good. We've set up contracts with the NOCs. The NOCs were not doing their job. Certainly the USOC really didn't do its job monitoring Salt Lake City [DeFrantz, 2001, p. 62].

Reflecting on those years of transition and scandal, Anita concluded,

> It was interesting that most people also didn't realize that from 1991 to 1994, I was the only IOC member in the United States of America. That was a very difficult period for me because

we had the right to host the Games and the responsibility of hosting the Centennial Games in Atlanta, and we had Salt Lake as a bid city. I had a lot of work to do, and I also had my full-time job as well [DeFrantz, 2001, p. 62].

Leadership led Anita into the next challenge. On February 4, 2001, she declared her candidacy to be president of the International Olympic Committee. She was the first woman in the 107-year history of the IOC to run for the office of president. She announced her candidacy in Dakar, Senegal, the day before an IOC Executive Board meeting. The timing was intentional: "I had decided to make my announcement in Dakar to honor the people of Africa for all the work they have done over the years on behalf of the Olympic Movement. There are so many volunteers, so many people who have given, and so many athletes; the many we know and the many we'll never know" (DeFrantz, 2001, p. 3).

On that day, Anita also stepped in as president pro tem for President Juan Samaranch, who had the flu and couldn't attend the meeting. The day's agenda included a visit to Île de Gorée, a major center for trading enslaved human beings during the 15th through early 19th centuries. "While I had fully intended to go there," Anita said, "I had not intended to go as president pro tem of the IOC.... I not only had to deal with the very personal emotional experience of Île de Gorée, but also the unplanned experience of acting as president pro tem. That made it very, very difficult" (DeFrantz, 2001, p. 1).

Despite the many leadership roles women had occupied, Anita still had to disprove the stereotype that women's emotions interfere with the ability to lead:

> On we went, taking a boat trip, which the people enslaved had to take. We were told these people had already traveled many miles as captives of war; that's how it was set up. These captives were already disoriented and exhausted, and who knows what had happened to them? Then they were put on some kind of boat, obviously wind aided, to take another horrific journey, this time much shorter. On our diesel-fueled boat ride to Île de Gorée, I'm already chatting with my colleagues. We're having polite discussions while I was going through all my personal set of emotions. I was dealing with emotions of profound sadness for these enslaved people: men, women and children. It was a very difficult time for me [DeFrantz, 2001, p. 1].

Throughout the visit, she struggled to maintain professional composure:

> I held it together until he showed us the very tiny space the captured men were kept in and told us the huge number of men and the length of days they were confined. He then showed us the room and started talking about what was done.... Clearly, in the U.S.A., we are the descendants of this process. When he got to where they kept the children, I just lost it. Fortunately I had on my shades. I didn't have enough Kleenex for that experience, and unfortunately I'd left my handkerchief back at the hotel. But here I am president pro tem. I just sort of melted to the back of the group. What they did to children was unthinkable. I had some reality of what had happened, but the physical presence of being at the actual site was overwhelming. To look out at the sea and know of the sharks, and how the sharks would follow the ships because they would just throw people off as they died, or got sick, or for punishment—there was absolutely no respect for human life—zero [DeFrantz, 2001, p. 2].

The visit ended with a ritual. As president pro tem, Anita was asked to sign the museum's guest book. She felt conflicted:

> This was a great honor, but for me, I had to struggle in my mind to understand that signing the book was an honor. The people were so proud, knowing that I was an African American and knowing that I was really more connected to them…. Standing in the room where the transactions were finalized was a really difficult struggle for me. I finally made it by thinking that signing the book meant that this practice had ended. But, at first, I had these images that I was signing one of these transactions, and I could not do that [DeFrantz, 2001, p. 3].

Anita's memory of the day she announced her candidacy for IOC presidency is inseparable from her recollections of visiting Île de Gorée, which is not surprising. Her lifelong will to defend human rights blurs the two into one experience.

Anita was not elected, and defeat generated this familiar tension of maintaining her composure as a high profile IOC member while experiencing overwhelming emotion. She confided that she had some forewarning: "The day before about 10 people who had promised to vote for me came to me and said they weren't going to vote for me. So I knew I'd lost those 10 votes" (A. DeFrantz, personal communication, March 5, 2012). After being eliminated during the multi-stage voting, she recalled, "there was a time when I just could not stop crying. But I was traveling from one place to another, and I didn't have a handkerchief or anything with me, which was ridiculous" (A. DeFrantz, personal communication, March 5, 2012). The days following the election, like the hours at Île de Gorée, demanded professional composure. Her stories demonstrate that while she could be tough, her spirit and empathy had not hardened. And that is the well of her leadership to which she returns again and again for renewal.

A Vision for the Future

To look ahead, Anita first looks back to Harriet Tubman, the historical woman whom she most admires:

> Harriet Tubman decided she would be free. She asked others to come along and no one did. She got to freedom herself and then she came back many times to lead others to freedom. I'm told through historical treatises that she helped free over 300 people, always at great personal risk. Then she became a scout for the Union Army. She was probably the first woman to carry a weapon in the army, and then finally they told her what she was doing was too dangerous. What could be more dangerous that what she had already accomplished? She then became a nurse for the Union Army. After the war was over and in her later years, she ran a home for the aged. She was always giving of herself [DeFrantz, 2001, p. 16].

This admiration reflects Anita's leadership style, which she described as inclusive: "I am a good decision-maker, which is important. I seek advice, I hear what people have to say on an issue, but I also make decisions before a problem becomes critical" (DeFrantz, 2001, p. 4). Considering how she would like others to perceive her, Anita stated, "I want other people to think of me as someone who provides opportunity. I'm about opportunity" (DeFrantz, 2001, p. 67).

Creating opportunity in sport means negotiating constant change. For example, the IOC dropped both baseball and softball from the 2012 and 2016 Olympic programs but added sports with opportunities for other athletes. Anita's personal commitment to equity for women in sport aligned with IOC's 1991 mandate that new sports added to an Olympic program must have events for women and men (IOC, 2016, Factsheet).

> In London [2012], we'll have women's boxing. I'm not going to put myself in the ring with those who might wish to harm me in some way, but that doesn't mean that other women shouldn't have that opportunity. Same with mountain biking. There are lots of injuries in mountain biking. But the thrill of it is something that both sexes enjoy [A. DeFrantz, personal communication, March 5, 2012].

The Summer Olympic Games in London were, in fact, the first Games in which every sport included women.

Anita has been looking ahead in many ways. In 2013, after a 12-year break from the IOC Executive Board, she was elected to another four-year term, her third term on the board. She is also a member of the Coordination Committee for the Tokyo 2020 Olympic Games. During her last months as president of LA84, she helped the organization prepare for the next president. She pointed out, "And that will be a real test of leadership. Because if you do something and it fails, then you've not done a good job" (A. DeFrantz, personal communication, March 5, 2012).

Decades after the U.S. boycott of the 1980 Summer Olympic Games, Anita tells her story in hopes that Olympic athletes will always have opportunities to compete. She returned to the U.S. rowing team's stickers, "We're here to make sure this will never happen again." She envisions a world of race and gender integration modeled on the Olympic village. "I do believe that the Olympic Games are a celebration of human excellence," she confirmed. "It proves to the world that we can come together. At the end of my days, I hope to have written on my tombstone, *She helped make the world more like an Olympic village* (DeFrantz, 2001, p. 65). As part of the genealogy of women who have supported women's rights as human rights, through Title IX, through sport, and through the Olympic Movement, Anita concluded, "In all these firsts, my job is to make sure that they are not the last" (A. DeFrantz, personal communication, March 5, 2012).

Chapter Notes

Chapter 2

1. In 1957, Mankato State Teachers College was renamed Mankato State College. In 1975, it became Mankato State University and in 1998 adopted its current name, Minnesota State University, Mankato.

2. ICHPER was founded in 1958. The Council expanded its name to ICHPER-SD in 1993 to include sport and dance (ICHPERD-SD).

Chapter 3

1. For primary documentation of AIAW principles and scholarship conflicts, see Mabel Lee's *A History of Physical Education and Sports in the U.S.A.*

Chapter 5

1. Dorothy McIntyre shared stories similar to anecdotes she wrote in "Reflections from the front of the bus" (2005). Where stories and language overlap, citation indicates reference to both "Reflections" and to our interview, although the interview was the primary source of information.

Chapter 6

1. The same information appears in a brief biography by S. Brody in *Sports Illustrated for Women*.

References

Ainsworth, D. (1975). "The history of physical education in college for women (USA)." In E. F. Zeigler (Ed.), *A history of physical education and sport in the United States and Canada* (167–180). Champaign, IL: Stipes.

Allen, C. (1956). *Fun for parties and programs.* Englewood Cliffs, NJ: Prentice-Hall.

American Alliance for Health, Physical Education, Recreation, and Dance [PDF file]. Retrieved from http://www.shapeamerica.org/about/upload/alliance_history.pdf.

Brody, S. (n.d.). Willye White, track and field. *Sports Illustrated for Women.* Retrieved from http://sportsillustrated.cnn.com/siforwomen/top_100/79/.

Carpenter, L. J., & Acosta, R.V. (2005). *Title IX.* Champaign, IL: Human Kinetics.

Carter, J. (1978, November 8). *Amateur Sports Act of 1978 statement on signing S. 2727 into law.* Retrieved from http://www.presidency.ucsb.edu/ws/?pid=30133.

Carter-Francique, A.R., & Richardson, F. M. (2015). Black female athlete experiences at historically black colleges and universities. In B. Hawkins, J. Cooper, A. Carter-Francique, & J. Kenyatta Cavil (Eds.), *The athletic experience at historically black colleges and universities: Past, present, and persistence* (pp. 61–83). Lanham, MD: Rowman & Littlefield.

Corbett, D. (1997). *Outstanding athletes of Congress.* Washington, D.C.: United States Capitol Historical Society.

Corbett, D. (2008, June 13). Personal communication. Interview and transcription by S. Van Oteghen.

Corbett, D. (2012). In memoriam. *Journal of Health, Physical Education, Recreation & Dance* 83(6), 9–56. doi: 10.1080/07303084.2012.10598787.

Corbett, D. (2016, March 4). Personal communication. Interview by D. LeBlanc.

Costa, D. M., & Guthrie, S. R. (1994). *Women and sport: Interdisciplinary perspectives.* Champaign, IL: Human Kinetics.

DeFrantz, A. (2001, May 13). An Olympian's oral history [Interview by A. Swanson]. LA84. Retrieved from http://library.la84.org/6oic/OralHistory/OHDeFrantz.pdf.

DeFrantz, A. (2012, March 5). Personal communication. Interview by A. Swanson.

Fox, C. (1992). Introduction. *JOPERD* 63(3), 3–35.

Freeman, W. H. (1987). *Physical education and sport in a changing society.* New York, NY: Macmillan.

Gerber, E. (1975). The controlled development of collegiate sport for women, 1923–1936. *Journal of Sport History* 2(1), 1–28.

Gulick, L. H. (1920). *The philosophy of play.* New York: Charles Scribner's Sons.

Hogshead-Makar, N., & Zimbalist, A. (2007). *Equal play: Title IX and social change.* Philadelphia, PA: Temple University Press.

ICHPER-SD Oceania Region. (n.d.). Retrieved from http://www.ichpersd-oceania.org/.

Institute of Medicine. *Fitness Measures and Health Outcomes in Youth.* (2012). Washington, D.C.: The National Academies Press. doi:10.17226/13483.

International Olympic Committee. (n.d.). *About. The Organisation.* Retrieved from http://www.olympic.org/about-ioc-institution.

International Olympic Committee. (n.d.). IOC crisis and reform chronology [PDF file]. Retrieved from http://www.olympic.org/documents/reports/en/en_report_590.pdf.

International Olympic Committee. (1996). Resolution of the 1st IOC World Conference on Women and Sport [PDF file]. Retrieved from http://www.olympic.org/Documents/Reports/EN/en_report_756.pdf.

International Olympic Committee. (2000). Resolution of the 2nd IOC World Conference on Women and Sport [PDF file]. Retrieved from http://www.olympic.org/Documents/Reports/EN/en_report_757.pdf.

International Olympic Committee. (2012). 5th World Conference on Women and Sport [PDF file]. Retrieved from http://www.olympic.org/Documents/Commissions_PDFfiles/women_and_sport/report_5th_conference_women_and_sport_EN.pdf.

International Olympic Committee. (2014) Factsheet: Women in the Olympic movement [PDF file]. Retrieved from http://www.olympic.org/Documents/Reference_documents_Factsheets/Women_in_Olympic_Movement.pdf.

International Olympic Committee (2016). Factsheet: Women in the Olympic movement [PDF file]. Retrieved from http://www.olympic.org/Documents/Reference_documents_Factsheets/Women_in_Olympic_Movement.pdf.

Jewett, A. E. (1975). Introducing Celeste Ulrich. *The Amy Morris Homans Lectures*. Normal, IL: The National Association for Physical Education of College Women.

Johnson, M. B., & McIntyre, D.E. (2005). *Daughters of the game: The first era of Minnesota girls high school basketball, 1891-194.2* St. Cloud, MN: McJohn Publishing.

Jordan, P. (1975, December 8). From the land of cotton. *Sports Illustrated*, 87-98.

LA84. (n.d.) *About*. Retrieved from http://www.la84.org/about/.

LA84. (2015, May 31). *News*. Statement from the LA 84 Foundation. Retrieved from http://www.la84.org/statement-from-the-la84-foundation/.

Lee, M. (1977). *Memories of a bloomer girl*. Washington, D.C.: American Alliance for Health, Physical Education, and Recreation.

Lee, M. (1983). *A history of physical education and sports in the U.S.A*. New York, NY: John Wiley and Sons.

Lipsyte, R. (1993, October 3). A practical woman with dreams intact. *New York Times*. Retrieved from http://www.nytimes.com.

Mallon, B. (2000). The Olympic bribery scandal [PDF file]. Retrieved from http://library.la84.org/SportsLibrary/JOH/JOHv8n2/johv8n2f.pdf.

McDonagh, E., & Pappano, L. (2008). *Playing with the boys: Why separate is not equal in sports*. New York, NY: Oxford University Press.

McIntyre, D. (2005). Reflections from the front of the bus. In K.C. Ridder, J.A. Brookins, & B. Stuhler (Eds.), *Stories by Minnesota women in sports: leveling the playing field* (pp. 139-152). St. Cloud, MN: North Star Press.

McIntyre, D. (2013, March 7). Personal communication. Interview by D. LeBlanc.

McIntyre, D.E., & and Johnson, M. B. (2012). *Two rings: A legacy of hope*. Mankato, MN: McJohn Publishing.

Miller, D. (2012). *The official history of the Olympic Games and the IOC: Athens to London, 1894-2012*. Edinburgh: Mainstream Publishing.

Minnesota State High School League. (2002). *Dorothy McIntyre: Pioneer for girls athletics retiring from League staff*. Minnesota State Girls Basketball Tournament program.

Nash, J. B. (1928). Athletics for girls. In A. S. Lockhart (Ed.), *Chronicle of American physical education: Selected readings, 1855-1930* (pp. 431-435). Dubuque, IA: William C. Brown.

North Carolina Central University. (n.d.) History of the University. Retrieved from http://www.nccu.edu/discover/history.cfm.

O'Reilly, J., & Cahn, S. K. (Eds.). (2007). *Women and sports in the United States: A documentary reader*. Lebanon, NH: Northeastern University Press. Retrieved from http://www.ebrary.com.

Office of the Law Revision Counsel. *United States Code*. Public Law 95-606 [PDF file]. Retrieved from http://uscode.house.gov/statutes/pl/95/606.pdf.

Our History. President's Council on Fitness, Sports & Nutrition. http://www.fitness.gov/about-pcfsn/our-history/.

Reddy, H. (n.d.) "I am woman." Retrieved from http://helenreddy.com/lyrics/i-am-woman/.

Schellberg, R. (1988, April 2). Personal communication. Interview by A. Swanson and

S. Van Oteghen. Transcription by S. Van Oteghen.

SHAPE America National Convention and Expo. (2015). Conference Prospectus [PDF file]. Retrieved from http://www.eppon line.com/pdf/AAHPERD-2015Prospectus-Seattle.pdf.

SHAPE America, National Standards. Retrieved from http://www.shapeamerica.org/standards/index.cfm.

SHAPE America, Recognition Awards. Retrieved from http://www.shapeamerica.org/recognition/awards/luther-halsey-gulick-award.cfm.

Sloan, M. (1994, January). *International Association of Physical Education and Sport for Girls and Women* [Bulletin].

Smith, R. T. (1982, March 21). *Minneapolis Tribune*, 2B.

Suggs, W. (2005). *A place on the team: The triumph and tragedy of Title IX*. Princeton, NJ: Princeton University Press.

Swanson, A., & Van Oteghen, S.L. (1989). "Oral history of retired American Alliance for Health, Physical Education, Recreation and Dance (AAHPERD) leaders: Presidents and/or national award recipients interview with Dr. Catherine Louise Allen." *Exercise & sports science faculty research.* Retrieved from http://sophia.stkate.edu/exsci_fac/5.

Swanson, A., & Van Oteghen, S.L. (1989). "Oral history of retired American Alliance for Health, Physical Education, Recreation and Dance (AAHPERD) leaders: Presidents and/or national award recipients interview with Dr. Fay Biles." *Exercise & sports science faculty research.* Retrieved from http://sophia.stkate.edu/exsci_fac/8.

Swanson, A., & Van Oteghen, S.L. (1990). "Oral history of retired American Alliance for Health, Physical Education, Recreation and Dance (AAHPERD) leaders: Presidents and/or national award recipients interview with Dr. Celeste Ulrich." *Exercise & sports science faculty research.* Retrieved from http://sophia.stkate.edu/exsci_fac/11.

Ulrich, Adele Celeste. (2014, October 14). In memoriam. *National Academy of Kinesiology*. Retrieved from http://www.nationalacademyofkinesiology.org/in-memoriam/in-memoriam/adele-celeste-ulrich.

United Nations Office on Sport for Development and Peace. (2010, February). *Why sport.* Sport and the millennium development goals [PDF file]. Retrieved from http://www.un.org/wcm/webdav/site/sport/shared/sport/pdfs/Backgrounders/Sport%20and%20the%20MDGs_FACT SHEET_February%202010.pdf.

United States Department of Education. Office for Civil Rights. (1998). Title IX and sex discrimination. Retrieved from http://www2.ed.gov/about/offices/list/ocr/docs/tix_dis.html.

United States Department of State. (n.d.). *Empowering girls and women through sport.* Retrieved from http://globalsportswomen.org/.

University Libraries Digital Collections. Papers of faculty administrators. University of Maryland. Retrieved from http://digital.lib.umd.edu/archivesum/rguide/umcpfac.jsp.

"Vacations." (1941, July 14). *Life* 11 (2), 66–75.

Vesper Boat Club. About. http://vesperboatclub.org/about-2/.

Ware, S. (2007). *Title IX: A brief history with documents*. Boston: Bedford/St. Martin's.

White, W. (1992, November 19). Personal communication. Interview by A. Swanson. Transcription by S. Van Oteghen.

Wiley, B. (1945, August 22). Three Southern bells wow soldiers on Guam. *The Evening Independent*. Retrieved from https://news.google.com/newspapers?nid=950&dat=19450822&id=4_5PAAAAIBAJ&sjid=H1U DAAAAIBAJ&pg=2328,6714174&hl=en.

Women's Sports Foundation. "Title IX and race in intercollegiate sport" [PDF file]. Retrieved from https://www.womenssportsfoundation.org/en/home/research/articles-and-reports/school-and-colleges/title-ix-and-race-in-intercollegiate-sport.

Wushanley, Y. (2004). *Playing nice and losing: The struggle for control of women's intercollegiate athletics, 1960–2000* (1st edition). Syracuse, NY: Syracuse University Press.

Index

Ainsworth, Dorothy 14, 26, 27, 146; see also Dorothy Sears Ainsworth Award
Allison, Lavonia 134–135
Amateur Athletic Union 4, 21, 117, 161, 174
Amateur Sports Act of 1978 173–174
American Alliance for Health, Physical Education and Recreation (AAHPER) 8, 25, 49, 52
American Alliance for Health, Physical Education, Recreation and Dance (AAHPERD) 1, 6, 8, 55, 56–57, 77–78, 85–86, 87, 100, 135, 137, 141, 144–145, 146, 153–154; see also American Alliance for Health, Physical Education and Recreation (AAHPER); American Physical Education Association (APEA); SHAPE America
American Physical Education Association (APEA) 8, 33
Applebee, Constance 64–65, 69
Association for Intercollegiate Athletics for Women (AIAW) 7, 8, 54, 55–56, 57, 61, 78, 138, 140, 141, 164

basketball: high school 13–15, 52, 69, 90, 92–96, 105, 107, 109–110, 112–113; intercollegiate 4, 52, 57, 136–37, 140, 142, 164; intramural 33, 133–134
Boston-Bouvé College 29; see also Bouvé-Boston School
Bouvé-Boston School 6, 24–25, 27, 45, 46, 53; see also Boston-Bouvé College

Camp Fire Girls of America 6, 31–32, 34, 37, 40
Carter, Pres. Jimmy 129, 173–75
Coleman, Mary Channing 47–48, 49, 54
Commission on Intercollegiate Athletics for Women (CIAW) 8, 54, 164
Connecticut College 7, 159, 163–167, 181, 187

Division for Girls' and Women's Sports (DGWS) 8, 53–54, 55, 78, 98–99, 100, 164
Dorothy Sears Ainsworth Award 27, 41
Duke University 65–67, 135

Eisenhower, Pres. Dwight D. 72, 133

field hockey 6, 23, 46, 52, 64–69, 96
Friedan, Betty 54, 67

Georgia State College for Women 12
Girl Scouts 44–45, 61
Gulick, Luther Halsey 40, 153; see also Luther Halsey Gulick Award
gymnastics 20, 96, 98–99

Howard University 130, 137–140, 142–43, 146, 148, 151, 154–55

ice hockey 108–109
International Association of Physical Education and Sport for Girls and Women (IAPESGW) 26, 27, 41
International Council on Health, Physical Education and Recreation (ICHPER) 26, 41, 87, 193; see also International Council on Health, Physical Education, Recreation, Sport and Dance (ICHPER-SD)
International Council on Health, Physical Education, Recreation, Sport and Dance (ICHPER-SD) 7, 144, 146, 148, 193
International Olympic Committee (IOC) 7, 122–123, 150, 153, 158, 177, 180–191; Women and Sport Commission 150, 183–84; World Conference on Women and Sport 183–186

Jump Rope for Heart 62, 85–86

Kent State University 6, 62, 65, 69–71, 73–79, 80–85, 88

LA 84 Foundation 7, 158–159, 177–80, 191
Lee, Mabel 2, 15, 33, 35, 37–38, 40, 50, 54, 193
Life magazine 36–37
Lockhart, Aileene 37, 51
Luther College 93–94
Luther Halsey Gulick Award 153
Lynn, Minnie 23–25, 53

Macalester College 36–37

Madison College 6, 49–50
Mankato State College 39, 193; see also Mankato State Teachers College; Mankato State University; Minnesota State University, Mankato
Mankato State Teachers College 37–38, 193; see also Mankato State College; Mankato State University; Minnesota State University, Mankato
Mankato State University 6, 39, 193; see also Mankato State College; Mankato State Teachers College; Minnesota State University, Mankato
Memories of a Bloomer Girl 15; see also Lee, Mabel
Metheny, Eleanor 51, 54
Millennium Development Goals 185
Minnesota State High School League 5, 6, 90, 101–108, 110–111
Minnesota State University, Mankato 40, 193; see also Mankato State College; Mankato State Teachers College; Mankato State University

Nash, Jay B. 20–22, 26, 35, 40, 51
National Association for Girls and Women in Sport (NAGWS) 7, 8, 141–143, 154
National Association for Sports and Physical Education (NASPE) 77, 85
National Association for the Advancement of Colored People (NAACP) 133, 159
National Collegiate Athletic Association (NCAA) 5, 8, 56, 57, 108, 141–142, 152–153, 164, 174
National Section for Girls and Women's Sports (NSGWS) 8, 51, 71–72
National Section on Women's Athletics (NSWA) 8, 52, 54
New York University 6, 20, 35, 37
North Carolina Central University 136; see also North Carolina College
North Carolina College 134–136; see also North Carolina Central University

Oberteuffer, Delbert 50
The Ohio State University 50, 70, 73
Olympic Games 5, 6, 7, 87, 98, 115, 117–124, 127–129, 147, 150, 162, 166, 168–173, 178–180, 191; illegal drug use 181–182; 1980 U.S. boycott 7, 174–177; Salt Lake City Organizing Committee scandal 186–189

Pennsylvania State University 167–168
Physical Education Public Information Project 77–78, 85, 86

play days 4, 15, 38, 71, 96, 98, 133–134, 136
President's Council on Physical Fitness 72, 145; see also President's Council on Physical Fitness and Health; President's Council on Youth Fitness
President's Council on Physical Fitness and Health 128; see also President's Council on Physical Fitness; President's Council on Youth Fitness
President's Council on Youth Fitness 151; see also President's Council on Physical Fitness; President's Council on Physical Fitness and Health
Princeton University 166, 168, 174–176, 179

Rudolph, Wilma 98, 117, 122, 129

Schellberg Gymnasium 39
SHAPE America 8, 145, 153–54

Teachers College, Columbia University 16, 20
Temple, Ed 117–118, 120
Tennessee State University 117–118, 120
track and field: Chicago 125; high school 5, 16, 90, 96, 102, 109, 117; intercollegiate 117, 120–124, 134–35; Olympic 7, 98, 115, 118

United States Olympic Committee 7, 77, 87, 98, 118, 173–178, 180–181, 188
United States Women's Rowing Team 166, 174–177
University of Maryland–College Park 137–139
University of Minnesota 35, 98, 109
University of Nebraska–Lincoln 32–33, 37–38, 40
University of North Carolina at Greensboro 6, 42, 46–49, 53, 58, 142
University of Northern Iowa 7, 155–157
University of Oregon 6, 57–59

Vietnam War 27–29, 75–76

Walker, LeRoy 57, 134–35, 141, 149, 154, 156
Williams, Jesse Feiring 20, 35, 49, 51
Women's Division of the National Amateur Athletic Foundation (NAAF-WD) 4, 13, 14, 98, 105, 111, 124
Women's Equity Action League 39
Women's Sports Foundation 152–154
World War I 12
World War II 5–7, 9, 16–20, 28, 36, 48, 66, 90, 91

Zagoria, Robert 175–176

www.ingramcontent.com/pod-product-compliance
Ingram Content Group UK Ltd.
Pitfield, Milton Keynes, MK11 3LW, UK
UKHW021845140426
5217IPUK00022B/1607